Sara Jeannette Duncan

A Daughter of Today

A Novel

Sara Jeannette Duncan

A Daughter of Today
A Novel

ISBN/EAN: 9783337029333

Printed in Europe, USA, Canada, Australia, Japan

Cover: Foto ©Thomas Meinert / pixelio.de

More available books at **www.hansebooks.com**

A DAUGHTER OF TO-DAY

A NOVEL

BY

MRS. EVERARD COTES
(SARA JEANNETTE DUNCAN)
AUTHOR OF A SOCIAL DEPARTURE, AN AMERICAN GIRL IN LONDON,
THE SIMPLE ADVENTURES OF A MEMSAHIB, ETC.

NEW YORK
D. APPLETON AND COMPANY
1894

A DAUGHTER OF TO-DAY

CHAPTER I.

MISS KIMPSEY dropped into an arm-chair in Mrs. Leslie Bell's drawing-room and crossed her small dusty feet before her while she waited for Mrs. Leslie Bell. Sitting there, thinking a little of how tired she was and a great deal of what she had come to say, Miss Kimpsey enjoyed a sense of consideration that came through the ceiling with the muffled sound of rapid footsteps in the chamber above. Mrs. Bell would be "down in a minute," the maid had said. Miss Kimpsey was inclined to forgive a greater delay, with this evidence of hasteful preparation going on overhead. The longer she had to ponder her mission the better, and she sat up nervously straight pondering it, tracing with her parasol a sage-green block in the elderly æstheticated pattern of the carpet.

Miss Kimpsey was thirty-five, with a pale, oblong

little face, that looked younger under its softening "bang" of fair curls across the forehead. She was a buff-and-gray-colored creature, with a narrow square chin and narrow square shoulders, and a flatness and straightness about her everywhere that gave her rather the effect of a wedge, to which the big black straw hat she wore tilted a little on one side somehow conduced. Miss Kimpsey might have figured anywhere as a representative of the New England feminine surplus—there was a distinct suggestion of character under her unimportant little features—and her profession was proclaimed in her person, apart from the smudge of chalk on the sleeve of her jacket. She had been born and brought up and left over in Illinois, however, in the town of Sparta, Illinois. She had developed her conscience there, and no doubt, if one knew it well, it would show peculiarities of local expansion directly connected with hot corn-bread for breakfast, as opposed to the accredited diet of legumes upon which consciences arrive at such successful maturity in the East. It was, at all events, a conscience in excellent controlling order. It directed Miss Kimpsey, for example, to teach three times a week in the boys' night-school through the winter, no matter how sharply the wind blew off Lake Michigan, in addition to her daily duties at the High School, where

for ten years she had imparted instruction in the
"English branches," translating Chaucer into the
modern dialect of Sparta, Illinois, for the benefit of
Miss Elfrida Bell, among others. It had sent her
on this occasion to see Mrs. Leslie Bell, and Miss
Kimpsey could remember circumstances under which
she had obeyed her conscience with more alacrity.

"It isn't," said Miss Kimpsey, with internal discouragement, "as if I knew her well."

Miss Kimpsey did not know Mrs. Bell at all well.
Mrs. Bell was president of the Browning Club, and
Miss Kimpsey was a member; they met, too, in the
social jumble of fancy fairs in aid of the new
church organ; they had a bowing acquaintance—
that is, Mrs. Bell had. Miss Kimpsey's part of it
was responsive, and she always gave a thought to
her boots and her gloves when she met Mrs. Bell.
It was not that the Spartan social circle which Mrs.
Bell adorned had any vulgar prejudice against the
fact that Miss Kimpsey earned her own living—
more than one of its ornaments had done the same
thing—and Miss Kimpsey's relations were all "in
grain" and obviously respectable. It was simply
that none of the Kimpseys, prosperous or poor, had
ever been in society in Sparta, for reasons which
Sparta itself would probably be unable to define;
and this one was not likely to be thrust among

the elect because she taught school and enjoyed life upon a scale of ethics.

Mrs. Bell's drawing-room was a slight distraction to Miss Kimpsey's nervous thoughts. The little school-teacher had never been in it before, and it impressed her. "It's just what you would expect her parlor to be," she said to herself, looking furtively round. She could not help her sense of impropriety; she had always been taught that it was very bad manners to observe anything in another person's house, but she could not help looking either. She longed to get up and read the names of the books behind the glass doors of the tall bookcase at the other end of the room, for the sake of the little quiver of respectful admiration she knew they would give her; but she did not dare to do that. Her eyes went from the bookcase to the photogravure of Doré's "Entry into Jerusalem," under which three Japanese dolls were arranged with charming effect. "The Reading Magdalen" caught them next, a colored photograph, and then a Magdalen of more obscure origin in much blackened oils and a very deep frame; then still another Magdalen, more modern, in monochrome. In fact, the room was full of Magdalens, and on an easel in the corner stood a Mater Dolorosa, lifting up her streaming eyes. Granting the capacity to take them seriously, they might have depressed some people, but they elevated Miss Kimpsey.

She was equally elevated by the imitation willow pattern plates over the door, and the painted yellow daffodils on the panels, and the orange-colored *Revue des Deux Mondes* on the corner of the table, and the absence of all bows or draperies from the furniture. Miss Kimpsey's own parlor was excrescent with bows and draperies. "She is above them," thought Miss Kimpsey, with a little pang. The room was so dark that she could not see how old the *Revue* was; she did not know either that it was always there, that unexceptionable Parisian periodical, with Dante in the original and red leather, *Academy Notes*, and the *Nineteenth Century*, all helping to furnish Mrs. Leslie Bell's drawing-room in a manner in accordance with her tastes; but if she had, Miss Kimpsey would have been equally impressed. It took intellect even to select these things. The other books, Miss Kimpsey noticed by the numbers labelled on their backs, were mostly from the circulating library—"David Grieve," "Cometh up as a Flower," "The Earthly Paradise," Ruskin's "Stones of Venice," Marie Corelli's "Romance of Two Worlds." The mantelpiece was arranged in geometrical disorder, but it had a gilt clock under a glass shade precisely in the middle.

When the gilt clock indicated, in a mincing way, that Miss Kimpsey had been kept waiting fifteen minutes, Mrs. Bell came in. She had fastened her last button and assumed the expression appropriate to Miss Kimpsey at the foot of the stair. She was a tall, thin woman, with no color and rather narrow brown eyes much wrinkled round about, and a forehead that loomed at you, and grayish hair twisted high into a knot behind—a knot from which a wispy end almost invariably escaped. When she smiled her mouth curved downward, showing a number of large even white teeth, and made deep lines which suggested various things, according to the nature of the smile, on either side of her face. As a rule one might take them to mean a rather deprecating acceptance of life as it stands—they seemed intended for that—and then Mrs. Bell would express an enthusiasm and contradict them. As she came through the door under the "Entry into Jerusalem," saying that she really must apologize, she was sure it was unpardonable keeping Miss Kimpsey waiting like this, the lines expressed an intention of being as agreeable as possible without committing herself to return Miss Kimpsey's visit.

"Why, no, Mrs. Bell," Miss Kimpsey said earnestly, with a protesting buff-and-gray smile, "I didn't mind waiting a particle—honestly I didn't.

Besides, I presume it's early for a call; but I thought I'd drop in on my way from school." Miss Kimpsey was determined that Mrs. Bell should have every excuse that charity could invent for her. She sat down again, and agreed with Mrs. Bell that they were having lovely weather, especially when they remembered what a disagreeable fall it had been last year; certainly this October had been just about perfect. The ladies used these superlatives in the tone of mild defiance that almost any statement of fact has upon feminine lips in America. It did not seem to matter that their observations were entirely in union.

"I thought I'd run in—" said Miss Kimpsey, screwing herself up by the arm of her chair.

"Yes?"

"And speak to you about a thing I've been thinking a good deal of, Mrs. Bell, this last day or two. It's about Elfrida."

Mrs. Bell's expression became judicial. If this was a complaint—and she was not accustomed to complaints of Elfrida—she would be careful how she took it.

"I hope—" she began.

"Oh, you needn't worry, Mrs. Bell. It's nothing about her conduct, and it's nothing about her school work."

"Well, that's a relief," said Mrs. Bell, as if she had expected it would be. "But I know she's bad at figures. The child can't help that, though; she gets it from me. I think I ought to ask you to be lenient with her on that account."

"I have nothing to do with the mathematical branches, Mrs. Bell. I teach only English to the senior classes. But I haven't heard Mr. Jackson complain of Elfrida at all." Feeling that she could no longer keep her errand at arm's length, Miss Kimpsey desperately closed with it. "I've come— I hope you won't mind—Mrs. Bell, Elfrida has been quoting Rousseau in her compositions, and I thought you'd like to know."

"In the original?" asked Mrs. Bell, with interest. "I didn't think her French was advanced enough for that."

"No, from a translation," Miss Kimpsey replied. "Her sentence ran: 'As the gifted Jean Jacques Rousseau told the world in his "Confessions"'—I forget the rest. That was the part that struck me most. She had evidently been reading the works of Rousseau."

"Very likely. Elfrida has her own subscription at the library," Mrs. Bell said speculatively. "It shows a taste in reading beyond her years, doesn't it, Miss Kimpsey? The child is only fifteen."

"Well, *I've* never read Rousseau," the little teacher stated definitely. "Isn't he—atheistical, Mrs. Bell, and improper every way?"

Mrs. Bell raised her eyebrows and pushed out her lips at the severity of this ignorant condemnation. "He was a genius, Miss Kimpsey—rather I should say he *is*, for genius cannot die. He is much thought of in France. People there make a little shrine of the house he occupied with Madame Warens, you know."

"Oh!" returned Miss Kimpsey, "*French* people."

"Yes. The French are peculiarly happy in the way they sanctify genius," said Mrs. Bell vaguely, with a feeling that she was wasting a really valuable idea.

"Well, you'll have to excuse me, Mrs. Bell. I'd always heard you entertained about as liberal views as there were going on any subject, but I didn't expect they embraced Rousseau." Miss Kimpsey spoke quite meekly. "I know we live in an age of progress, but I guess I'm not as progressive as some."

"Many will stay behind," interrupted Mrs. Bell impartially, "but many more will advance."

"And I thought maybe Elfrida had been reading that author without your knowledge or approval, and that perhaps you'd like to know."

"I neither approve nor disapprove," said Mrs. Bell, poising her elbow on the table, her chin upon her hand, and her judgment, as it were, upon her chin. "I think her mind ought to develop along the lines that nature intended; I think nature is wiser than I am"—there was an effect of condescending explanation here—"and I don't feel justified in interfering. I may be wrong—"

"Oh no!" said Miss Kimpsey.

"But Elfrida's reading has always been very general. She has a remarkable mind, if you will excuse my saying so; it devours everything. I can't tell you *when* she learned to read, Miss Kimpsey—it seemed to come to her. She has often reminded me of what you see in the biographies of distinguished people about their youth. There are really a great many points of similarity sometimes. I shouldn't be surprised if Elfrida did anything. I wish *I* had had her opportunities!"

"She's growing very good-looking," remarked Miss Kimpsey.

"It's an interesting face," Mrs. Bell returned. "Here is her last photograph. It's full of soul, I think. She posed herself," Mrs. Bell added unconsciously.

It was a cabinet photograph of a girl whose eyes looked definitely out of it, dark, large, well shaded, full of a desire to be beautiful at once expressed and fulfilled. The nose was a trifle heavily blocked, but the mouth had sensitiveness and charm. There was a heaviness in the chin, too, but the free springing curve of the neck contradicted that, and the symmetry of the face defied analysis. It was turned a little to one side, wistfully; the pose and the expression suited each other perfectly.

"*Full* of soul!" responded Miss Kimpsey. "She takes awfully well, doesn't she? It reminds me—it reminds me of pictures I've seen of Rachel, the actress, really it does."

"I'm afraid Elfrida has no talent *that* way." Mrs. Bell's accent was quite one of regret.

"She seems completely wrapped up in her painting just now," said Miss Kimpsey, with her eyes still on the photograph.

"Yes; I often wonder what her career will be, and sometimes it comes home to me that it *must* be art. The child can't help it—she gets it straight from me. But there were no art classes in my day." Mrs. Bell's tone implied a large measure of what the world had lost in consequence. "Mr. Bell doesn't agree with me about Elfrida's being predestined for art," she went on, smiling; "his whole idea is that she'll marry like other people."

"Well, if she goes on improving in looks at the

rate she has, you'll find it difficult to *prevent*, I should think, Mrs. Bell." Miss Kimpsey began to wonder at her own temerity in staying so long. "Should you be opposed to it?"

"Oh, I shouldn't be *opposed* to it exactly. I won't say I don't expect it. I think she might do better, myself; but I dare say matrimony will swallow her up as it does everybody—almost everybody—else." A finer ear than Miss Kimpsey's might have heard in this that to overcome Mrs. Bell's objections matrimony must take a very attractive form indeed, and that she had no doubt it would. Elfrida's instructress did not hear it; she might have been less overcome with the quality of these latter-day sentiments if she had. Little Miss Kimpsey, whom matrimony had not swallowed up, had risen to go. "Oh, I'm sure the most gifted couldn't do *better!*" she said, hardily, in departing, with a blush that turned her from buff-and-gray to brick color.

Mrs. Bell picked up the *Revue* after she had gone, and read three lines of a paper on the climate and the soil of Poland. Then she laid it down again at the same angle with the corner of the table which it had described before.

"Rousseau!" she said aloud to herself. "*C'est un peu fort mais—*" and paused, probably for maturer reflection upon the end of her sentence.

CHAPTER II.

"LESLIE," said Mrs. Bell, making the unnecessary feminine twist to get a view of her back hair from the mirror with a hand-glass, "aren't you *delighted?* Try to be candid with yourself now, and own that she's tremendously improved."

It would not have occurred to anybody but Mrs. Bell to ask Mr. Leslie Bell to be candid with himself. Candor was written in large letters all over Mr. Leslie Bell's plain, broad countenance. So was a certain obstinacy, not of will, but of adherence to prescribed principles, which might very well have been the result of living for twenty years with Mrs. Leslie Bell. Otherwise he was a thick-set man with an intelligent bald head, a fresh-colored complexion, and a well-trimmed gray beard. Mr. Leslie Bell looked at life with logic, or thought he did, and took it with ease, in a plain way. He was known to be a good man of business, with a leaning toward generosity, and much independence of opinion. It was not a custom among election candidates to ask Leslie Bell for his vote. It was pretty well understood that nothing would influence it except his "views," and that none of the ordinary considerations in use with refractory electors would influence his views. He was a man of large, undemonstrative affections, and it was a matter of private regret with him that there should have been only one child, and that a daughter, to bestow them upon. His simplicity of nature was utterly beyond the understanding of his wife, who had been building one elaborate theory after another about him ever since they had been married, conducting herself in mysterious accordance, but had arrived accurately only at the fact that he preferred two lumps of sugar in his tea.

Mr. Bell did not allow his attention to be taken from the intricacies of his toilet by his wife's question until she repeated it.

"Aren't you charmed with Elfrida, Leslie? Hasn't Philadelphia improved her beyond your wildest dreams?"

Mr. Bell reflected. "You know I don't think Elfrida has ever been as pretty as she was when she was five years old, Maggie."

"*Do* say Margaret," interposed Mrs. Bell plaintively. She had been suffering from this for twenty years.

"It's of no use, my dear; I never remember unless there's company present. I was going to say

Elfrida had certainly grown. She's got to her full size now, I should think, and she dwarfs you, moth— Margaret."

Mrs. Bell looked at him with tragic eyes. "Do you see no more in her than *that?*" she exclaimed.

"She looks well, I admit she looks well. She seems to have got a kind of style in Philadelphia."

"*Style!*"

"I don't mean fashionable style—a style of her own; and according to the professors, neither the time nor the money has been wasted. But she's been a long year away, Maggie. It's been considerably dull without her for you and me. I hope she won't take it into her head to want to leave home again."

"If it should be necessary to her plan of life—"

"It won't be necessary. She's nineteen now, and I'd like to see her settle down here in Sparta, and the sooner the better. Her painting will be an interest for her all her life, and if ever she should be badly off she can teach. That was my idea in giving her the training."

"Settle down in *Sparta!*" Mrs. Bell repeated, with a significant curve of her superior lip. "Why, who is there—"

"Lots of people, though it isn't for me to name them, nor for you either, my dear. But speaking generally, there isn't a town of its size in the Union with a finer crop of go-ahead young men in it than Sparta."

Mrs. Bell was leaning against the inside shutter of their bedroom window, looking out, while she waited for her husband. As she looked, one of Sparta's go-ahead young men, glancing up as he passed in the street below and seeing her there behind the panes, raised his hat.

"Heavens, *no!*" said Mrs. Bell. "You don't understand, Leslie."

"Perhaps not," Mr. Bell returned. "We must get that packing-case opened after dinner. I'm anxious to see the pictures." Mr. Bell put the finishing touches to his little finger-nail and briskly pocketed his penknife. "Shall we go downstairs now?" he suggested. "Fix your brooch, mother; it's just on the drop."

Elfrida Bell had been a long year away—a year that seemed longer to her than it possibly could to anybody in Sparta, as she privately reflected when her father made this observation for the second and the third time. Sparta accounted for its days chiefly in ledgers, the girl thought; there was a rising and a going down of the sun, a little eating and drinking and speedy sleeping, a little discussion of the newspapers. Sparta got over its days by strides and stretches, and the strides and stretches seemed afterward to have been made over gaps and gulfs full of emptiness. The year divided itself and got its painted leaves, its white silences, its rounding buds, and its warm fragrances from the winds of heaven, and so there were four seasons in Sparta, and people talked of an early spring or a late fall; but Elfrida told herself that time had no other division, and the days no other color. Elfrida seemed to be unaware of the opening of the new South Ward Episcopal Methodist Church. She overlooked the municipal elections too, the plan for overhauling the town waterworks, and the reorganization of the public library. She even forgot the Browning Club.

Whereas—though Elfrida would never have said "whereas"—the days in Philadelphia had been long and full. She had often lived a week in one of them, and there had been hours that stretched themselves over an infinity of life and feeling, as Elfrida saw it, looking back. In reality, her experience had been usual enough and poor enough; but it had fed her in a way, and she enriched it with her imagination, and thought, with keen and sincere pity, that she had been starved till then. The question that preoccupied her when she moved out of the Philadelphia station in the Chicago train was that of future sustenance. It was under the surface of her thoughts when she kissed her father and mother and was made welcome home; it raised a mute remonstrance against Mr. Bell's cheerful prophecy that she would be content to stay in Sparta for a while now, and get to know the young society; it neutralized the pleasure of the triumphs in the packing-box. Besides, their real delight had all been exhaled at the students' exhibition in Philadelphia, when Philadelphia looked at them. The opinion of Sparta, Elfrida thought, was not a matter for anxiety. Sparta would be pleased in advance.

Elfrida allowed one extenuating point in her indictment of Sparta: the place had produced her as she was at eighteen, when they sent her to Philadelphia. This was only half conscious—she was able to formulate it later—but it influenced her sincere and vigorous disdain of the town correctively, and we may believe that it operated to except her father and mother from the general wreck of her opinion to a greater extent than any more ordinary feeling did. It was not in the least a sentiment of affection for her birthplace; if she could have chosen she would very much have preferred to be born somewhere else. It was simply an important qualifying circumstance. Her actual and her ideal self, her most mysterious and interesting self, had originated in the air and the opportunities of Sparta. Sparta had even done her the service of showing her that she was unusual, by contrast, and Elfrida felt that she ought to be thankful to somebody or something for being as unusual as she was. She had had a comfortable, spoiled feeling of gratitude for it before she went to Philadelphia, which had developed in the meantime into a shudder at the mere thought of what it meant to be an ordinary person. "I could bear not to be charming," said she sometimes to her Philadelphia looking-glass, "but I could *not* bear not to be clever."

She said "clever," but she meant more than that. Elfrida Bell believed that something other than cleverness entered into her personal equation. She looked sometimes into her very soul to see what, but the writing there was in strange characters that faded under her eyes, leaving her uncomprehending but tranced. Meanwhile art spoke to her from all sides, finding her responsive and more responsive. Some books, some pictures, some music brought her a curious exalted sense of double life. She could not talk about it at all, but she could slip out into the wet streets on a gusty October evening, and walk miles exulting in it, and in the light on the puddles and in the rain on her face, coming back, it must be admitted, with red cheeks and an excellent appetite. It led her into strange absent silences and ways of liking to be alone, which gratified her mother and worried her father. When Elfrida burned the gas of Sparta late in her own room, it was always her father who saw the light under the door, and who came and knocked and told her that it was after eleven, and high time she was in bed. Mrs. Bell usually protested. "How can the child reach any true development," she asked, "if you interfere with her like this?" to which Mr. Bell usually replied that whatever she developed, he didn't want it to be headaches and hysteria. Elfrida invariably answered, "Yes, papa," with complete docility; but it must be said that Mr. Bell generally knocked in vain, and the more perfect the submission of the daughterly reply the later the gas would be apt to burn. Elfrida was always agreeable to her father. So far as she thought of it she was appreciatively fond of him, but the relation pleased her, it was one that could be so charmingly sustained. For already out of the other world she walked in—the world of strange kinships and insights and recognitions, where she saw truth afar off and worshipped, and as often met falsehood in the way and turned raptly to follow—the girl had drawn a vague and many-shaped idea of artistic living which embraced the filial attitude among others less explicable. It gave her pleasure to do certain things in certain ways. She stood and sat and spoke, and even thought, at times, with a subtle approval and enjoyment of her manner of doing it. It was not actual artistic achievement, but it was the sort of thing that entered her imagination as such achievement's natural corollary. Her self-consciousness was a supreme fact of her personality; it began earlier than any date she could remember, and it was a channel of the most unfailing and intense satisfaction to her from many sources. One was her beauty, for she had developed an elusive beauty that served her moods. When she was dull she called herself ugly—unfairly, though her face lost tremendously in value then—and her general dislike of dullness and ugliness became particular and acute in connection with herself. It is not too much to say that she took a keen enjoying pleasure in the flush upon her own cheek and the light in her own eyes no less than in the inward sparkle that provoked it—an honest delight, she would not have minded confessing it. Her height, her symmetry, her perfect abounding health were separate joys to her; she found absorbing and critical interest in the very figment of her being. It was entirely preposterous that a young woman should kneel at an attic window in a flood of spring moonlight, with her hair about the shoulders of her nightgown, repeating Rossetti to the wakeful budding garden, especially as it was for herself she did it—nobody else saw her. She knelt there partly because of a vague desire to taste the essence of the spring and the garden and Rossetti at once, and partly because she felt the romance of the foolish situation. She knew of the shadow her hair made around her throat, and that her eyes were glorious in the moonlight. Going back to bed, she paused before the looking-glass and wafted a kiss, as she blew the candle out, to the face she saw there. It was such a pretty face, and so full of the spirit of Rossetti and the moonlight, that she couldn't help it. Then she slept, dreamlessly, comfortably, and late; and in the morning she had never taken cold.

Philadelphia had pointed and sharpened all this. The girl's training there had vitalized her brooding dreams of producing what she worshipped, had given shape and direction to her informal efforts, had concentrated them upon charcoal and canvas. There was an enthusiasm for work in the Institute, a canonization of names, a blazing desire to imitate that tried hard to fan itself into originality. Elfrida kindled at once, and felt that her soul had lodged forever in her fingers, that art had found for her, once for all, a sacred embodiment. She spoke with subdued feeling of its other shapes; she was at all points sympathetic; but she was no longer at all points desirous. Her aim was taken. She would not write novels or compose operas; she would paint. There was some renunciation in it and some humility. The day she came home, looking over a dainty sandalwood box full of early verses, twice locked against her mother's eye, "The desire of the moth for the star," she said to herself; but she did not tear them up. That would have been brutal.

Elfrida wanted to put off opening the case that held her year's work until next day. She quailed somewhat in anticipation of her parents' criticisms as a matter of fact; she would have preferred to postpone parrying them. She acknowledged this to herself with a little irritation that it should be so, but when her father insisted, chisel in hand, she went down on her knees with charming willingness to help him. Mrs. Bell took a seat on the sofa and clasped her hands with the expression of one who prepares for prayer.

One by one Mr. Leslie Bell drew out his daughter's studies and copies, cutting their strings, clearing them of their paper wrappings, and standing each separately against the wall in his crisp, business-like way. They were all mounted and framed; they stood very well against the wall; but Mr. Bell, who began hopefully, was presently obliged to try to hide his disappointment, the row was so persistently black and white. Mrs. Bell, on the sofa, had the look of postponing her devotions.

"You seem to have done a great many of these—etchings," said Mr. Bell.

"Oh, papa! They're not etchings, they're subjects in charcoal—from casts and things."

"They do you credit—I've no doubt they do you credit. They're very nicely drawn," returned her father, "but they're a good deal alike. We won't be able to hang more than two of them in the same room. Was *that* what they gave you the medal for?"

Mr. Bell indicated a drawing of Psyche. The lines were delicate, expressive, and false; the relief was imperfect, yet the feeling was undeniably caught. As a drawing it was incorrect enough, but its charm lay in a subtle spiritual something that had worked into it from the girl's own fingers, and made the beautiful empty classic face modernly interesting. In view of its inaccuracy the committee had been guilty of a most irregular proceeding in recognizing it with a medal; but in a very young art school this might be condoned.

"It's a perfectly lovely thing," interposed Mrs. Bell from the sofa. "I'm sure it deserves one."

Elfrida said nothing. The study was ticketed, it had obviously won a medal.

Mr. Bell looked at it critically. "Yes, it's certainly well done. In spite of the frame—I wouldn't give ten cents for the frame—the effect is fine. We must find a good light for that. Oh, now we come to the oil-paintings. We both presumed you would do well at the oil-paintings; and for my part," continued Mr. Bell definitely, "I like them best. There's more variety in them." He was holding at arm's-length, as he spoke, an oblong scrap of filmy blue sky and marshy green fields in a preposterously wide, flat, dull gold frame, and looking at it in a puzzled way. Presently he reversed it and looked again.

"No, papa," Elfrida said, "you had it right side up before." She was biting her lip, and struggling with a desire to pile them all back into the box and shut the lid and stamp on it.

"That's exquisite!" murmured Mrs. Bell, when Mr. Bell had righted it again.

"It's one of the worst," said Elfrida briefly.

Mr. Bell looked relieved. "Since that's your own opinion, Elfrida," he said, "I don't mind saying that I don't care much about it either. It looks as if you'd got tired of it before you finished it."

"Does it?" Elfrida said.

"Now this is a much better thing, in my opinion," her father went on, standing the picture of an old woman behind an apple-stall along the wall with the rest. "I don't pretend to be a judge, but I know what I like, and I like that. It explains itself."

"It's a lovely bit of color," remarked Mrs. Bell.

Elfrida smiled. "Thank you, mamma," she said, and kissed her.

When the box was exhausted, Mr. Bell walked up and down for a few minutes in front of the row against the wall, with his hands in his pockets, reflecting, while Mrs. Bell discovered new beauties to the author of them.

"We'll hang this lot in the dining-room," he said at length, "and those black-and-whites with the oak mountings in the parlor. They'll go best with the wall-paper there."

"Yes, papa."

"And I hope you won't mind, Elfrida," he added, "but I've promised that they shall have one of your paintings to raffle off in the bazar for the alterations in the Sunday-school next week."

"Oh no, papa. I shall be delighted."

Elfrida was sitting beside her mother on the sofa, and at the close of this proposition Mr. Bell came and sat there too. There was a silence for a moment while they all three confronted the line of pictures leaning against the wall. Then Elfrida began to laugh, and she went on laughing, to the astonishment of her parents, until the tears came into her eyes. She stopped as suddenly, kissed her mother and father, and went upstairs. "I'm afraid you've hurt her feelings, Leslie," said Mrs. Bell, when she had well gone.

But Elfrida's feelings had not been hurt, though one might say that the evening left her sense of humor rather sore. At that moment she was dallying with the temptation to describe the whole scene in a letter to a valued friend in Philadelphia, who would have appreciated it with mirth. In the end she did not write. It would have been too humiliating.

CHAPTER III.

"*Pas mal, parbleu!*" Lucien remarked, with pursed-out lips, running his fingers through his shock of coarse hair, and reflectively scratching the top of his big head as he stepped closer to Nádie Palicsky's elbow, where she stood at her easel in his crowded atelier. The girl turned and looked keenly into his face, seeking his eyes, which were on her work with a considering, interested look. Satisfied, she sent a glance of joyous triumph at a somewhat older woman, whose place was next, and who was listening with the amiable effacement of countenance that is sometimes a more or less successful disguise for chagrin. On this occasion it seemed to fail, for Mademoiselle Palicsky turned her attention to Lucien and her work again with a slight raising of the eyebrows and a slighter sigh. Her face assumed a gentle melancholy, as if she were pained at the exhibition of a weakness of her sex; yet it was unnecessary to be an acute observer to read there the hope that Lucien's significant phrase had not by any chance escaped her neighbor.

"The drawing of the neck," Lucien went on, "is excellently brutal." Nádie wished he would speak a little louder, but Lucien always arranged the carrying power of his voice according to the susceptibilities of the atelier. He thrust his hands into his pockets and still stood beside her, looking at her study of the nude model who posed upon a table in the midst of the students. "In you, mademoiselle," he added in a tone yet lower, "I find the woman and the artist divorced. That is a vast advantage—an immense source of power. I am growing more certain of you; you are not merely cleverly eccentric as I thought. You have a great deal that no one can teach you. You have finished that—I wish to take it downstairs to show the men. It will not be jeered at, I promise you."

"*Cher maître!* You mean it?"

"But certainly!"

The girl handed him the study with a look of almost doglike gratitude in her narrow gray eyes. Lucien had never said so much to her before, though the whole atelier had noticed how often he had been coming to her easel lately, and had disparaged her in corners accordingly. She looked at the tiny silver watch she wore in a leather strap on her left wrist—he had spent nearly five minutes with her this time, watching her work and talking to her, in itself a triumph. It was almost four o'clock, and the winter daylight was going; presently they would all stop work. Partly for the pleasure of being chaffed and envied and complimented in the anteroom in the general washing of brushes, and partly to watch Lucien's rapid progress among the remaining easels, Mademoiselle Palicsky deliberately sat down in a prematurely vacant chair, slung one slender little limb over the other, and waited. As she sat there a generous thought rose above her exultation. She hoped everybody else in the atelier had guessed what Lucien was saying to her all that while, and had seen him carry off her day's work, but not the little American. The little American, who was at least thirteen inches taller than Mademoiselle Palicsky, was sufficiently discouraged already, and it was pathetic, in view of almost a year of failure, to see how she clung to her ghost of a talent. Besides, the little American admired Nádie Palicsky, her friend, her comrade, quite enough already.

Elfrida had heard, nevertheless. She listened eagerly, tensely, as she always did when Lucien opened his lips in her neighborhood. When she saw him take the sketch to show in the men's atelier downstairs, to exhibit to that horde of animals below, whose studies and sketches and compositions were so constantly brought up for the stimulus and instruction of Lucien's women students, she grew suddenly so white that the girl who worked next her, a straw-colored Swede, asked her if she were ill, and offered her a little green bottle of salts of lavender. "It's that beast of a calorifère," the Swede said, nodding at the hideous black cylinder that stood near them; "they will always make it too hot."

Elfrida waved the salts back hastily—Lucien was coming her way. She worked seated, and as he seemed on the point of passing with merely a casual glance and an ambiguous "H'm!" she started up. The movement effectually arrested him, unintentional though it seemed. He frowned slightly, thrusting his hands deep into his coat-pockets, and looked again.

"We must find a better place for you, mademoiselle; you can make nothing of it here so close to the model, and below him thus." He would have gone on, but in spite of his intention to avert his eyes he caught the girl's glance, and something infinitely appealing in it stayed him again. "Mademoiselle," he said, with visible irritation, "there is nothing to say that I have not said many times already. Your drawing is still ladylike, your color is still pretty, and, *sapristi!* you have worked with me a year! Still," he added, recollecting himself

—Lucien never lost a student by over-candor—"considering your difficult place the shoulders are not so bad. *Continuez*, mademoiselle."

The girl's eyes were fastened immovably upon her work as she sat down again, painting rapidly in an ineffectual, meaningless way, with the merest touch of color in her brush. Her face glowed with the deepest shame that had ever visited her. Lucien was scolding the Swede roundly; she had disappointed him, he said. Elfrida felt heavily how impossible it was that *she* should disappoint him. And they had all heard—the English girl in the South Kensington gown, the rich New Yorker, Nádie's rival the Roumanian, Nádie herself; and they were all, except the last, working more vigorously for hearing. Nádie had turned her head away, and so far as the back of a neck and the tips of two ears could express oblivion of what had passed, it might have been gathered from hers. But Elfrida knew better, and she resented the pity of the pretence more than if she had met Mademoiselle Palicsky's long light gray eyes full of derisive laughter.

For a year she had been in it and of it, that intoxicating life of the Quartier Latin: so much in it that she had gladly forgotten any former one; so much of it that it had become treason to believe existence supportable under any other conditions. It was her pride that she had felt everything from the beginning; her instinctive apprehension of all that is to be apprehended in the passionate, fantastic, vivid life on the left side of the Seine had been a conscious joy from the day she had taken her tiny appartement in the Rue Porte Royale, and bought her colors and sketching-block from a dwarf-like little dealer in the next street, who assured her proudly that he supplied Henner and Dagnan-Bouveret, and moreover knew precisely what she wanted from experience. "*Moi aussi, mademoiselle, je suis artist!*" She had learned nothing, she had absorbed everything. It seemed to her that she had entered into her inheritance, and that in the possessions that throng the Quartier Latin she was born to be rich. In thinking this she had an overpowering realization of the poverty of Sparta, so convincing that she found it unnecessary to tell herself that she would never go back there. That was the unconscious pivotal supposition in everything she thought or said or did. After the first bewildering day or two when the exquisite thrill of Paris captured her indefinitely, she felt the full tide of her life turn and flow steadily in a new direction with a delight of revelation and an ecstasy of promise that made nothing in its sweep of every emotion that had not its birth and growth in art, and forbade the mere consideration of anything that might be an obstacle, as if it were a sin. She entered her new world with proud recognition of its unwritten laws, its unsanctified morale, its riotous overflowing ideals; and she was instant in gathering that to see, to comprehend these was to be thrice blessed, as not to see, not to comprehend them was to dwell in outer darkness with the bourgeois, and the "sandpaper" artists, and others who are without hope. It gave her moments of pure delight to reflect how little "the people" suspected the reality of the existence of such a world notwithstanding all they read and all they professed, and how absolutely exclusive it was in the very nature of nature; how it had its own language untranslatable, its own creed unbelievable, its own customs unfathomable by outsiders, and yet among the true-born how divinely simple recognition was. Her allegiance had the loyalty of every fibre of her being; her scorn of the world she had left was too honest to permit any posing in that regard. The life at Sparta assumed the colors and very much the significance depicted on a bit of faded tapestry; when she thought of it, it was to groan that so many of her young impressionable years had been wasted there. She hoarded her years, now that every day and every hour was suffused with its individual pleasure or interest, or that keen artistic pain which also had its value, as a sensation, in the Quartier Latin. It distressed her to think that she was almost twenty-one.

The interminable year that intervened between Elfrida's return from Philadelphia and her triumph in the matter of being allowed to go to Paris to study, she had devoted mainly to the society of the Swiss governess in the Sparta Seminary for young ladies—Methodist Episcopal—with the successful object of getting a working knowledge of French. There had been a certain amount of "young society" too, and one or two incipient love-affairs, watched with anxious interest by her father and with a harrowed conscience by her mother, who knew Elfrida's capacity for amusing herself; and unlimited opportunities had occurred for the tacit exhibition of her superiority to Sparta, of which she had not always taken advantage. But the significance of the year gathered into the French lessons; it was by virtue of these that the time had a place in her memory. Mademoiselle Joubert supplemented her instruction with a violent affection, a great deal of her society, and the most entertainingly modern of the French novels, which Brentano sent her monthly in enticing packets, her single indulgence. So that after the first confusion of a multitude of tongues in the irrelevant Parisian key Elfrida found herself reasonably fluent and fairly at ease. The illumined jargon of the atelier staid with her naturally; she never forgot a word or a phrase, and in two months she was babbling and mocking with the rest.

She lived alone; she learned readily to do it on eighty francs a month, and her appartement became charming in three weeks. She divined what she should have there, and she managed to get extraordinary bargains in mystery and history out of the dealers in such things, so cracked and so rusty, so moth-eaten and of such excellent color, that the escape of the combined effect from *banalité* was a marvel. She had a short, sharp struggle with her American taste for simple elegance in dress, and overthrew it, aiming, with some success, at originality instead. She found it easy in Paris to invest her striking personality in a distinctive costume, sufficiently becoming and sufficiently odd, of which a broad soft felt hat, which made a delightful brigand of her, and a Hungarian cloak formed important features. The Hungarian cloak suited her so extremely well that artistic considerations compelled her to wear it occasionally, I fear, when other people would have found it uncomfortably warm. In nothing that she said or did or admired or condemned was there any trace of the commonplace, except, perhaps, the desire to avoid it; it had become her conviction that she owed this to herself. She was thoroughly popular in the atelier, her *petits soupers* were so good, her enthusiasms so generous, her drawing so bad. The other pupils declared that she had a head *divinement tragique*, and for those of them she liked she sometimes posed, filling impressive parts in their weekly compositions. They all knew the little appartement in the Rue Porte Royale, more or less well according to the favor with which they were received. Nádie Palicsky perhaps knew it best—Nádie Palicsky and her friend Monsieur André Vambéry, who always accompanied her when she came to Elfrida's in the evening, finding it impossible to allow her to be out alone at night, which Nádie confessed agreeable to her vanity, but a bore.

Elfrida found it difficult in the beginning to admire the friend. He was too small for dignity, and Nádie's inspired comparison of his long black hair to "*serpents noirs*" left her unimpressed. Moreover she thought she detected about him a personal odor which was neither that of sanctity nor any other abstraction. It took time and conversation and some acquaintance with values as they obtain at the École des Beaux Arts, and the knowledge of what it meant to be "selling," to lift Monsieur Vambéry to his proper place in her regard. After that she blushed that he had ever held any other. But from the first Elfrida had been conscious of a kind of pride in her unshrinking acceptance of the situation. She and Nádie had exchanged a pledge of some sort, when Mademoiselle Palicsky bethought herself of the unconfessed fact. She gave Elfrida a narrow look, and then leaned back in her low chair and bent an imperturbable gaze upon the slender spiral of blue smoke that rose from the end of her cigarette.

"It is necessary now that you should know, petite—nobody else does, Lucien would be sure to make a fuss, but—I have a lover, and we have decided about marriage that it is ridiculous. It is a *brave âme*. You ought to know him; but if it makes any difference—"

Elfrida reflected afterward with satisfaction that she had not even changed color, though she had found the communication electric. It seemed to her that there had been something dignified, noble almost, in the answer she had made, with a smile that acknowledged the fact that the world had scruples on such accounts as these:

"*Cela m'est absolument égal!*"

So far as the life went it was perfect. The Quartier spoke and her soul answered it, and the world had nothing to compare with a conversation like that. But the question of production, of achievement, was beginning to bring her moments when she had a terrible sensation that the temperature of her passion was chilled. She had not yet seen despair, but she had now and then lost her hold of herself, and she had made acquaintance with fear. There had been no vivid realization of failure, but a problem was beginning to form in her mind, and with it a distinct terror of the solution, which sometimes found a shape in her dreams. In waking, voluntary moments she would see her problem only as an unanswerable enigma.

Yet in the beginning she had felt a splendid confidence. Her appropriation of theory had been so brilliant and so rapid, her instructive appreciation had helped itself out so well with the casual formulas of the schools, she seemed to herself to have an absolute understanding of expression. She held her social place among the others by her power of perception, and that, with the completeness of her repudiation of the bourgeois, had given her Nádie Palicsky, whom the rest found difficult, variable, unreasonable. Elfrida was certain that if she might only talk to Lucien she could persuade him of a great deal about her talent that escaped him—she was sure it escaped him—in the mere examination of her work. It chafed her always that her personality could not touch the master; that she must day after day be only the dumb, submissive pupil. She felt sometimes that there were things she might say to Lucien which would be interesting and valuable for him to hear.

Lucien was always non-committal for the first few months. Everybody said so, and it was natural enough. Elfrida set her teeth against his silences, his casual looks and ambiguous encouragements for a length of time which did infinite credit to her determination. She felt herself capable of an eternity of pain; she was proudly conscious of a willingness to oppose herself to innumerable discouragements—to back her talent, as it were, against all odds. That was historic, dignified, to be expected! But in the inmost privacy of her soul she had conceived the character of the obstacles she was prepared to face, and the list resolutely excluded any idea that it might not be worth while. Indifference and contempt cut at the very roots of her pledges to herself. As she sat listening on this afternoon to the vivid terms of Lucien's disapproval of what the Swede had done, she had a sharp consciousness of this severance.

She had nothing to say to any one in the general babble of the anteroom, and nobody noticed

her white face and resolute eyes particularly—
the Americans were always so pale and so *exalté*.
Nádie kept away from her. Elfrida had to cross
the room and bring her, with a little touch of angry
assertion upon the arm, from the middle of the
group she had drawn around her, on purpose, as her
friend knew.

"I want you to dine with me—really *dine*," she
said, and her voice was both eager and repressed.
"We will go to Babaudin's—one gets an excellent
haricot there—and you shall have that little white
cheese that you love. Come! I want you particularly. I will even make him bring champagne—
anything."

Nádie gave her a quick look and made a little
theatrical gesture of delight.

"*Quel bonheur!*" she cried for the benefit of the
others; and then in a lower tone: "But not Babaudin's, petite. André will not permit Babaudin's;
he says it is not *convenable*," and she threw up her
eyes with mock resignation. "Say Papaud's. They
keep their feet off the table at Papaud's—there are
fewer of those *bêtes des Anglais*."

"Papaud's is cheaper," Elfrida returned darkly.
"The few Englishmen who dine at Babaudin's behave perfectly well. I will not be insulted about
the cost. I'll be answerable to André. You don't

lie as a general thing, and why now? I can afford it, truly. You need not be distressed."

Mademoiselle Palicsky looked into the girl's tense face for an instant, and laughed a gay assent. But to herself she said, as she finished drying her brushes on an inconceivably dirty bit of cotton: "She has found herself out, she has come to the truth. She has discovered that it is not in her, and she is coming to me for corroboration. Well, I will not give it, me! It is extremely disagreeable, and I have not the courage. *Pourquoi donc!* I will send her to Monsieur John Kendal; she may make him responsible. He will break her, but he will not lie to her; they sacrifice all to their consciences, those English! And now, you good-natured fool, you are in for a devil of an evening!"

CHAPTER IV.

"THREE months more," Elfrida Bell said to herself next morning, in the act of boiling an egg over a tiny kerosene stove in the cupboard that served her as a kitchen, "and I will put it to every test I know. Three unflinching months! John Kendal will not have gone back to England by that time. I shall still get his opinion. If he is only as encouraging as Nádie was last night, dear thing! I almost forgave her for being so much, much cleverer than I am. Oh, letters!" as a heavy knock repeated itself upon the door of the room outside.

There was only one; it was thrust beneath the door, showing a white triangle to her expectancy as she ran out to secure it, while the fourth flight creaked under Madame Vamousin descending. She picked it up with a light heart—she was young and she had slept. Yesterday's strain had passed; she was ready to count yesterday's experience among the things that must be met. Nádie had been so sensible about it. This was a letter from home, and the American mail was not due until next day. Inside there would be news of a little pleasure trip to New York, which her father and mother had been planning lately—Elfrida constantly urged upon her parents the necessity of amusing themselves—and a remittance. The remittance would be more than usually welcome, for she was a little in debt—a mere trifle, fifty or sixty francs; but Elfrida hated being in debt. She tore the end of the envelope across with absolute satisfaction, which was only half chilled when she opened out each of the four closely written sheets of foreign letter-paper in turn and saw that the usual postal order was not there.

Having ascertained this however, she went back to her egg; in another ten seconds it would have been hard-boiled, a thing she detested. There was the egg, and there was some apricot-jam—the egg in a slender-stemmed Arabian silver cup, the jam golden in a little round dish of wonderful old blue. She set it forth, with the milk-bread and the butter and the coffee, on a bit of much mended damask with a pattern of rosebuds, and a coronet in one corner. Her breakfast gave her several sorts of pleasure.

Half an hour after it was over she was still sitting with the letter in her lap. It is possible to imagine that she looked ugly. Her dark eyes had a look of persistence in spite of fear, a line or two shot up from between her brows, her lips were pursed a little and drawn down at the corners, her chin thrust forward. Her face and her attitude helped each other to express the distinctest possible negative. Her neck had an obstinate bend; she leaned forward clasping her knees, for the moment a creature of rigid straight lines. She had hardly moved since she read the letter.

She was sorry to learn that her father had been unfortunate in business, that the Illinois Indubitable Insurance Company had failed. At his age the blow would be severe, and the prospect, after a life of comparative luxury, of subsisting even in Sparta on eight hundred dollars a year could not be an inviting one for either of her parents. When she thought of their giving up the white brick house in Columbia Avenue and going to live in Cox Street, Elfrida was thoroughly grieved. She felt the sincerest gratitude, however, that the misfortune had not come sooner, before she had learned the true significance of living, while yet it might have placed her in a state of blind irresolution which would probably have lasted indefinitely. After a year in Paris she was able to make up her mind, and this she could not congratulate herself upon sufficiently, since a decision at the moment was of such vital importance. For one point upon which Mrs. Leslie's letter insisted, regretfully but strongly, was that the next remittance, which they hoped to be able to send in a week or two, would necessarily be the last. It would be as large as they could make it; at all events it would amply cover her passage and railway expenses to Sparta, and of course she would sail as soon as it reached her. It was an elaborate letter, written in phrases which Mrs. Leslie thought she evolved, but probably remembered from a long and comprehensive course of fiction as appropriate to the occasion, and Elfrida read between the lines with some impatience how largely their trouble was softened to her mother by the consideration that it would inevitably bring her back to them. "We can bear it well if we bear it together," wrote Mrs. Bell. "You have always been our brave daughter, and your young courage will be invaluable to us now. Your talents will be our flowers by the way-side. We shall take the keenest possible delight in watching them expand, as, even under the cloud of financial adversity, we know they will."

"Dear over-confident parent," Elfrida reflected grimly at this point, "I must yet prove that I have any."

Along with the situation she studied elaborately the third page of the *Sparta Sentinel*. When it had arrived, months before, containing the best part of a long letter describing Paris, which she had

written to her mother in the first freshness of her
delighted impressions, she had glanced over it with
half-amused annoyance at the foolish parental pride
that suggested printing it. She was already too remote from the life of Sparta to care very much one
way or another, but such feeling as she had was of
that sort. And the compliments from the minister,
from various members of the Browning Club, from
the editor himself, that filtered through her mother's
letters during the next two or three weeks, made
her shrug with their absolute irrelevance to the only
praise that could thrill her and the only purpose
she held dear. Even now, when the printed lines
contained the significance of a possible resource,
she did not give so much as a thought to the flatter-
ing opinion of Sparta as her mother had conveyed it
to her. She read them over and over, relying desperately on her own critical sense and her knowledge
of what the Paris correspondent of the *Daily Dial*
thought of her chances in that direction. He, Frank
Parke, had told her once that if her brush failed she
had only to try her pen, though he made use of no
such commonplace as that. He said it, too, at the
end of half an hour's talk with her, only half an hour.
Elfrida, when she wished to be exact with her vanity, told herself that it could not have been more
than twenty-five minutes. She wished for particu-

lar reasons to be exact with it now, and she did not fail to give proper weight to the fact that Frank Parke had never seen her before that day. The Paris correspondent of the *Daily Dial* was well enough known to be of the *monde*, and rich enough to be as bourgeois as anybody. Therefore some of the people who knew him thought it odd that at his age this gentleman should prefer the indelicacies of the Quartier to those of "tout Paris," and the bad vermouth and cheap cigars of the Rue Luxembourg to the peculiarly excellent quality of champagne with which the president's wife made her social atonement to the Faubourg St. Germain. But it was so, and its being so rendered Frank Parke's opinion that Miss Bell could write if she chose to try, not only supremely valuable to her, but available for the second time if necessary, which was perhaps more important.

There would be a little more money from Sparta, perhaps one hundred and fifty dollars. It would come in a week, and after that there would be none. But a supply of it, however modest, must be arranged somehow—there were the "frais" of the atelier, to speak of nothing else. The necessity was irritatingly absolute. Elfrida wished that her scruples were not so acute about arranging it by writing for the press. "If I could think for a moment that

I had any right to it as a means of expression!" she reflected. "But I haven't. It is an art for others. And it *is* an art, as sacred as mine. I have no business to degrade it to my uses." Her mental position when she went to see Frank Parke was a cynical compromise with her artistic conscience, of which she nevertheless sincerely regretted the necessity.

The correspondent of the *Daily Dial* had a club for one side of the river and a café for the other. He dined oftenest at the café, and Elfrida's card, with "urgent" inscribed in pencil on it, was brought to him that evening as he was finishing his coffee. She had no difficulty in getting it taken in. Mr. Parke's theory was that a newspaper man gained more than he lost by accessibility. He came out immediately, furtively returning a toothpick to his waistcoat pocket—a bald, stout gentleman of middle age, dressed in loose gray clothes, with shrewd eyes, a nose which his benevolence just saved from being hawk-like, a bristling white mustache, and a pink double chin. It rather pleased Frank Parke, who was born in Hammersmith, to be so constantly taken for an American—presumably a New Yorker.

"Monsieur—" began Elfrida a little formally. She would not have gone on in French, but it was her way to use this form with the men she knew in

Paris, irrespective of their nationality, just as she invariably addressed letters which were to be delivered in Sparta, Illinois, "à madame Leslie Bell, Avenue Columbia," of that municipality.

"Miss Elfrida, I am delighted to see you," he interrupted her, stretching out one hand and looking at his watch with the other. "I am fortunate in having fifteen whole minutes to put at your disposal. At the end of that time I have an appointment with a cabinet minister, who would rather see the devil. So I must be punctual. Shall we walk a bit along these dear boulevards, or shall I get a fiacre? No? You're quite right—Paris was made for eternal walking. Now, what is it, my dear child?"

Mr. Parke had already concluded that it was money, and had fixed the amount he would lend. It was just half of what Mademoiselle Knike, of Paolo Rossi's, had succeeded in extracting from him last week. He liked having a reputation for amiability among the ateliers, but he must not let it cost too much.

Elfrida felt none of that benumbing shame which sometimes seizes those who would try literature confessing to those who have succeeded in it, and the occasion was too important for the decorative diffidence that might have occurred to her if it had been trivial. She had herself well gathered together, and she would have been concise and direct even if there had been more than fifteen minutes.

"One afternoon last September, at Nádie Palicsky's—there is no chance that you will remember, but I assure you it is so—you told me that I might, if I tried—write, monsieur."

The concentration of her purpose in her voice made itself felt where Frank Parke kept his acuter perceptions, and put them at her service.

"I remember perfectly," he said.

"*Je m'en félicite.* It is more than I expected. Well, circumstances have made it so that I must either write or scrub. Scrubbing spoils one's hands, and besides, it isn't sufficiently remunerative. So I have come to ask you whether you seriously thought so, or whether it was only politeness—*blague*—or what? I know it is horrible of me to insist like this, but you see I must." Her big dark eyes looked at him without a shadow of appeal, rather as if he were destiny and she were unafraid.

"Oh, I meant it," he returned ponderingly. "You can often tell by the way people talk that they would write well. But there are many things to be considered, you know."

"Oh, I know—whether one has any real right to write, anything to say that makes it worth while. I'm afraid I can't find that I have. But there must be scullery-maid's work in literature—in journalism, isn't there? I could do that, I thought. After all, it's only one's own art that one need keep sacred." She added the last sentence a little defiantly.

But the correspondent of the *Daily Dial* was not thinking of that aspect of the matter. "It's not a thing you can jump into," he said shortly. "Have you written anything, anywhere, for the press before?"

"Only one or two things that have appeared in the local paper at home. They were more or less admired by the people there, so far as that goes."

"Were you paid for them?"

Elfrida shook her head. "I've often heard the editor say he paid for nothing but his telegrams," she said.

"There it is, you see."

"I want to write for *Raffini's Chronicle*," Elfrida said quickly. "You know the editor of *Raffini*, of course, Mr. Parke. You know everybody. Will you do me the very great favor to tell him that I will report society functions for him at one half the price he is accustomed to pay for such writing, and do it more entertainingly?"

Frank Parke smiled. "You are courageous indeed, Miss Elfrida. That is done by a woman who is invited everywhere in her proper person, and knows 'tout Paris' like her alphabet. I believe she holds stock in *Raffini;* anyway, they would double her pay rather than lose her. You would have more chance of ousting their leader-writer."

"I should be sorry to oust anybody," Elfrida returned with dignity.

"How do you propose to help it, if you go in for doing better or cheaper what somebody else has been doing before?"

Miss Bell thought for a minute, and demonstrated her irresponsibility with a little shrug. "Then I'm very sorry," she said. "But, monsieur, you haven't told me what to do."

The illuminator of European politics for the *Daily Dial* wished heartily that it had been a matter of two or three hundred francs.

"I'm afraid I—well, I don't see how I *can* give you any very definite advice. The situation doesn't admit of it, Miss Bell. But—have you given up Lucien?"

"No. It is only that—that I must earn money to pay him."

"Oh! Home supplies stopped?"

"My people have lost all their money except barely enough to live on. I can't expect another sou."

"That's hard lines!"

"I'm awfully sorry for them. But it isn't enough, being sorry, you know. I must do something. I thought I might write for *Raffini,* for—for practice, you know—the articles they print are really very bad—and afterward arrange to send Paris letters to some of the big American newspapers. I know a woman who does it. I assure you she is quite stupid. And she is paid—but enormously!" Mr. Parke repressed his inclination to smile.

"I believe that sort of thing over there is very much in the hands of the syndicates—McClure and those fellows," he said, "and they won't look at you unless you're known. I don't want to discourage you, Miss Bell, but it would take you at least a year to form a connection. You would have to learn Paris about five times as well as you fancy you know it already, and then you would require a special course of training to find out what to write about. And then, remember, you would have to compete with people who know every inch of the ground. Now if I can be of any assistance to you *en camarade,* you know, in the matter of your passage home—"

"Thanks," Elfrida interposed quickly, "I'm not going home. If I can't write I can scrub, as I said. I must find out." She put out her hand. "I am sure there are not many of those fifteen minutes left," she said, smiling and quite undismayed. "I have to thank you very sincerely for—for sticking to the opinion you expressed when it was only a matter of theory. As soon as I justify it in practice I'll let you know."

The correspondent of the *Daily Dial* hesitated, looked at his watch and hesitated again. "There's plenty of time," he fibbed, frowning over the problem of what might be done.

"Oh no!" Elfrida said. "You are very kind, but there can't be. You will be very late, and perhaps his Excellency will have given the audience to the devil instead—or to Monsieur de Pommitz." Her eyes expressed perfect indifference. Frank Parke laughed outright. De Pommitz was his rival for every political development, and shone dangerously in the telegraphic columns of the London *World*.

"De Pommitz isn't in it this time," he said. "I'll tell you what I *might* do, Miss Elfrida. How long have you got for this—experiment?"

"Less than a week."

"Well, go home and write me an article—something locally descriptive. Make it as bright as you can, and take a familiar subject. Let me have it in three days, and I'll see if I can get it into *Raffini* for you. Of course, you know, I can't promise that they'll look at it."

"You are very good," Elfrida returned hastily, seeing his real anxiety to be off. "Something locally descriptive. I've often thought the atelier would make a good subject."

"Capital, capital! Only be very careful about personalities and so forth. *Raffini* hates giving offence. Good-bye! Here you, *cocher!* Boulevard Haussmann!"

CHAPTER V.

JOHN KENDAL had only one theory that was not received with respect by the men at Lucien's. They quoted it as often as other things he said, but always in a spirit of derision, while Kendal's ideas as a rule got themselves discussed seriously, now and then furiously. This young man had been working in the atelier for three years with marked success almost from the beginning. The first things he did had a character and an importance that brought Lucien himself to admit a degree of soundness in the young fellow's earlier training, which was equal to great praise. Since then he had found the line in the most interesting room in the Palais d'Industrie, the *cours* had twice medalled him, and Albert Wolff was beginning to talk about his *coloration délicieuse*. Also it was known that he had condescended for none of these things. His success in Paris added piquancy to his preposterous notion that an Englishman should go home and paint England and hang his work in the Academy, and made it even more unreasonable than if he had failed.

"For me," remarked André Vambéry, with a finely curled lip, "I never see an English landscape without thinking of what it would bring *par hectare*. It is *trop arrangée*, that country, all laid out in a pattern of hedges and clumps, for the pleasure of the milords. And every milord has the taste of every other milord. He will go home to perpetuate that!"

"*Si, si! Mais c'est pour sa patrie.*"

Nádie defended him. Women always did.

"Bah!" returned her lover. "*Pour nous autres artists la France est la patrie, et la France seule!* Every day he is in England he will lose—lose—lose. Enfin, he will paint the portraits of the wives and daughters of Sir Brown and Sir Smith, and he will do it as Sir Brown and Sir Smith advise. *Avec son talent unique, distinctive! Oh, je suis à bout de patience!*"

When Kendal's opinion materialized and it became known that he meant to go back in February, and would send nothing to the Salon that year, the studio tore its hair and hugged its content. All but the master, who attempted to dissuade his pupil with literal tears, of which he did not seem in the least ashamed and which annoyed Kendal very much. In fact, it was a dramatic splash of Lucien's which happened to fall upon his coat-sleeve that decided Kendal finally about the impossibility of living always in Paris. He could not take life seriously where the emotions lent themselves so easily. And Kendal thought that he ought to take life seriously, because his natural tendency was otherwise. Kendal was an Englishman with a temperament which multiplied his individuality. If his father, who was once in the Indian Staff Corps, had lived, Kendal would probably have gone into the Indian Staff Corps too. And if his mother, who was of clerical stock, had not died about the same time, it is more than likely that she would have persuaded him to the bar. With his parents the obligation to be anything in particular seemed to Kendal to have been removed, however, and he followed his inclination in the matter instead, which made him an artist. He would have found life too interesting to confine his observation of it within the scope of any profession, but of course he could have chosen none which presents it with greater fascination. To speak quite baldly about him, his intelligence and his sympathies had a wider range than is represented by any one power of expression, even the catholic brush. He had the analytical turn of the age, though it had been denied him to demonstrate what he saw except through an art which is synthetic. With a more comprehensive conception of modern tendencies and a subtler descriptive vocabulary, Kendal might have divided his allegiance between Lucien and the magazines, and ended a light-handed fiction-maker of the more refined order of realists. As it was, he made his studies for his own pleasure, and if the people he met ministered to him further than they knew, nothing came of it more than that. What he liked best to achieve was an intimate knowledge of his fellow-beings from an outside point of view. Where intimate knowledge came of intimate association he found that it usually compromised his independence of criticism, which in the Quartier Latin was a serious matter. So he rather cold-bloodedly aimed at keeping his own personality independent of his observation of other people's, and as a rule he succeeded.

That Paris had neither made Kendal nor marred him may be gathered for the first part from his contentment to go back to paint in his native land, for the second from the fact that he had a relation with Elfrida Bell which at no point verged toward the sentimental. He would have found it difficult to explain in which direction it did verge—in fact, he would have been very much surprised to know that he sustained any relation at all toward Miss Bell important enough to repay examination. The red-armed, white-capped proprietress of a *crèmerie* had effected their introduction by regretting to them jointly that she had only one helping of *compote de cerises* left, and leaving them to arrange its consumption between them. And it is safer than it would be in most similar cases to say that neither Elfrida's heavy-lidded beauty nor the smile that gave its instant attraction to Kendal's delicately eager face had much to do with the establishment of their acquaintance, such as it was. Kendal, though his virtue was not of the heroic order, would have turned a contemptuous heel upon any imputation of the sort, and Elfrida would have stared it calmly out of countenance.

To Elfrida it soon became a definite and agreeable fact that she and the flower of Lucien's had things to say to each other—things of the rare temperamental sort that say themselves seldom. Within a fortnight she had made a niche for him in that private place where she kept the images of those toward whom she sustained this peculiarly sacred obligation, and to meet him had become one of those pleasures which were in Sparta so notably unattainable. I cannot say that considerations which from the temperamental point of view might be described as ulterior had never suggested themselves to Miss Bell. She had thought of them, with a little smile, as a possible development on Kendal's part that might be amusing. And then she had invariably checked the smile, and told herself that she would be sorry, very sorry. Instinctively she separated the artist and the man. For the artist she had an admiration none the less sincere for its exaggerations, and a sympathy which she thought the best of herself; for the man, nothing, except the half-contemptuous reflection that he was probably as other men.

If Elfrida stamped herself less importantly upon the surface of Kendal's mind than he did upon hers, it may be easily enough accounted for by the multiplicity of images there before her. I do not mean to imply that all or many of these were feminine, but, as I have indicated, Kendal was more occupied with impressions of all sorts than is the habit of his fellow-countrymen, and at twenty-eight he had managed to receive quite enough to make a certain seriousness necessary in a fresh one. There was no seriousness in his impression of Elfrida. If he had gone so far as to trace its lines he would have found them to indicate a more than sl'ghtly fantastic young woman with an appreciation of certain artistic verities out of all proportion to her power to attain them. But he had not gone so far. His encounters with her were among his casual amusements; and if the result was an occasional dinner together or first night at the Folies Dramatiques, his only reflection was that a girl who could do such things and not feel compromised was rather pleasant to know, especially so clever a girl as Elfrida Bell. He did not recognize in his own mind the mingled beginnings of approval and disapproval which end in a personal theory. He was quite unaware, for instance, that he liked the contemptuous way in which she held at arm's length the moral laxities of the Quartier, and disliked the cool cynicism with which she flashed upon them there the sort of *jeu de mot* that did not make him uncomfortable on the lips of a Frenchwoman. He understood that she had nursed Nádie Palicsky through three weeks of diphtheria, during which time Monsieur Vambéry took up his residence fourteen blocks away, without any special throb of enthusiasm; and he heard her quote Voltaire on the miracles—some of her ironies were a little old-fashioned—without conscious disgust. He was willing enough to meet her on the special plane she constituted for herself—not as a woman, but as an artist and a Bohemian. But there were others who made the same claim with whom it was an affectation or a pretence, and Kendal granted it to Elfrida without any special conviction that she was more sincere than the rest. Besides, it is possible to grow indifferent, even to the unconventionalities, and Kendal had been three years in the Quartier Latin.

CHAPTER VI.

If Lucien had examined Miss Bell's work during the week of her experiment with Anglo-Parisian journalism, he would have observed that it grew gradually worse as the days went on. The devotion of the small hours to composition does not steady one's hand for the reproduction of the human muscles, or inform one's eye as to the correct manipulation of flesh tints. Besides, the model suffered from Elfrida an unconscious diminution of enthusiasm. She was finding her first serious attempt at writing more absorbing than she would have believed possible, and she felt that she was doing it better than she expected. She was hardly aware of the moments that slipped by while she dabbled aimlessly in unconsidered color meditating a phrase, or leaned back and let nothing interfere with her apprehension of the atelier with the other reproductive instinct. She did not recognize the deterioration in her work, either; and at the very moment when Nádie Palicsky, observing Lucien's neglect of her, inwardly called him a brute, Elfrida was planning to leave the atelier an hour earlier for the sake of the more urgent thing which she had to do. She finished it in five days, and addressed it to Frank Parke with a new and uplifting sense of accomplishment. The ever fresh miracle happened to her, too, in that the working out of one article begot the possibilities of half a dozen more, and the next day saw her well into another. In posting the first she had a premonition of success. She saw it as it would infallibly appear in a conspicuous place in *Raffini's Chronicle*, and heard the people of the American Colony wondering who in the world could have written it. She conceived that it would fill about two columns and a half. On Saturday afternoon, when Kendal joined her crossing the courtyard of the atelier, she was preoccupied with the form of her rebuff to any inquiries that might be made as to whether she had written it.

They walked on together, talking casually of casual things. Kendal, glancing every now and then at the wet study Elfrida was carrying home, felt himself distinctly thankful that she did not ask his opinion of it, as she had, to his embarrassment once or twice before; though it was so very bad that he was half disposed to abuse it without permission. Miss Bell seemed persistently interested in other things, however—the theatres, the ecclesiastical bill before the Chamber of Deputies, the new ambassador, even the recent improvement of the police system. Kendal found her almost tiresome. His half-interested replies interpreted themselves to her after a while, and she turned their talk upon trivialities, with a gay exhilaration which was not her frequent mood.

She asked him to come up when they arrived, with a frank cordiality which he probably thought of as the American way. He went up, at all events, and for the twentieth time admired the dainty chic of the little apartment, telling himself, also for the twentieth time, that it was extraordinary how agreeable it was to be there—agreeable with a distinctly local agreeableness whether its owner happened to be also there or not. In this he was altogether sincere, and only properly discriminating. He spent fifteen minutes wondering at her whimsical interest, and when she suddenly asked him if he really thought the race *had* outgrown its physical conditions, he got up to go, declaring it was too bad, she must have been working up back numbers of the *Nineteenth Century*. At which she consented to turn their talk into its usual personal channel, and he sat down again content.

"Doesn't the Princess Bobaloff write a charming

hand!" Elfrida said presently, tossing him a square white envelope.

"It isn't hers if it's an invitation. She has a wretched relation of a Frenchwoman living with her who does all that. May I light a cigarette?"

"You know you may. It is an invitation, but I didn't accept."

"Her soirée last night? If I'd known you had been asked I should have missed you."

" I ought to tell you," Elfrida went on, coloring a little, "that I was invited through Leila Van Camp—that ridiculously rich girl, you know, they say Lucien is in love with. The Van Camp has been affecting me a good deal lately. She says my manners are so pleasing, and besides, Lucien once told her she painted better than I did. The princess is a great friend of hers."

"Why didn't you go?" Kendal asked, without any appreciable show of curiosity. If he had been looking closely enough he would have seen that she was waiting for his question.

"Oh, it lies somehow, that sort of thing, outside my idea of life. I have nothing to say to it, and it has nothing to say to me."

Kendal smiled introspectively. He saw why he had been shown the letter. "And yet," he said, "I venture to hope that if we had met there we might have had some little conversation."

Elfrida leaned back in her chair and threw up her head, locking her slender fingers over her knee. "Of course," she said indifferently. "I understand why you should go. You must. You have arrived at a point where the public claims a share of your personality. That's different."

Kendal's face straightened out. He was too much of an Englishman to understand that a personally agreeable truth might not be flattery, and Elfrida never knew how far he resented her candor when it took the liberty of being gracious.

"I went in the humble hope of getting a good supper and seeing some interesting people," he told her. "Loti was there, and Madame Rives-Chanler, and Sargent."

"And the supper?" Miss Bell inquired, with a touch of sarcasm.

"Disappointing," he returned seriously. "I should say bad—as bad as possible." She gave him an impatient glance.

"But those people—Loti and the rest—it is only a serio-comic game to them to go the Princess Bobaloff's. They wouldn't if they could help it. They don't live their real lives in such places—among such people!"

Kendal took the cigarette from his mouth and laughed. "Your Bohemianism is quite Arcadian in its quality—deliciously fresh," he declared. "I think they do. Genius clings to respectability after a time. A most worthy and amiable lady, the Princess."

Elfrida raised the arch of her eyebrows. "Much too worthy and amiable," she ventured, and talked of something else, leaving Kendal rasped, as she sometimes did, without being in any degree aware of it.

"How preposterous it is," he said, moved by his irritation to find something preposterous, "that girls like Miss Van Camp should come here to work."

"They can't help being rich. It shows at least the germ of a desire to work out their own salvation. I think I like it."

"It shows the germ of an affectation in rather an advanced stage of development. I give her three months more to tire of snubbing Lucien and distributing caramels to the less fortunate young ladies of the studio. Then she will pack up those pitiful attempts of hers and take them home to New York, and spend a whole season in glorious apology for them."

Elfrida looked at him steadily for an instant. Then she laughed lightly. "Thanks," she said. "I see you had not forgotten my telling you that Lucien said she painted better than I did."

Kendal wondered whether he had really meant to go so far. "I am sorry," he said, "but I am afraid I had not forgotten it."

"Well, you would not say it out of ill-nature. You must have wanted me to know—what you thought."

"I think," he said seriously, "that I did—at least that I do—want you to know. It seems a pity that you should work on here—mistakenly—when there are other things that you could do well."

"'Other things' have been mentioned to me before," she returned, with a strain in her voice that she tried to banish. "May I ask what particular thing occurs to you?"

He was already remorseful. After all, what business of his was it to interfere, especially when he knew that she attached such absurd importance to his opinion? "I hardly know," he said, "but there must be something; I am convinced that there is something."

Elfrida put her elbows on a little table, and shadowed her face with her hands.

"I wish I could understand," she said, "why I should be so willing to—to go on at any sacrifice, if there is no hope in the end."

Kendal's mood of grim frankness overcame him again. "I believe I know," he said, watching her. Her hands dropped from her face, and she turned it toward him mutely.

"It is not achievement you want, but success. That is why," said he.

There was silence for a moment, broken by light footsteps on the stair and a knock. "My good friends," cried Mademoiselle Palicsky from the doorway, "have you been quarrelling?" She made a little dramatic gesture to match her words, which brought out every line of a black velvet and white corduroy dress, which would have been a horror upon an Englishwoman. Upon Mademoiselle Palicsky it was simply an admiration-point of the kind never seen out of Paris, and its effect was instantaneous. Kendal acknowledged it with a bow of exaggerated deference. "*C'est parfait!*" he said with humility, and lifted a pile of studies off the nearest chair for her.

Nádie stood still, pouting. "Monsieur is amused," she said. "Monsieur is always amused. But I have that to tell which monsieur will graciously take *au grand serieux.*"

"What is it, Nádie?" Elfrida asked, with something like dread in her voice. Nádie's air was so important, so rejoiceful.

"*Ecoutez donc!* I am to send two pictures to the Salon this year. Carolus Duran has already seen my sketch for one, and he says there is not a doubt —*not a doubt*—that it will be considered. Your congratulations, both of you, or your hearts' blood! For on my word of honor I did not expect it this year."

"A thousand and one!" cried Kendal, trying not to see Elfrida's face. "But if you did not expect it this year, mademoiselle, you were the only one who had so little knowledge of affairs," he added gaily.

"And now," Nádie went on, as if he had interrupted her, "I am going to drive in the Bois to see what it will be like when the people in the best carriages turn and say, 'That is Mademoiselle Nádie Palicsky, whose picture has just been bought for the Luxembourg.'"

She paused and looked for a curious instant at Elfrida, and then slipped quickly behind her chair. "*Embrasse moi, chérie!*" she said, bringing her face with a bird-like motion close to the other girl's.

Kendal saw an instinctive momentary aversion in the backward start of Elfrida's head, and from the bottom of his heart he was sorry for her. She pushed her friend away almost violently.

"No!" she said. "No! I am sorry, but it is too childish. We never kiss each other, you and I. And listen, Nádie: I am delighted for you, but I have a sick headache—*la migraine,* you understand. And you must go away, both of you—both of you!" Her voice raised itself in the last few words to an almost hysterical imperativeness. As they went down the stairs together Mademoiselle Palicsky remarked to Mr. John Kendal, repentant of the good that he had done:

"So she has consulted her oracle and it has barked out the truth. Let us hope she will not throw herself into the Seine!"

"Oh no!" Kendal replied. "She's horribly hurt but I am glad to believe that she hasn't the capacity for tragedy. Somebody," he added gloomily, "ought to have told her long ago."

Half an hour later the postman brought Elfrida a letter from Mr. Frank Parke, and a packet containing her manuscript. It was a long letter, very kind, and appreciative of the article, which Mr. Parke called bright and gossipy, and, if anything, too cleverly unconventional in tone. He did not take the trouble to criticise it seriously, and left Elfrida under the impression that, from his point of view at least, it had no faults. Mr. Parke had offered the article to *Raffini,* but while they might have printed it upon his recommendation, it appeared that even his recommendation could not induce them to promise to pay for it. And it was a theory with him that what was worth printing was invariably worth paying for, so he returned the manuscript to its author in the sincere hope that it might yet meet its deserts. He had been thinking over the talk they had had together, and he saw more plainly than ever the hopelessness of her getting a journalistic start in Paris, however, and he would distinctly advise her to try London instead. There were a number of ladies' papers published in London—he regretted that he did not know the editors of any of them—and amongst them, with her freshness of style, she would be sure to find an opening. Mr. Parke added the address of a lodging-house off Fleet Street, where Elfrida would be in the thick of it, and the fact that he was leaving Paris for three months or so, and hoped she would write to him when he came back. It was a letter precisely calculated to draw an unsophisticated amateur mind away from any other mortification, to pour balm upon any unrelated wound. Elfrida felt herself armed by it to face a sea of troubles. Not absolutely, but almost, she convinced herself on the spot that her solemn choice of an art had been immature, and to some extent groundless and unwarrantable; and she washed all her brushes with a mechanical and melancholy sense that it was for the last time. It was easier than she would have dreamed for her to decide to take Frank Parke's advice and go to London. The life of the Quartier had already vaguely lost in charm since she knew that she must be irredeemably a failure in the atelier, though she told herself, with a hot tear or two, that no one loved it better, more comprehendingly, than she did. Her impulse was to begin packing at once; but she put that off until the next day, and wrote two or three letters instead. One was to John Kendal. This is the whole of it:

"Please believe me very grateful for your frankness this afternoon. I have been most curiously blind. But I agree with you that there is something else, and I am going away to find it out and to do it. When I succeed I will let you know, but you shall not tell me that I have failed again.

"ELFRIDA BELL."

The other was addressed to her mother, and when it reached Mr. and Mrs. Bell in Sparta they said it was certainly sympathetic and very well written. This was to disarm one another's mind of the suspicion that its last page was doubtfully daughterly.

"In view of what are now your very limited resources, I am sure dear mother, you will understand my unwillingness to make any additional drain upon them, as I should do if I followed your wishes and came home. I am convinced of my ability to support myself, and I am not coming home. To avoid giving you the pain of repeating your request, and the possibility of your sending me money which you cannot afford to spare, I have decided not to let you know my whereabouts until I can write to you that I am in an independent position. I will only say that I am leaving Paris, and that no letters sent to this address will be forwarded. I sincerely hope you will not allow yourself to be in any way anxious about me, for I assure you that there is not the slightest need. With much love to papa and yourself,

"Always your affectionate daughter,

"ELFRIDA.

"P. S.—I hope your asthma has again succumbed to Dr. Paley."

CHAPTER VII.

THERE was a scraping and a stumbling sound in the second floor front bedroom of Mrs. Jordan's lodgings in a by-way of Fleet Street, at two o'clock in the morning. It came up to Elfrida mixed with the rattle of a departing cab over the paving-stones below, outside where the fog was lifting and showing one street-lamp to another. Elfrida in her attic had been sitting above the fog all night; her single candle had not been obscured by it. The cab had been paid and the andirons were being disturbed by Mr. Golightly Ticke, returned from the Criterion Restaurant, where he had been supping with the leading lady of the Sparkle Company, at the leading lady's expense. She could afford it better than he could, she told him, and that was extremely true, for Mr. Ticke had his capacities for light comedy still largely to prove, while Mademoiselle Phyllis Fane had almost disestablished herself upon the stage, so long and so prosperously had she pirouetted there. Mr. Golightly Ticke's case excited a degree of the large compassion which Mademoiselle Phyllis had for incipient genius of the interesting sex, and which served her instead of virtue of the more ordinary sort. He had a double claim upon it, because, in addition to being tall and fair and misunderstood by most people, with a thin nose that went beautifully with a mediæval costume, he was such a gentleman. Phyllis loosened her purse-strings instinctively, with genuine gratification, whenever this young man approached. She believed in him; he had ideas, she said, and she gave him more; in the end he would be sure to "catch on." Through the invariable period of obscurity which comes before the appearance of any star, she was in the habit of stating that he would have no truer friend than Filly Fane. She "spoke to" the manager, she pointed out Mr. Ticke's little parts to the more intimate of her friends of the press. She sent him delicate little presents of expensive cigars, scents, and soaps; she told him often that he would infallibly "get there." The fact of his having paid his own cab-fare from the Criterion on this particular morning gave him, as he found his way upstairs, almost an injured feeling of independence.

As the sounds defined themselves more distinctly, troublous and uncertain, Elfrida laid down her pen and listened.

"What an absurd boy it is!" she said. "He's trying to go to bed in the fireplace."

As a matter of fact, Mr. Ticke's stage of intoxication was not nearly so advanced as that; but Elfrida's mood was borrowed from her article, and she felt the necessity of putting it graphically. Besides, a picturesque form of stating his condition was almost due to Mr. Ticke. Mr. Ticke lived the unfettered life; he was of the elect; Elfrida reflected, as Mr. Ticke went impulsively to bed, how easy it was to discover the elect. A glance would do it, a word, the turning of an eyelid; she knew it of Golightly Ticke days before he came up in an old velvet coat, and without a shirt collar, to borrow a sheet of note paper and an envelope from her. On that occasion Mr. Ticke had half apologized for his appearance, saying, "I'm afraid I'm rather a Bohemian," in his sympathetic voice. To which Elfrida had responded, handing him the note paper, "Afraid!" and the understanding was established at once. Elfrida did not consider Mr. Ticke's other qualifications or disqualifications; that would have been a bourgeois thing to do. He was a *belle âme*, that was sufficient. He might find life difficult, it was natural and probable. She, Elfrida Bell, found it difficult. He had not succeeded yet; neither had she; therefore they had a comradeship—they and a few others—of revolt against the dull conventional British public that barred the way to success. Yesterday she had met him at the street-door, and he had stopped to remark that along the Embankment nature was making a bad copy of one of Vereschagin's pictures. When people could say things like that, nothing else mattered much. It is impossible to tell whether Miss Bell would have found room in this philosophy for the godmotherly benevolence of Mademoiselle Fane, if she had known of it, or not.

It was a long, low-roofed room in which Elfrida Bell meditated, biting the end of her pen, upon the difference it made when a fellow-being was not a Philistine; and it was not in the least like any other apartment Mrs. Jordan had to let. It was the atelier of the Rue Porte Royale transported. Elfrida had brought all her possessions with her, and took a nameless comfort in arranging them as she liked them best. "Try to feel at home," she said whimsically to her Indian zither as she hung it up. "We shall miss Paris, you and I, but one day we shall go back together." A Japanese screen wandered across the room and made a bedroom of the end. Elfrida had to buy that, and spent a day in finding a cheap one which did not offend her. The floor was bare except for a little Afghan prayer-carpet, Mrs. Jordan having removed, in suspicious astonishment, an almost new tapestry of as nice a pattern as she ever set eyes on, at her lodger's request. A samovar stood on a little square table in the corner, and beside it a tin box of biscuits. The dormer-windows were hung with Eastern stuffs, a Roman lamp stood on the mantel, a Koran-holder held Omar Khayyam second-hand, and Meredith's last novel, and "Anna Karenina," and "Salammbô," and two or three recent numbers of the *Figaro*. Here and there on the wall a Salon photograph was fastened. A study of a girl's head that Nádie had given her was stuck with a Spanish dagger over the fireplace. A sketch of Vambéry's and one of Kendal's, sacredly framed, hung where she could always see them. There was a vague suggestion of roses about the room, and a mingled fragrance of joss-sticks and cigarettes. The candle shone principally upon a little bronze Buddha, who sat lotus-shrined on the writing-table among Elfrida's papers, with an ineffable, inscrutable smile. On the top shelf of a closet in the wall a small pile of canvases gathered dust, face downward. Not a brush-mark of her own was visible. She told herself that she had done with that.

The girl sat with her long cloak about her and a blanket over her knees. Her fingers were almost nerveless with cold; as she laid down her manuscript she tried to wring warmth into them. Her face was white, her eyes were intensely wide open and wide awake; they had black dashes underneath, an emphasis they did not need. She lay back in her chair and gave the manuscript a little push toward Buddha smiling in the middle of the table. "Well?" she said, regarding him with defiant inquiry, cleverly mocked.

Buddha smiled on. The candle sputtered, and his shadow danced on three or four long thick envelopes lying behind him. Elfrida's eyes followed it.

"Oh!" said she, "you refer me to those, do you? *Ce n'est pas poli*, Buddha dear, but you are always honest, aren't you?" She picked up the envelopes and held them fanwise before her. "Tell me, Buddha, why have they all been sent back? I myself read them with interest, I who wrote them, and surely that proves something!" She pulled a page or two out of one of them, covered with her clear, conscious, handwriting, a handwriting with a dainty pose in it suggestive of inscrutable things behind the word. Elfrida looked at it affectionately, her eyes caressed the lines as she read them. "I find here true things and clever things," she went on; "Yes, and original, *quite* original things. That about Balzac has never been said before—I assure you, Buddha, it has never been said before! Yet the editor of the *Athenian* returns it to me in two days with a printed form of thanks—exactly the same printed form of thanks with which he would return a poem by Arabella Jones! Is the editor of the *Athenian* a dolt, Buddha? The *Decade* typewrites his regrets—that's better—but the *Bystander* says nothing at all but 'Declined with thanks' inside the flap of the envelope." The girl stared absently into the candle. She was not in reality greatly discouraged by these refusals; she knew that they were to be expected; indeed, they formed part of the picturesqueness of the situation in which she saw herself, alone in London, making her own fight for life as she found it worth living, by herself, for herself, in herself. It had gone on for six weeks; she thought she knew all its bitterness, and she saw nowhere the faintest gleam of coming success; yet the idea of giving it up did not even occur to her. At this moment she was reflecting that after all it was something that her articles had been returned—the editors had evidently thought them worth that much trouble—she would send them all off again in the morning, trying the *Athenian* article with the *Decade*, and the rejected of the *Decade* with the *Bystander;* they would see that she did not cringe before one failure or many. Gathering up the loose pages of one article to put them back, her eyes ran mechanically again over its opening sentences. Suddenly something magnetized them, a new interest flashed into them; with a little nervous movement she brought the page closer to the candle and looked at it carefully. As she looked she blushed crimson, and dropping the paper, covered her face with her hands.

"Oh, *Buddha!*" she cried softly, struggling with her mortification, "no wonder they rejected it! There's a mistake in the very second line— a mistake in *spelling!*" She felt her face grow hotter as she said it, and instinctively she lowered her voice. Her vanity was pricked as with a sword; for a moment she suffered keenly. Her fabric of hope underwent a horrible collapse; the blow was at its very foundation. While the minute hand of her mother's old-fashioned gold watch travelled to its next point, or for nearly as long as that, Elfrida was under the impression that a person who spelled "artificially" with one *l* could never succeed in literature. She believed she had counted the possibilities of failure. She had thought of style, she had thought of sense—she had never thought of spelling! She began with a penknife to make the word right, and almost fearfully let herself read the first few lines. "There are no more!" she said to herself, with a sigh of relief. Turning the page, she read on, and the irritation began to fade out of her face.

She turned the next page and the next, and her eyes grew interested, absorbed, enthusiastic. There were some more, one or two, but she did not see them. Her house of hope built itself again. "A mere slip," she said, reassured; and then, as her eye fell on a little fat dictionary that held down a pile of papers, "But I'll go over them all in the morning, to make sure, with *that*."

Then she turned with new pleasure to the finished work of the night, settled the sheets together, put them in an envelope, and addressed it:

>   *The Editor,*
>   *The Consul,*
>   *6 Tibby's Lane,*
>   *Fleet Street, E. C.*

She hesitated before she wrote. Should she write "The Editor" only, or "George Alfred Curtis, Esq.," first, which would attract his attention perhaps, as coming from somebody who knew his name. She had a right to know his name, she told herself; she had met him once in the happy Paris days. Kendal had introduced him to her, in a brief encounter at the Salon, and she remembered the appreciativeness of the glance that accompanied the stout middle-aged English gentleman's bow. Kendal had told her then that Mr. Curtis was the editor of the *Consul*. Yes, she had a right to know his name. And it might make the faintest shadow of a difference—but no, "The Editor" was more dignified, more impersonal; her article should go in upon its own merits, absolutely upon its own merits; and so she wrote.

It was nearly three o'clock, and cold, shivering cold. Mr. Golightly Ticke had wholly subsided. The fog had climbed up to her, and the candle showed it clinging to the corners of the room. The water in the samovar was hissing. Elfrida warmed her hands upon the cylinder and made herself some tea. With it she disposed of a great many sweet biscuits from the biscuit box, and thereafter lighted a cigarette. As she smoked she re-read an old letter, a long letter in a flowing foreign hand, written from among the haymakers at Barbizon, that exhaled a delicate perfume. Elfrida had read it thrice for comfort in the afternoon; now she tasted it, sipping here and there with long enjoyment of its deliciousness. She kissed it as she folded it up, with the silent thought that this was the breath of her life, and soon—oh, passably soon—she could bear the genius in Nádie's eyes again.

Then she went to bed. "You little brute," she said to Buddha, who still smiled as she blew out the candle, "can't you forget it?"

CHAPTER VIII.

MISS BELL arose late the next morning, which was not unusual. Mrs. Jordan had knocked three times vainly, and then left the young lady's chop and coffee outside the door on the landing. If she *would* 'ave it cold, Mrs. Jordan reasoned, she would, and more warnin' than knockin' three times no livin' bean could expect. Mrs. Jordan went downstairs uneasy in her mind, however. The matter of Miss Bell's breakfast generally left her uneasy in her mind. It was not in reason, Mrs. Jordan thought, that a young littery lady should keep that close, for Elfrida's custom of having her breakfast deposited outside her door was as invariable as it was perplexing. Miss Bell was as charming to her landlady as she was to everybody else, but Mrs. Jordan found a polite pleasantness that permitted no opportunity for expansion whatever more stimulating to the curiosity and irritating to the mind generally than the worst of bad manners would have been. That was the reason she knocked three times when she brought up Miss Bell's breakfast. At Mr.

Ticke's door she wrapped once, and cursorily at that. Mr. Ticke was as conversational as you please on all occasions, and besides, Mr. Ticke's door was usually half open. The shroud of mystery in which Mrs. Jordan wrapped her "third floor front" grew more impenetrable as the days went by. Her original theory, which established Elfrida as the heroine of the latest notorious divorce case, was admirably ingenious, but collapsed in a fortnight with its own weight. "Besides," Mrs. Jordan reasoned, "if it 'ad been that person, ware is the corrispondent all this time? There's been nothin' in the shape of a corrispondent hangin' round *this* house, for I've kep' my eye open for one. I give 'er up," said Mrs. Jordan darkly, "that's wot I do, an' I only 'ope I won't find 'er suicided on charcoal some mornin' like that pore young poetiss in yesterday's paper."

Another knock, half an hour later, found Elfrida finishing her coffee. Out-of-doors the world was gray, the little square windows were beaten with rain. Inside the dreariness was redeemed to the extent of a breath, a suggestion. An essence came out of the pictures and the trappings, and blended itself with the lingering fragrance of the joss-sticks and the roses and the cigarettes in a delightful manner. The room was almost warm with it. It seemed to centre in Elfrida; as she sat beside the writing-table, whose tumultuous papers had been pushed away to make room for the breakfast dishes, she was instinct with it.

Miss Bell glanced hurriedly around the room. It was unimpeachable—not so much as a strayed collar interfered with its character as an apartment where a young lady might receive. "Come in," she said. She knew the knock.

The door opened slowly to a hesitating push, and disclosed Mr. Golightly Ticke by degrees. Mr. Ticke was accustomed to boudoirs less rigid in their exclusiveness, and always handled Miss Bell's door with a certain amount of embarrassment. If she wanted a chance to whisk anything out of the way he would give her that chance. Fully in view of the lady and the coffee-pot Mr. Ticke made a stage bow. "Here is my apology," he said, holding out a letter; "I found it in the box as I came in."

It was another long thick envelope, and in its upper left-hand corner was printed, in early English lettering, *The St. George's Gazette*. Elfrida took it with the faintest perceptible change of countenance. It was another discomfiture, but it did not prevent her from opening her dark eyes with a remote effect of pathos entirely disconnected with its reception. "And you climbed all these flights to give it to me!" she said, with gravely smiling plaintiveness. "Thank you. Why should you have been so good? Please, please sit down."

Mr. Ticke looked at her expressively. "I don't know, Miss Bell, really. I don't usually take much trouble for people. I say it without shame. Most people are not worth it. You don't mind my saying that you're an exception, though. Besides, I'm afraid I had my eye on my reward."

"You're reward!" Elfrida repeated. Her smiling comprehension insisted that it did not understand.

"The pleasure of saying good-morning to you. But that is an inanity, Miss Bell, and unworthy of me. I should have left you to divine it."

"How could I divine an inanity in connection with you?" she answered, and her eyes underlined her words. When he returned, "Oh, you always parry!" she felt a little thrill of pleasure with herself. "How did it go—last night?" she asked.

"Altogether lovely. Standing room only, and the boxes taken for a week. I find myself quite adorable in my little part now. I *feel* it, you know. I am James Jones, a solicitor's clerk, to my fingers' ends. My nature changes, my environment changes, the instant I go on. But a little thing upsets me. Last night I had to smoke a cigar—the swell of the piece gives me a cigar—and he gave me a poor one. It wasn't in tone—the unities required that he should give me a good cigar. See? I felt quite confused for the moment."

Elfrida's eyes had strayed to the corner of her letter. "If you want to read that," continued Mr. Ticke, "I know you won't mind me."

"Thanks," said Elfrida calmly. "I've read it already. It's a rejected article."

"My play came back again yesterday for the thirteenth time. The fellow didn't even look at it. I know, because I stuck the second and third pages together as if by accident, and when it came back they were still stuck. And yet these men pretend to be on the lookout for original work! It's a thrice beastly world, Miss Bell."

Elfrida widened her eyes again and smiled with a vague impersonal winningness. "I suppose one ought not to care," said she, "but there is the vulgar necessity of living."

"Yes," agreed Mr. Ticke; and then sardonically: "Waterloo Bridge at ebb tide is such a nasty alternative. I could never get over the idea of the drainage."

"Oh, I know a better way than that." She chose her words deliberately. "A much better way. I keep it here," holding up the bent little finger of her left hand. It had a clumsy silver ring on it, square and thick in the middle, bearing deep-cut

Sanskrit letters. "It is a dear little alternative," she went on, "like a bit of brown sugar. Rather a nice taste, I believe,—and no pain. When I am quite tired of it all I shall use this, I think. My idea is that it's weak to wait until you can't help it. Besides, I could never bear to become—less attractive than I am now."

"Poison!" said Mr. Golightly Ticke, with an involuntarily horrified face. Elfrida's hand was hanging over the edge of the table, and he made as if he would examine the ring without the formality of asking leave.

She drew her fingers away instantly. "In the vernacular," she answered coolly. "You may not touch it."

"I beg your pardon. But how awfully chic!"

"It *is* chic, isn't it? Not so very old, you know." Elfrida raised her eyebrows and pursed her lips a little. "It came from Persia. They still do things like that in those delightful countries. And I've had it tested. There's enough to—satisfy—three people. When you are quite sure you want it I don't mind sharing with you. If you are going out, Mr. Ticke, will you post this for me? It's a thing about American social ideals, and I'm trying the *Consul* with it."

"Delighted. But if I know the editor of the *Consul*, it won't get two minutes' consideration."

"No?"

"Being the work of a lady, no. Doesn't matter how good it is. The thing to know about the *Consul* man is this. He's very nice to ladies—can't resist ladies; consequence is, the paper's half full of ladies' copy every week. I know, because a cousin of mine writes for him, and most unsympathetic stuff it is. Yet it always goes in, and she gets her three guineas a week as regularly as the day comes. But her pull is that she knows him personally, and she's a damned pretty woman."

Elfrida followed him with interest. "Is she as pretty as I am?" she asked, purely for information.

"Lord, no!" Mr. Ticke responded warmly. "Besides, you've got style, and distinction, and ideas. Any editor would appreciate your points, once you saw him. But you've got to see him first. My candid advice is *take* this to the *Consul* office."

Elfrida looked at him in a way which baffled him to understand. "I don't think I can do that," she said slowly; and then added, "I don't know."

"Well," he said, "I'll enter my protest against the foolishness of doing it this way by refusing to post the letter." Mr. Ticke was tremendously in earnest, and threw it dramatically upon the table. "You may be a George Eliot or a—an Elizabeth Barrett Browning, but in these days you want every advantage, Miss Bell, and women who succeed understand that."

Elfrida's face was still enigmatic, so engimatic that Mr. Ticke felt reluctantly constrained to stop. "I must pursue the even tenor of my way," he said airily, looking at his watch. "I've an engagement to lunch at one. *Don't* ask me to post that article, Miss Bell. And by the way," as he turned to go, "I haven't a smoke about me. Could you give me a cigarette?"

"Oh yes," said Elfrida, without looking at him, "as many as you like," and she pushed an open box toward him; but she had an absent, considering air that did not imply any idea of what she was doing.

"Thanks, only one. Or perhaps two—there now, two! How good these little Hafiz fellows are! Thanks awfully. Good-bye!"

"Good-bye," said Elfrida, with her eyes on the packet addressed to the editor of the *Consul;* and Mr. Golightly Ticke tripped downstairs. She had not looked at him again.

She sat thinking, thinking. She applied herself first to stimulate the revolt that rose within her against Golightly Ticke's advice—his intolerably, no, his forgetfully presumptuous advice. She would be just to him: he talked so often to women with whom such words would carry weight, for an instant he might fail to recognize that she was not one of those. It was absurd to be angry, and not at all in accordance with any theory of life that operated in Paris. Instinctively, at the thought of a moral indignation upon such slender grounds in Paris she gave herself the benefit of a thoroughly expressive Parisian shrug. And how they understood success in Paris! Beasts!

And yet it was all in the game. It was a matter of skill, of superiority, of puppet-playing. One need not soil one's hands—in private one could always laugh. She remembered how Nádie had laughed when three bunches of roses from three different art critics had come in together—how inextinguishably Nádie had laughed. It was in itself a success of a kind. Nádie had no scruples, except about her work. She went straight to her end, believing it to be an end worth arriving at by any means. And now Nádie would presently be *très en vue—très en vue!* After all, it was a much finer thing to be scrupulous about one's work—that was the real morality, the real life. Elfrida closed her eyes and felt a little shudder of consciousness of how real it was. When she opened them again she was putting down her protest with a strong hand, crushing her rebellious instincts unmercifully. She did not allow herself a moment's self-deception. She did not insult her intelligence by the argument that it was a perfectly harmless and proper thing to offer a piece of work to an editor in person—that everybody did it—that she might thereby obtain some idea of what would suit his paper if her article did not. She was perfectly straightforward in confronting Golightly Ticke's idea, and she even disrobed it, to her own consciousness, of any garment of custom and conventionality it might have had to his. Another woman might have taken it up and followed it without an instant's hesitation, as a matter concerning which there could be no doubt, a matter of ordinary expediency—of course a man would be nicer to a woman than to another man; they always were; it was natural. But Elfrida, with her merciless insight, had to harden her heart and ply her self-respect with assurances that it was all in the game, and it was a superb thing to be playing the game. Deliberately she chose the things she looked best in, and went out.

CHAPTER IX.

THE weather had cleared to a compromise. The dome of St. Paul's swelled dimly out of the fog as Elfrida turned into Fleet Street, and the railway bridge that hangs over the heads of the people at the bottom of Ludgate Hill seemed a curiously solid structure connecting space with space. Fleet Street, wet and brown, and standing in all unremembered fashions, lifted its antiquated head and waited for more rain; the pavements glistened briefly, till the tracking heels of the crowd gave them back their squalor; and there was everywhere that newness of turmoil that seems to burst even in the turbulent streets of the City when it stops raining. The girl made her way toward Charing Cross with the westward-going crowd. It went with a steady, respectable jog-trot, very careful of its skirts and umbrellas and the bottoms of its trousers; she took pleasure in hastening past it with her light gait. She would walk to the *Consul* office, which was in the vicinity of the Haymarket; indeed, she must, for the sake of economy. "I ought really to be *very* careful," thought Elfrida. "I've only eight sovereigns left, and I can't—oh, I *can't* ask them for any more at home." So she went swiftly on, pausing once before a picture-dealer's in the Strand to make a mocking mouth at the particularly British quality of the art which formed the day's exhibit, and once to glance at a news-stand where two women of the street, one still young and pretty, the other old and foul, were buying the *Police Gazette* from a stolid-faced boy. "What a subject for Nádie," she said to herself, smiling, and hurried on. Twenty yards further a carter's horse lay dying with its head upon the pavement. She made an impulsive détour of nearly half a mile to avoid passing the place, and her thoughts recurred painfully to the animal half a dozen times. The rain came down again before she reached the *Consul* office; a policeman misinformed her, she had a difficulty in finding it. She arrived at last, with damp skirts and muddy boots. It had been a long walk, and the article upon American social ideals was limp and spotted. A door confronted her, flush with the street. She opened it, and found herself at the bottom of a flight of stairs, steep, dark, and silent. She hesitated a moment, and then went up. At the top another closed door met her, with *The Consul* painted in black letters on the part of it that consisted of ground glass somewhat the worse for pencil-points and finger-nails. Elfrida lifted her hand to knock, then changed her mind and opened the door.

It was a small room lined on two sides with deal compartments bulging with dusty papers. There were two or three shelves of uninteresting-looking books, and a desk which extended into a counter. The upper panes of the window were ragged with cobwebs, and the air of the place was redolent of stale publications. A thick-set little man in spectacles sat at the desk. It was not Mr. Curtis.

The thick-set man rose as Elfrida entered, and came forward a dubious step or two. His expression was not encouraging.

"I have called to see the editor, Mr. Curtis," said she.

"The editor is not here."

"Oh, isn't he? I'm sorry for that. When is he likely to be in? I want to see him particularly."

"He only comes here once a week, for about an hour," replied the little man, reluctant even to say so much. "But I could see that he got a letter."

"Thanks," returned Elfrida. "At what time and on what day does he usually come?"

"That I'm not at liberty to say," the occupant of the desk replied briefly, and sat down again.

"Where *is* Mr. Curtis?" Elfrida asked. She had

not counted upon this. To the physical depression of her walk there added itself a strong disgust with the unsuccessful situation. She persisted, knowing what she would have to suffer from herself if she failed.

"Mr. Curtis is in the country. I cannot possibly give you his address. You can write to him here, and the letter will be forwarded. But he only sees people by appointment—especially ladies," the little man added, with a half-smile which had more significance in it than Elfrida could bear. Her face set itself against the anger that burned up in her, and she walked quickly from the door to the desk, her wet skirts swishing with her steps. She looked straight at the man, and began to speak in a voice of constraint and authority.

"You will be kind enough to get up," she said, "and listen to what I have to say." The man got up instantly.

"I came here," she went on, "to offer your editor an article—this article;" she drew out the manuscript and laid it before him. "I thought from the character of the contributions to last week's number of the *Consul* that he might very well be glad of it."

Her tone reduced the man to silence. Mechanically he picked up the manuscript and fingered the leaves.

"Read the first few sentences, please," said Elfrida.

"I've nothing to do with that department, miss—"

"I have no intention whatever of leaving it with you. But I shall be obliged if you will read the first few sentences." He read them, the girl standing watching him.

"Now," said she, "do you understand?" She took the pages from his hand and returned them to the envelope.

"Yes, miss—it's certainly interesting, but—"

"Be quite sure you understand," said Elfrida, as the ground-glass door closed behind her.

Before she reached the foot of the staircase she was in a passion of tears. She leaned against the wall in the half darkness of the passage, shaking with sobs, raging with anger and pity, struggling against her own contempt. Gradually she gained a hold upon herself, and as she dried her eyes finally she lost all feeling but a heavy sense of failure. She sat down faintly on the lowest step, remembering that she had eaten nothing since breakfast, and fanned her flushed face with the sheets of her manuscript. She preferred that even the unregarding London streets should not see the traces of her distress. She was still sitting there, ten minutes later, when the door opened and threw the gray light from outside over her. She had found her feet before Mr.

Curtis had fairly seen her. He paused, astonished, with his gloved hand upon the knob. The girl seemed to have started out of the shadows, and the emotion of her face dramatized its beauty. She made a step toward the door.

"Can I do anything for you?" asked the editor of the *Consul*, taking off his hat.

"Nothing, thank you," Elfrida replied, looking beyond him. "Unless you will kindly allow me to pass."

It was still raining doggedly, as it does in the the late afternoon. Elfrida thought with a superlative pang of discomfort of the three or four blocks that lay between her and the nearest bake-shop. She put up her umbrella, gathered her skirts up behind, and started wearily for the Haymarket. She had never in her life felt so tired. Suddenly a thrill of consciousness went up from her left hand —the hand that held her skirts—such a thrill as is known only to the sex that wills to have its pocket there. She made one or two convulsive confirmatory clutches at it from the outside, then, with a throe of actual despair, she thrust her hand into her pocket. It was a crushing fact, her purse was gone— her purse that held the possibilities of her journalistic future molten and stamped in eight golden sovereigns—her purse!

Elfrida cast one hopeless look at the pavement behind her before she allowed herself to realize the situation. Then she faced it, addressing a dainty French oath to the necessity. "Come," she said to herself, "now it begins to be really amusing—*la vraie comédie.*" She saw herself in the part—it was an artistic pleasure—alone, in a city of melodrama, without a penny, only her brains. Besides, the sense of extremity pushed and concentrated her; she walked on with new energy and purpose. As she turned into the Haymarket a cab drew up almost in front of her. Through its rain-beaten glass front she recognized a face—Kendal's. His head was thrown back to speak to the driver through the roof. In the instant of her glance Elfrida saw that he wore a bunch of violets in his button-hole, and that he was looking splendidly well. Then, with a smile that recognized the dramatic value of his appearance at the moment, she lowered her umbrella and passed on, unseen.

Almost gaily she walked into a pawnbroker's shop, and obtained with perfect nonchalance five pounds upon her mother's watch. She had no idea that she ought to dispute the dictum of the bald young man with the fishy eyes and the high collar. It did not occur to her that she was paid too little. What she realized was that she had wanted to pawn something all her life—it was a deliciously effective extremity. She reserved her rings with the distinct purpose of having the experience again. Then she made a substantial lunch at a rather expensive restaurant. "It isn't time yet," she thought, "for crusts and dripping," and tipped the waiter a shilling, telling him to get her a cab. As she turned into the Strand she told the cabman to drive slowly, and made him stop at the first newspaper office she saw. As she alighted a sense of her extravagance dawned upon her, and she paid the man off. Then she made a resolutely charming ascent to the editorial rooms of the *Illustrated Age.*

Twenty minutes later she came down again, and the door was opened for her by Mr. Arthur Rattray, one of the sub-editors, a young man who had already distinguished himself on the staff of the *Age* by his intelligent perception of paying matter, and his enterprise in securing it. Elfrida continued to carry her opinions upon the social ideals of her native democracy in their much-stained envelope, but there was a light in her eyes which seemed to be the reflection of success.

"It's still raining," said the young man cheerfully.

"So it is," Elfrida responded. "And—oh, how atrocious of me!—I've left my umbrella in the cab!"

"Hard luck!" exclaimed Mr. Rattray; "an umbrella is an organic part of one in London. Shall I stop this 'bus?"

"Thanks, no. I'll walk, I think. It's only a little way. I shan't get wet. Good-afternoon!" Elfrida nodded to him brightly and hurried off; but it could not have occasioned her surprise to find Mr. Rattray beside her a moment later with a careful and attentive umbrella, and the intention of being allowed to accompany her that little way. By the time they arrived Mr. Rattray had pledged himself to visit Scotland Yard next day in search of a dark brown silk *en tout cas* with a handle in the similitude of an ivory mummy.

"Are these your diggings?" he asked, as they reached the house. "Why, Ticke lives here too—the gentle Golightly—do you know him?" Elfrida acknowledged her acquaintance with Mr. Ticke, and Mr. Rattray hastened to deprecate her thanks for his escort. "Remember," he said, "no theories, no fine writing, no compositions. Describe what you've seen and know, and give it a tang, an individuality. And so far as we are concerned, I think we could use that thing you proposed about the Latin Quarter, with plenty of anecdote, very well. But you must make it short."

CHAPTER X.

KENDAL mounted to Elfrida's *appartement* in the Rue Porte Royale to verify the intimation of her departure, or happily to forestall its execution, the morning after her note reached him. He found it bare and dusty. A workman was mending the stove; the concierge stood looking on, with her arms folded above the most striking feature of her personality. Every vestige of Elfrida was gone, and the tall windows were open, letting the raw February air blow through. Outside the sunlight lay in squares and triangles on the roofs, and gave the place its finishing touch of characterlessness. Yes, truly, mademoiselle had gone, the evening before. Was monsieur then not aware? The concierge was of opinion that mademoiselle had had bad news, but her tone implied that no news could be quite bad enough to justify the throwing up of such desirable apartments upon such short notice. Mademoiselle had left in such haste that she had forgotten both to say where she was going and to leave an address for letters; and it would not be easy to surpass the consciousness of injury with which the concierge demanded what she was to say to the *facteur* on the day of the post from America, when there were always four or five letters for mademoiselle. Monsieur would be *bien amiable* if he would allow that they should be directed to him. Upon reflection monsieur declined this responsibility. With the faintest ripple of resentment at being left out of Elfrida's confidence, he stated to himself that it would be intrusive. He advised the concierge to keep them for a week or two, during which Miss Bell would be sure to remember to send for them, and turned to go.

"*Mademoiselle est allée à la Gare du Nord,*" added the concierge, entirely aware that she was contributing a fact to Kendal's mental speculation, and wishing it had a greater intrinsic value. But Kendal merely raised his eyebrows in polite acknowledgment of unimportant information. "En effet!" he said, and went away. Nevertheless he could not help reflecting that *Gare du Nord* probably meant Calais, and Calais doubtless meant England, probably London. As he thought of it he assured himself that it was London, and his irritation vanished at the thought of the futility of Elfrida in London. It gave him a half curious, half solicitous amusement instead. He pictured her with her Hungarian peasant's cloak and any one of her fantastic hats in the conventional highways he knew so well, and smiled. "She will have to take herself differently there," he reflected, without pausing to consider exactly what he meant by it, "and she'll find that a bore." As yet he himself had never taken her differently so far as he was aware, and in spite of the obvious provocation of her behavior it did not occur to him to do it now. He reflected with a shade of satisfaction that she knew his London address. When she saw quite fit she would doubtless inform him as to what she was doing and where she might be found. He smiled again at the thought of the considerations which Elfrida would put into the balance against the pleasure of seeing him. They were not humiliating; he was content to swing high on the other side indefinitely; but he admitted to himself that she had taken a pleasure out of Paris for him, and went back to his studio missing it. He went on missing it for quite two days, at the end of which he received an impetuous visit—excessively impetuous considering the delay—from Nádie Palicsky. In its course Mademoiselle Palicsky declared herself robbed and wronged by "*cette incomprise d'Americaine*," whom she loved— but *loved*, did he understand? No, it was not probable that he understood—what did a man know of love? As much perhaps as that flame—Kendal permitted himself the luxury of an open fire. Nádie stared into it for a moment with cynical eyes. Under the indirect influence of Kendal's regard they softened.

"She always understood! It was a joy to show her anything. She interpreted Bastien Lepage better than I—indeed that is true—but only with her soul, she had no hands. Yes, I loved her, and she was good for me. I drew three breaths in her presence for one in her absence. And she has taken herself away; even in her letter—I had a line too—she was as remote as a star! I hope," continued Nádie, with innocent candor, as she swung her little feet on the corner of Kendal's table, "that you do not love her too. I say prayers to *le bon Dieu* about it. I burn candles."

"And why?" Kendal asked, with a vigorous twist of his palette knife.

"Because you are such a beast," she responded calmly, watching his work with her round cleft chin in the shell of her hand. "That's not bad, you know. That nearest girl sitting on the grass is almost felt. But if you show it to the English they will be so shocked that they will use lorgnettes to hide their confusion. Ah!" she said, jumping down, "here am I wasting myself upon you, with a carriage *à l'heure!* You are not worth it," and she went. After that it seemed to Kendal that he did not miss Elfrida so much. Certainly it never occurred to him to hasten his departure by a day on her account, and there came a morning when he drove through Bloomsbury and realized that he had not thought about her for a fortnight. The British Museum suggested her to him there—the British Museum, and the certainty that within its massive walls a number of unimaginative young women in collarless sage-green gowns were copying casts of antique sculptures at that moment. But he did not allow himself to suppose that she could possibly be among them.

He sniffed London all day with a home-returning satisfaction in her solidity and her ugliness and her low-toned fogs and her great throbbing unostentatious importance, which the more flippant capital seemed to have intensified in him. He ordered the most British luncheon he could think of, and reflected upon the superiority of the beer. He read the leaders in the *Standard* through to the bitter end, and congratulated himself and the newspaper that there was no rag of an absurd *feuilleton* to distract his attention from the importance of the news of the day. He remembered all sorts of acquaintances that Paris had foamed over for months; his heart warmed to a certain whimsical old couple who lived in Park Street and went out to walk every morning after breakfast with their poodle. He felt disposed to make a formal call upon them and inquire after the poodle. It was perhaps with an unconscious desire to make rather more of the idyl of his homecoming that he went to see the Cardiffs instead, who were his very old friends, and lived in Kensington Square.

As he turned out of Kensington High Street into a shoppy little thoroughfare, and through it to this quiet, neglected high-nosed old locality, he realized with an added satisfaction that he had come back to Thackeray's London. One was apt, he reflected, with a charity which he would not have allowed himself always, to undervalue Thackeray in these days. After all, he once expressed London so well that now London expressed him, and that was something.

Kendal found the Cardiffs—there were only two, Janet and her father—at tea, and the Halifaxes there, four people he could always count on to be glad to see him. It was written candidly in Janet's face—she was a natural creature—as she asked him how he dared to be so unexpected. Lady Halifax cried out robustly from the sofa to know how many pictures he had brought back; and Miss Halifax, full of the timid enthusiasm of the well-brought-up elderly English girl, gave him a sallow but agreeable regard from under her ineffective black lace hat, and said what a surprise it was. When they had all finished, Lawrence Cardiff took his elbow off the mantelpiece, changed his cup into his other hand to shake hands, and said, with his quiet, clean-shaven smile, "So you're back!"

"Daddy has been hoping you would be here soon," said Miss Cardiff. "He wants the support of your presence. He's been daring to enumerate 'Our Minor Artists' in the *Brown Quarterly*, and his position is perfectly terrible. Already he's had forty-one letters from friends, relatives, and picture-dealers suggesting names he has 'doubtless forgotten.' Poor daddy says he never knew them."

"Has he mentioned me?" asked Kendal, sitting down squarely with his cup of tea.

"He has not."

"Then it's in the character of the uncomplaining left-over that I'm wanted, the modest person who waits until he's better. I refuse to act. I'll go over to the howling majority."

"*You* will never be a minor artist, Mr. Kendal," ventured Miss Halifax.

"Certainly not. You will rise to greatness at a bound," said Lady Halifax, with substantial conviction and an illustrative wave of a fat well-gloved hand with a doubled-up fragment of bread and butter between the thumb and forefinger, "or we shall be much disappointed in you."

"It's rapidly becoming a delicate compliment to have been left out," Mr. Cardiff remarked, with melancholy.

"Some of those you've honored with your recognition are the maddest of all, aren't they, daddy, as we say in America! Dear old thing, you *are* in a perilous case, and who is to take you round at the Private Views this year—that's the question of the hour! You needn't depend upon me. There won't be a soul on the line that you haven't either put in or left out!"

"It was a fearful thing to write about," Kendal responded comfortably. "He deserves all the consequences. Let him go round alone." Under the surface of his thoughts was a pleased recognition of how little a fresh-colored English girl changes in three years. Looking at Miss Halifax's hat, it occurred to him that it was an agreeable thing not to be eternally "struck" by the apparel of women—so forcibly that he almost said it. "What have you been doing?" he asked Janet.

"Wonders," Lady Halifax responded for her. "I can't think where she gets the energy or the brains—"

"Can't you?" her father interrupted. "Upon my word!" Mr. Cardiff had the serious facial muscles of a comedian, and the rigid discipline he was compelled to give them as a professor of Oriental tongues of London University intensified their effect when it was absurd. The rest laughed, and his cousin went on to say that she wished *she* had the gift. Her daughter echoed her, looking at Janet in a way that meant she would say it, whatever the consequences might be.

"I must see something," said Kendal, "immediately."

"*See* something!" exclaimed Lady Halifax. "Well, look in the last number of the *London Magazine*. But you'll please show something first."

"Yes, indeed!" Miss Halifax echoed.

"When will you be ready for inspection?" Mr. Cardiff asked.

"Come on Thursday, all of you. I'll show you what there is."

"Will you give us our tea?" Miss Halifax inquired, with a nervous smile.

"Of course. And there will be buns. You will do me the invaluable service of representing the opinion of the British public in advance. Will Thursday suit?"

"Perfectly," Lady Halifax replied. "The old rooms in Bryanston Street, I suppose?"

"Thursday won't suit us," Janet put in decisively. "No, papa; I've got people coming here to tea. Besides, Lady Halifax is quite equal to representing the whole British public by herself, aren't you, dear?" That excellent woman nodded with a pretence of loftily consenting, and her daughter gave Janet rather a suspicious glance. "Daddy and I will come another day," Janet went on in reassuring tones; "but we shall expect buns too, remember."

Then they talked of the crocuses in Kensington Gardens; and of young Skeene's new play at the Princess's—they all knew young Skeene, and wished him well; and of Framley's forthcoming novel—Framley, who had made his noble reputation by portrait-painting—good old Framley—how would it go?

"He knows character," Kendal said.

"That's nothing now," retorted Lawrence Cardiff. "Does he know where it comes from and where it's going to? And can he choose? And has he the touch? And hasn't he been too long a Royal Academician and a member of the Church of England, and a believer in himself? Oh no! Framley hasn't anything to tell this generation that he couldn't say best on canvas."

"Well," said Lady Halifax disconcertingly, "I suppose the carriage is at the door, Lawrence, but you might just send to inquire. The horses stand so badly, I told Peters he might take them round and round the square."

Cardiff looked at her with amused reproach, and rang the bell; and Janet begged somebody or anybody to have another cup of tea. The Halifaxes always tried Janet.

They went at last, entreating Cardiff, to his annoyance, not to come down the narrow winding stair with them to their carriage. To him no amount of familiar coming and going could excuse the most trivial of such negligences. He very often put Janet into her cab, always if it rained.

The moment they left the room a new atmosphere created itself there for the two that remained. They sought each other's eyes with the pleasantest sense of being together in reality for the first time, and though Janet marked it by nothing more significant than a suggestion that Kendal should poke the fire, there was an appreciable admission in her tone that they were alone and free to talk, which he recognized with great good-will. He poked the fire, and she on her low chair, clasping her knee with both hands, looked almost pretty in the blaze. There had always been between them a distinct understanding, the understanding of good-fellowship and ideas of work, and Kendal saw with pleasure that it was going to be renewed.

"I am dying to tell you about it," he said.

"Paris?" she asked, looking up at him. "I am dying to hear. The people, especially the people. Lucien, what was he like? One hears so much of Lucien – they make him a priest and a king together. And did you go to Barbizon?"

Another in her place might have added, "And why did you write so seldom?" There was something that closed Janet's lips to this. It was the same thing that would not permit her to call Kendal "Jack," as several other people did, though her Christian name had been allowed to him for a long time. It made an awkwardness sometimes, for she would not say "Mr. Kendal" either—that would be a rebuke or a suggestion of inferiority, or what not —but she bridged it over as best she could with a jocose appellative like "signor," "monsieur," or "Mr. John Kendal," in full. "Jack" was impossible, "John" was worse. Yes, with a little nervous shudder, *much* worse.

He told her about Paris to her fascination; she had never seen it: about the boulevards and the cafés and the men's ateliers, and the vagrant pathos of student life there—he had seen some clean bits of it—and to all of this old story he gave such life as a word or a phrase can give. Even his repressions were full of meaning, and the best—she felt it was the best—he had to offer her he offered in fewest words, letting her imagination riot with them. He described Lucien and the American Colony. He made her laugh abundantly over the American amateur as Lucien managed him. They had no end of fun over these interesting, ingenious, and prodigal people in their relation to Parisian professional circles. He touched on Nádie Palicsky lightly, and perhaps it was because Janet insisted upon an accentuation of the lines—he had sent her a photograph of one of Nádie's best things—that he refrained from mentioning Elfrida altogether. Elfrida, he thought, he would keep till another time. She would need so much explanation; she was too interesting to lug in now, it was getting late. Besides, Elfrida was an exhausting subject, and he was rather done.

CHAPTER XI.

INDIVIDUALLY a large number of Royal Academicians pronounced John Kendal's work impertinent, if not insulting, meaningless, affected, or flippant. Collectively, with a corporate opinion that might be discussed but could not be identified, they received it and hung it, smothering a distressful doubt, where it would be least likely to excite either the censure of the right-minded or the admiration of the unorthodox. The Grosvenor gave him a discreet appreciation, and the New received him with joy and thanksgiving. If he had gone to any of the Private Views, which temptation he firmly resisted, he would have heard the British public—for after all the British public is always well represented at a Private View—say discontentedly how much better it would like his pictures if they were only a little more finished. He might even have had the cruel luck to hear one patron of the arts, who began by designing the pictorial advertisements for his own furniture-polish, state that he would buy that twilight effect with the empty fields, if only the trees in the foreground weren't so blurred. Other things, too, he might have heard that would have amused him more as being less commonplace, but pleased him no better, said by people who cast furtive glances over their shoulders to see if anybody that might be the artist was within reach of their discriminating admiration; and here and there, if he had listened well, a vigorous word that meant recognition and reward. It was not that he did not long for the tritest word of comment from the oracle before which he had chosen to lay the fruit of his labors; indeed, he was so conscious of his desire to know this opinion, not over clever as he believed it, that he ran away on the evening of varnishing-day. If he staid he felt that he would inevitably compromise his dignity, so he hid himself with some amiable people in Hampshire, who could be relied upon not to worry him, for a week. He did not deny himself the papers, however. They reached him in stacks, with the damp chill of the afternoon post upon them; and in their solid paragraphs he read the verdict of the British public written out in words of proper length and much the same phrases that had done duty for Eastlake and Sir Martin Shee. Fortunately, the amiable people included some very young people, so young that they could properly compel Kendal to go into the fields with them and make cowslip balls, and some robust girls of eighteen and twenty, who mutely demanded the pleasure of beating him at tennis every afternoon. He was able in this way to work off the depression that visited him daily with the damp odor of London art criticism, quite independently of its bias toward himself. He told himself that he had been let off fairly easily, though he winced considerably under the adulation of the *Daily Mercury*, and found himself breathing most freely when least was said about him. The day of his triumph in the *Mercury* he made monstrous cowslip balls, and thought that the world had never been sufficiently congratulated upon possessing the ideal simplicity of children.

Thereafter for two days nothing came, and he began to grow restless. Then the *Decade* made its weekly slovenly appearance, without a wrapper. He opened it with the accumulated interest of forty-eight hours, turned to "Fine Arts," and girded himself to receive the *Decade's* ideas. He read the first sentence twice—the article opened curiously, for the *Decade*. He looked at the cover to see whether he had not been mistaken. Then he sat down beside the open window, where a fine rain came in and smote upon the page, and read it through, straining his eyes in the gathering darkness over the last paragraph. After that he walked up and down the room among the shadows for half an hour, not ringing for lights, because the scented darkness of the garden, where the rain was dripping, and the half outlines of the things in the room were so much more grateful to his imagination as the *Decade's* critic had stimulated it with the young, mocking, brilliant voice that spoke in the department of "Fine Arts." It stirred him all through. In the pleasure it gave him he refused to reflect how often it dismissed with contempt where it should have considered with respect, how it was sometimes inconsistent, sometimes exaggerated and obscure. He was rapt in the delicacy and truth with which the critic translated into words the recognizable souls of a certain few pictures—it could not displease him that they were very few, since three of his were among them. When it spoke of these the voice was strong and gentle, with an uplifted tenderness, and all the suppressed suggestion that good pictures themselves have. It made their quality felt in the lines, and it spoke with a personal joy.

"A new note!" Kendal thought aloud. "A voice crying in the wilderness, by Jove! Wolff might have done it if it had been in French, but Wolff would have been fairer and more technical and less sympathetic."

A fine energy crept all through him and burned at

his finger-ends. The desire to work seized him deliciously with the thrill of being understood, a longing to accomplish to the utmost of his limitations—he must reasonably suppose his limitations. Sometimes they were close and real; at this moment they were far off and vague, and almost dissolved by the force of his joyous intention. He threw himself mentally upon a half-finished canvas that stood against the wall in Bryanston Street, and spent ten exalted minutes in finishing it. When it was done he found it ravishing, and raged because he could not decently leave for town before four o'clock next day. He worked off the time before dinner by putting his things together, and the amiable people had never found him so delightful as he was that evening. After amusing one of the robust young ladies for half an hour at prodigious cost, he found himself comparing their conversation with the talk he might have had in the time with Elfrida Bell, and a fresh sense of injury visited him at having been high-handedly debarred from that pleasure for so many weeks. It staid with him and pricked him all the way to town next day. He was a fool, he thought, to have missed the chance of meeting her upon the opening days of the London exhibitions; she was sure to have gone, if it were only to scoff, and her scoffing would have been so amusing to listen to. He thought gloomily of the impossibility of finding her in London if she didn't wish to be found, and he concluded that he really wanted to see her, that he must see her soon—to show her that article.

The desire had not passed from him three days later, when the boy from below-stairs brought him up a card. Kendal was in his shirt-sleeves, and had just established a relation of great intimacy with an entirely new subject. Before the boy reached him he recognized with annoyance that it was a lady's card, and he took it between his thumb and his palette with the most brutal impatience. "You are to say—" he began, and stopped. "Show the lady up," he said in substitution, while his face cleared with a puzzled amusement, and he looked at the card again. It read "Miss Elfrida Bell," but the odd thing was down in one corner, where ran the statement, in small square type, "*The Illustrated Age.*"

There was a sweet glory of May sunlight in the streets outside, and she seemed to bring some of it in with her, as well as the actual perfume of the bunch of violets which she wore in her belt. Her eyes, under the queerest of hats, were bright and soft, there was a faint color in her cheeks. Her shapely hands were in gray gloves with long gauntlets, and in one of them she carried a business-like little black notebook.

She came in with a shy hesitation that became her very well, and as she approached, their old understanding immediately arranged itself between them. "I should be perfectly justified in sulking," he declared gaily, disencumbering a chair of a battered tin box of empty twisted tubes for her, "and asking you to what I might attribute the honor of this visit." He put up his eye-glass and stared through it with an absurd affectation of dignified astonishment. "But I'll magnanimously admit that I'm delighted to see you. I'll even lay aside my wounded sensibilities enough to ask you where you've been."

"I!" faltered Elfrida softly, with her wide-eyed smile. "Oh! as if that were of any consequence!" She stepped back a pace or two to look at an unpacked canvas, and her expression changed. "Ah!" she said gravely, "how good it is to see that! I wish I could remember by myself so much, half so much, of the sunlight of that country. In three days of these fogs I had forgotten it. I mean the reality of it. Only a pale theory staid with me. Now it comes back."

"Then you *have* been in London?" he probed, while she looked wistfully at the fringe of a wood in Brittany that stood upon his canvas. Her eyes left the picture and wandered around the room.

"I!" she said again. "In London? Yes, I have been in London. How *splendidly* different you are!" she said, looking straight at him as if she stated a falling of the thermometer or a quotation from the Stock Exchange. "But are you sure, *perfectly* sure," she went on, with dainty emphasis, "that you can stay different? Aren't you the least bit afraid that in the end your work may become—pardon me—commercial, like the rest? Is there no danger?"

"I wish you would sit down," Kendal said ruefully. "I shouldn't feel it so much, perhaps, if you sat down. And pending my acknowledgment of a Londoner's sin in painting in London, it seems to me that you have put yourself under pretty much the same condemnation."

"I have not come to paint," Elfrida answered quickly. "I have put away the insanity of thinking I ever could. I told you that, I think, in a letter. But there are—other things. You may remember that you thought there were."

She spoke with so much repressed feeling that Kendal reproached himself with not having thought carefully enough about it to take her at her letter's word. He took up the card that announced her, and looked again at the lower left-hand corner. "I do remember, but I don't understand. Is this one of them?" he asked.

Something, something absolutely unintentional and of the slightest quality, in his voice operated to lower her estimate of the announcement on the card, and she flushed a little.

"It's—it's a way," she said. "But it was stupid—bourgeois—of me to send up a card—such a card. With most of these people it is necessary; with you, of course, it was hideous! Give it to me, please," and she proceeded to tear it slowly into little bits. "You must pardon me," she went on, "but I thought, you know—we are not in Paris now—and there might be people here. And then, after all, it explains me."

"Then I should like another," Kendal interrupted.

"I'm going to do a descriptive article for the *Age;* the editor wants to call it 'Through the Studios,' or something of that sort—about the artists over here and their ways of working, and their places, and their ideas, and all that, and I thought, if you didn't mind, I should like to begin with you. Though it's rather like taking an advantage."

"But are you going in for this sort of thing seriously? Have you ever done anything of the sort before? Isn't it an uncommon grind?" Kendal asked, with hearty interest. "What made you think of it? Of course you may say any mortal thing you want to about me—though I call it treachery, your going over to the critics. And I'm afraid you won't find anything very picturesque here. As you say, we're not in Paris."

"Oh yes, I shall," she replied sweetly, ignoring his questions. "I like pipes and cobwebs and old coats hanging on a nail, and plenty of litter and dust and confusion. It's much better for work than tapestries and old armour and wood-carvings."

Miss Bell did not open her little black notebook to record these things, however. Instead, she picked up a number of the *London Magazine* and looked at the title of an article pencil-marked on the pale green cover. It was Janet Cardiff's article, and Lady Halifax had marked it. Elfrida had read it before. It was a fanciful recreation of the conditions of verse-making when Herrick wrote, very pleasurably ironical in its bearing upon more modern poetry-making. It had quite deserved the praise she gave it in the corner which the *Age* reserved for magazines. "I want you to understand," she said slowly, "that it is only a way. I shall not be content to stick at this—ordinary—kind of journalistic work. I shall aim at something better—something perhaps even as good as that," she held up the marked article. "I wonder if she realizes how fortunate she is—to appear between the same covers as Swinburne!"

"It is not fortune altogether," Kendal answered; "she works hard."

"Do you know her? Do you see her often? Will you tell her that there is somebody who takes a special delight in every word she writes?" asked Elfrida impulsively. "But no, of course not! Why should she care—she must hear such things so often. Tell me, though, what is she like, and particularly how old is she?"

Kendal had begun to paint again; it was a compliment he was able to pay only to a very few people. "I shall certainly repeat it to her," he said. "She can't hear such things often enough—nobody can. How shall I tell you what she is like! She is tall, about as tall as you are, and rather thin. She has a good color, and nice hair and eyes."

"What colored eyes?"

"Brown, I think. No—I don't know, but not blue. And good eyebrows. Particularly good eyebrows."

"She must be plain," Elfrida thought, "if he has to dwell upon her eyebrows. And how old?" she asked again. "Much over thirty?"

"Oh dear, no! Not thirty. Twenty-four, I should say."

Elfrida's face fell perceptibly. "Twenty-four!"

she exclaimed. "And I am already twenty! I shall never catch up to her in four years. Oh, you have made me so unhappy! I thought she must be *quite* old—forty perhaps. I was prepared to venerate her. But twenty-four and good eyebrows! It is too much."

Kendal laughed. "Oh, I say!" he exclaimed, jumping up and bringing a journal from the other side of the room, "if you're going in for art criticism, here's something! Do you see the *Decade?* The *Decade's* article on the pictures in last week's number fairly brought me back to town." He held his brush between his teeth and found the place for her. "There! I don't know who did it, and it was the first thing Miss Cardiff asked me when I put in my appearance there yesterday, so she doesn't either, though she writes a good deal for the *Decade.*"

Kendal had gone back to work, and did not see that Elfrida was making an effort of self-control, with a curious exaltation in her eyes. "I—I have seen this," she said presently.

"Capital, isn't it?"

"Miss Cardiff asked you who wrote it?" she repeated hungrily.

"Yes; she commissioned me to find out, and if he was respectable to bring him there. Her father said I was to bring him anyway. So I don't propose to find out. The Cardiffs have burned their fingers once or twice already handling obscure genius, and I won't take the responsibility. But it's adorably savage, isn't it?"

"Do you really like it?" she asked. It was her first taste of success, and the savor was very sweet. But she was in an agony of desiré to tell him, to tell him immediately, but gracefully, delicately, that she wrote it. How could she say it, and yet seem uneager, indifferent? But the occasion must not slip. It was a miserable moment.

"Immensely," he replied.

"Then," she said, with just a little more significance in her voice than she intended, "you would rather not find out?"

He turned and met her shining eyes. She smiled, and he had an instant of conviction. "You," he exclaimed—"you did it! Really?"

She nodded, and he swiftly reflected upon what he had said. "Now criticise!" she begged impatiently.

"I can only advise you to follow your own example," he said gravely. "It's rather exuberantly cruel in places."

"Adorably savage, you *said!*"

"I wasn't criticising then. And I suppose," he went on, with a shade of awkwardness, "I ought to thank you for all the charming things you put in about me."

"Ah!" she returned, with a contemptuous pout and shrug, "don't say that—it's like the others. But," she clinched it notwithstanding, and rather quickly, "will you take me to see Miss Cardiff? I mean," she added, noting his look of consternation, "will you ask her if I may come? I forget—we are in London."

At this moment the boy from below-stairs knocked with tea and cakes, little Italian cakes in iced jackets and paper boats. "Yes, certainly—yes, I will," said Kendal, staring at the tray, and trying to remember when he had ordered it; "but it's your plain duty to make us both some tea, and to eat as many of these pink-and-white things as you possibly can. They seem to have come down from heaven for you."

They ate and drank and talked and were merry for quite twenty minutes. Elfrida opened her note-book and threatened absurdities of detail for publication in the *Age;* he defied her, tilted his chair back, put his feet on a packing-box, and smoked a cigarette. He placed all the studies he had made after she left Paris before her, and as she finished the last but one of the Italian cakes, they discussed these in the few words from which they both drew such large and satisfying meanings as do not lie at all in the vocabulary of outsiders. Elfrida felt the keenest pleasure of her whole life in the knowledge that Kendal was talking to her more seriously, more carefully, because of that piece of work in the *Decade;* the consciousness of it was like wine to her, freeing her thoughts and her lips. Kendal felt, too, that the plane of their relations was somehow altered. He was not sure that he liked the alteration. Already she had grown less amusing, and the real *camaraderie* which she constantly suggested her desire for he could not, at the bottom of his heart, truly tolerate with a woman. He was an artist, but he was also an Englishman, and he told himself that he must not let her get into the way of coming there. He felt an obscure inward irritation, which he did not analyze, that she should talk so well and be so charming personally at the same time.

Elfrida, still in the flush of her elation, was putting on her gloves to go, when the room resounded to a masterful double rap. The door almost simultaneously opened far enough to disclose a substantial gloved hand upon the outer handle, and in the tones of confident aggression which habit has given to many middle-aged ladies, a feminine voice said, "May we come in?"

It is not probable that Lady Halifax had ever

been so silently, surely, and swiftly damned before. In the fraction of an instant that followed Kendal glanced at the dismantled tray and felt that the situation was atrocious. He had just time to put his foot upon his half-smoked cigarette, and to force a pretence of unconcern into his "Come in! Come in!" when the lady and her daughter entered with something of unceremoniousness.

"Those are appalling stairs—" Lady Halifax observed Elfrida, and came to an instant's astonished halt—"of yours, Mr. Kendal, appalling!" Then as Kendal shook hands with Miss Halifax she faced round upon him in a manner which said definitely, "Explain!" and behind her sharp good-natured little eyes Kendal read, "If it is possible!" He looked at Elfrida in the silent hope that she would go, but she appeared to have no such intention. He was pushed to a momentary wish that she had got into the cupboard, which he dismissed, turning a deeper brick color as it came and went. Elfrida was looking up with calm inquiry, buttoning a last glove-button.

"Lady Halifax," he said, seeing nothing else for it, "this is Miss Bell, from America, a fellow-student in Paris. Miss Bell has deserted art for literature, though," he went on bravely, noting an immediate change in his visitor's expression, and the fact that her acknowledgment was quite as polite as was necessary. "She has done me the honor to look me up this afternoon in the formidable character of a representative of the press."

Lady Halifax looked as if the explanation was quite acceptable, though she reserved the right of criticism.

Elfrida took the first word, smiling prettily straight into Lady Halifax's face.

"Mr. Kendal pretends to be very much frightened," she said, with pleasant, modest coolness, and looked at Kendal.

"From America," Lady Halifax repeated, as if for the comfort of the assurance. "I am sure it is a great advantage nowadays to have been brought up in America." This was quite as delicately as Lady Halifax could possibly manage to inform Kendal that she understood the situation. Miss Halifax was looking absorbedly at Elfrida. "Are you really a journalist?" Miss Halifax asked. "How nice! I didn't know there were any ladies on the London press, except, of course, the fashion-papers, but that isn't quite the same, is it?"

When Miss Halifax said "How nice!" it indicated a strong degree of interest. The threads of Miss Halifax's imagination were perpetually twisting themselves about incidents that had the least unusualness, and here was a most unusual incident, with beauty and genius thrown in! Whether she could approve it or not in connection with Kendal, Miss Halifax would decide afterward. She told herself that she ought to be sufficiently devoted to Kendal to be magnanimous about his friends. Her six years of seniority gave her the candor to confess that she was devoted to Kendal—to his artistic personality, that is, and to his pictures. While Kendal turned a still uncomfortable back upon them, showing Lady Halifax what he had done since she had been there last—she was always pitiless in her demands for results—Elfrida talked a little about "the press" to Miss Halifax. Very lightly and gracefully she talked about it, so lightly and gracefully that Miss Halifax obtained an impression which she has never lost, that journalism for a woman had ideal attractions, and privately resolved if ever she were thrown upon the bleak world to take it up. As the others turned toward them again Elfrida noticed the conscience-stricken glance which Kendal gave to the tea-tray.

"Oh," she said, with a slight enhancement of her pretty Parisian gurgle, "I am very guilty—you must allow me to say that I am very guilty indeed! Mr. Kendal did not expect to see me to-day, and in his surprise he permitted me to eat up all the cakes! I am so sorry! Are there no more—anywhere?" she asked Kendal, with such a gay pretence of tragic grief that they all laughed together. She went away then, and while they waited for a fresh supply of tea, Kendal did his best to satisfy the curiosity of the Halifaxes about her. He was so more than thankful she had convinced them that she was a person about whom it was proper to be curious.

CHAPTER XII.

It was Arthur Rattray who generally did the art criticism for the *Decade*, and when a temporary indisposition interfered between Mr. Rattray and this duty early in May, he had acquired so much respect for Elfrida's opinion in artistic matters, and so much good-will toward her personally, that he wrote and asked her to undertake it for him with considerable pleasure. This respect and regard had dawned upon him gradually, from various sources, in spite of the fact that the Latin Quarter article had not been a particular success. That, to do Miss Bell justice, as Mr. Rattray said in mentioning the matter to the editor-in-chief, was not so much the fault of the article as the fault of their public. Miss Bell wrote the graphic naked truth about the Latin Quarter. Even after Rattray had sent her copy back to be amended for the third time, she did not seem able to realize that their public wouldn't stand *unions libres* when not served up with a moral purpose—that no artistic apology for them would do. In the end, therefore, Rattray was obliged to mutilate the article himself, and to neutralize it here and there. He was justified in taking the trouble, for it was matter they wanted, on account of some expensive drawings of the locality that had been in hand a long time. Even then the editor-in-chief had grumbled at its "tone," though the wrath of the editor-in-chief was nothing to Miss Bell's. Mr. Rattray could not remember ever having had before a conversation with a contributor which approached in liveliness or interest the one he sustained with Miss Bell the day after her copy appeared. If he imparted some ideas of expediency, he received some of obligation to artistic truth, which he henceforth associated with Elfrida's expressive eyes and what he called her foreign accent. On the whole, therefore, the conversation was agreeable, and it left him with the impression that Miss Bell, under proper guidance, could very possibly do some fresh unconventional work for the *Age*. Freshness and unconventionality for the *Age* was what Mr. Rattray sought as they seek the jewel in the serpent's head in the far East. He talked to the editor-in-chief about it, mentioning the increasing lot of things concerning women that had to be touched, which only a woman could treat "from the inside," and the editor-in-chief agreed sulkily, because experience told him it was best to agree with Mr. Rattray, that

Miss Bell should be taken on the staff on trial, at two pounds a week. "But the paper doesn't want a female Zola," he growled; "you can tell her that."

Rattray did not tell her precisely that, but he explained the situation so that she quite understood it, the next afternoon when he called to talk the matter over with her. He could not ask her to come to the office to discuss it, he said, they were so full up, they had really no place to receive a lady. And he apologized for his hat, which was not a silk one, in the uncertain way of a man who has heard of the proprieties in these things. She made him tea with her samovar, and she talked to him about Parisian journalism and the Parisian stage in a way that made her a further discovery to him; and his mind, hitherto wholly devoted to the service of the *Illustrated Age*, received an impetus in a new direction. When he had gone Elfrida laughed a little, silently, thinking first of this, for it was quite plain to her. Then, contrasting what the *Age* wanted her to write with her ideal of journalistic literature, she stated to Buddha that it was "worse than *panade*." "But it means two pounds a week, Buddha," she said; "fifty francs! Do you understand that? It means that we shall be able to stay here, in the world— that I shall not be obliged to take you to Sparta. You don't know, Buddha, how you would *loathe*

Sparta! But understand, it is at *that* price that we are going to despise ourselves for a while—not for the two pounds!"

And next day she was sent to report a distribution of diplomas to graduating nurses by the Princess of Wales.

Buddha was not an adequate confidant. Elfrida found him capable of absorbing her emotions indefinitely, but his still smile was not always responsive enough, so she made a little feast, and asked Golightly Ticke to tea, the Sunday after the Saturday that made her a salaried member of the London press. Golightly's felicitations were sincere and spasmodically sympathetic, but he found it impossible to conceal the fact that of late the world had not smiled equally upon him. In spite of the dramatic fervor with which the part of James Jones, a solicitor's clerk, had been rendered every evening, the piece at the Princess's had to come to an unprofitable close, the theatre had been leased to an American company, Phyllis had gone to the provinces, and Mr. Ticke's abilities were at the service of chance. By the time he had reached his second cigarette he was so sunk in cynicism that Elfrida applied herself delicately to discover these facts. Golightly made an elaborate effort to put her off. He threw his head back in his chair and watched the faint rings of his cigarette curling into indistinguishability against the ceiling, and said he was only the dust that blew about the narrow streets of the world, and why should she care to know which way the wind took him! Lighting his third, he said, as bitterly as that engrossment would permit him, that the sooner—puff—it was over—puff—the sooner—puff —to sleep; and when the lighting was quite satisfactorily accomplished he laughed harshly. "I shall think," said Elfrida earnestly, "if you do not tell me how things are with you, since they are bad, that you are not a true Bohemian—that you have scruples."

"You know better—at least I hope you do—than to charge me with that," Golightly returned, with an inflection full of reproachful meaning. "I—I drank myself to sleep last night, Miss Bell. When the candle flickered out I thought that it was all over— curious sensation. This morning," he added, looking through his half-closed eyelashes with sardonic stage effect, "I wished it had been."

"Tell me," Elfrida insisted gently; and looking attentively at his long, thin fingers Mr. Ticke then told her. He told her tersely, it did not take long; and in the end he doubled up his hand and pulled a crumpled cuff down over it. "To me," he said, "a thing like that represents the worst of it. When I look at that I feel capable of crime. I don't know whether you'll understand, but the consideration of what my finer self suffers through sordidness of this sort sometimes makes me think that to rob a bank would be an act of virtue."

"I understand," said Elfrida.

"Washerwomen as a class are callous. I suppose the alkalies they use finally penetrate to their souls. I said to mine last Thursday, 'But I must be clean, Mrs. Binkley!' and the creature replied, 'I don't see at all, Mr. Ticks'—she has an odious habit of calling me Mr. Ticks—'why you shouldn't go dirty occasional.' She seemed to think she had made a joke!"

"They live to be paid," Elfrida said, with hard philosophy, and then she questioned him delicately about his play. Could she induce him to show it to her, some day? Her opinion was worth nothing really—oh no, absolutely nothing—but it would be a pleasure if Golightly were *sure* he didn't mind.

Golightly found a difficulty in selecting phrases repressive enough to be artistic, in which to tell her that he would be delighted.

When Mr. Ticke came in that evening he found upon his dressing-table a thick square envelope addressed to him in Elfrida's suggestive hand. With his fingers and thumb he immediately detected a round hardness in one corner, and he took some pains to open the letter so that nothing should fall out. He postponed the pleasure of reading it until he had carefully extracted the two ten-shilling pieces, divested them of their bits of tissue-paper, and put them in his waistcoat pocket. Then he held the letter nearer to the candle and read: "I have thought about this for a whole hour. You must believe, please, that it is no vulgar impulse. I acknowledge it to be a very serious liberty, and in taking it I rely upon not having misinterpreted the scope of the freedom which exists between us. In Bohemia—our country—one may share one's luck with a friend, *n'est ce pas?* I will not ask to be forgiven."

"Nice girl," said Mr. Golightly Ticke, taking off his boots. He went to bed rather resentfully conscious of the difference there was in the benefactions of Miss Phyllis Fane.

Shortly after this Mr. Ticke's own luck mended, and on two different occasions Elfrida found a bunch of daffodils outside her door in the morning, that made a mute and graceful acknowledgment of the financial bond Mr. Ticke did not dream of offering to materialize in any other way. He felt his gratitude finely; it suggested to him a number of little directions in which he could make himself useful to Miss Bell, putting aside entirely the question of repayment.

One of these resolved itself into an invitation from the Arcadia Club, of which Mr. Ticke was a member in impressive arrears, to their monthly *soirée* in the Landscapists' rooms in Bond Street. The Arcadia Club had the most liberal scope of any in London, he told Elfrida, and included the most interesting people. Painters belonged to it, and sculptors, actors, novelists, musicians, journalists, perhaps above all, journalists. A great many ladies were members, Elfrida would see, and they were always glad to welcome a new personality. The club recognized how the world had run to types, and how scarce and valuable personalities were in consequence. It was not a particularly conventional club, but he would arrange that, if Elfrida would accept his escort, Mrs. Tommy Morrow should meet her in the dressing-room, as a concession to the prejudices of society.

"Mrs. Tommy is a brilliant woman in her way," Mr. Ticke added; "she edits the *Boudoir*—I might say she created the *Boudoir*. They call her the Queen of Arcadia. She has a great deal of manner."

"What does Mr. Tommy Morrow do?" Elfrida asked. But Golightly could not inform her as to Mr. Tommy Morrow's occupation.

The rooms were half full when they arrived, and as the man in livery announced them, "Mrs. Morrow, Miss Bell, and Mr. Golightly Ticke," it seemed to Elfrida that everybody turned simultaneously to look. There was nobody to receive them; the man in livery published them, as it were, to the company, which she felt to be a more effective mode of entering society, when it was the society of the arts. She could not possibly help being aware that a great many people were looking in her direction over Mrs. Tommy Morrow's shoulder. Presently it became obvious that Mrs. Tommy Morrow was also aware of it. The shoulder was a very feminine shoulder, with long lines curving forward into the sulphur-colored gown that met them not too prematurely. Mrs. Tommy Morrow insisted upon her shoulder, and upon her neck, which was short behind but long in front in effect, and curved up to a chin which was somewhat too persistently thrust forward. Mrs. Tommy had a pretty face with an imperious expression. "Just the face," as Golightly murmured to Elfrida, "to run the *Boudoir*." She seemed to know everybody, bowed right and left with varying degrees of cordiality, and said sharply, "No shop to-night!" to a thin young woman in a high black silk, who came up to her exclaiming, "Oh, Mrs. Morrow, that function at Sandringham has been postponed." Presently Mrs. Morrow's royal progress was interrupted by a gentleman who wished to present Signor Georgiadi, "the star of the evening," Golightly said hurriedly to Elfrida. Mrs. Morrow was very gracious, but the little fat Italian with the long hair and the drooping eyelids was atrociously embarrassed to respond to her compliments in English. He struggled so violently that Mrs. Morrow began to smile with a compassionate patronage which turned him a distressing terra-cotta. Elfrida looked on for a few minutes, and then, as one of the group, she said quietly in French, "And Italian opera in England, how do you find it, Signor?"

The Italian thanked her with every feature of his expressive countenance, and burst with polite enthusiasm into his opinion of the Albert Hall concerts. When he discovered Elfrida to be an American, and therefore not specially susceptible to praise of English classical interpretations, he allowed himself to become critical, and their talk increased in liveliness and amiability.

Mrs. Morrow listened with an appreciative air for a few minutes, playing with her fan; then she turned to Mr. Ticke.

"Golightly," she said acidly, "I am dying of thirst. You shall take me to the refreshment-table."

So the star of the evening was abandoned to

Elfrida, and finding in her a refuge from the dreadful English tongue, he clung to her. She was so occupied with him in this character that almost all the other distinguished people who attended the *soirée* of the Arcadia Club escaped her. Golightly asked her reproachfully afterward how he could possibly have pointed them out to her, absorbed as she was—and some of them would have been so pleased to be introduced to her! She met a few notwithstanding; they were chiefly rather elderly unmarried ladies, who immediately mentioned to her the paper they were connected with, and one or two of them, learning that she was a newcomer, kindly gave her their cards, and asked her to come and see them any second Tuesday. They had indefinite and primitive ideas of doing their hair, and they were certainly *mal tournée;* but Elfrida saw that she made an impression on them— that they would remember her and talk of her; and seeing that, other things became less noteworthy. She felt that these ladies were more or less emancipated, on easy terms with the facts of life, free from the prejudices that tied the souls of people she saw shopping at the Stores, for instance. That, and a familiarity with the exigencies of copy at short notice, was discernible in the way they talked and looked about them, and the readiness with which they produced a pencil to write the second Tuesday on their cards. Almost every lady suggested that she might have decorated the staff of her journal an appreciable number of years, if that supposition had not been forbidden by the fact that the feminine element in journalism is of comparatively recent introduction. Elfrida wondered what they occupied themselves with before. It did not detract from her sense of the success of the evening—Golightly Ticke went about telling everybody that she was the new American writer on the *Age*—to feel herself altogether the youngest person present, and manifestly the most effectively dressed, in her cloudy black net and daffodils. Her spirits rose with a keen instinct that assured her she would win, if it were only a matter of a race with *them*. She had never had the feeling, in any security, before; it lifted her and carried her on in a wave of exhilaration. Golightly Ticke, taking her in turn to the buffet for lemonade and a sandwich, told her that he knew she would enjoy it—she must be enjoying it, she looked in such capital form. It was the first time she had been near the buffet; so she had not had the opportunity of observing how important a feature the lemonade and sandwiches formed in the entertainment of the evening—how persistently the representatives of the arts, with varying numbers of buttons off their gloves, returned to this light refreshment.

Elfrida thanked Mrs. Tommy Morrow very sweetly for her chaperonage in the cloak-room when the hour of departure came. "Well," said Mrs. Morrow, "you can say you have seen a characteristic London literary gathering."

"Yes, thanks!" said Elfrida; and then, looking about her for a commonplace, "How much taller the women seem to be than the men," she remarked.

"Yes," returned Mrs. Tommy Morrow, "Du Maurier drew attention to that in *Punch*, some time ago."

CHAPTER XIII.

JANET CARDIFF, running downstairs to the drawing-room from the top story of the house in Kensington Square with the knowledge that a new American girl, who wrote very clever things about pictures, awaited her there, tried to remember just what sort of description John Kendal had given of her visitor. Her recollection was vague as to detail; she could not anticipate a single point with certainty, perhaps because she had not paid particular attention at the time. She had been given a distinct impression that she might expect to be interested, however, which accounted for her running downstairs. Nothing hastened Janet Cardiff's footsteps more than the prospect of anybody interesting. She and her father declared that it was their great misfortune to be thoroughly respectable, it cut them off from so much. It was in particular the girl's complaint against their life that humanity as they knew it was rather a neutral-tinted, carefully woven fabric too largely "machine-made," as she told herself, with a discontent that the various Fellows of the Royal Society and members of the Athenæum Club, with whom the Cardiffs were in the habit of dining, could hardly have thought themselves capable of inspiring. It seemed to Janet that nobody crossed their path until his or her reputation was made, and that by the time people had made their reputations they succumbed to them, and became uninteresting.

She told herself at once that nothing Kendal could have said would have prepared her for this American, and that certainly nothing she had seen or read of other Americans did. Elfrida was standing beside the open window looking out. As Janet came in a breeze wavered through and lifted the fluffy hair about her visitor's forehead, and the scent of the growing things in the little square came with it into the room. She turned slowly, with grave wide eyes and a plaintive indrawing of her pretty underlip, and held out three full-blown gracious Marechal Neil roses on long slender stems. "I have brought you these," she said, with a charming effect of simplicity, "to make me welcome. There was no reason, none whatever, why I should be welcome, so I made one. You will not be angry—perhaps?"

Janet banished her conventional "Very glad to see you" instantly. She took the roses with a quick thrill of pleasure. Afterward she told herself that she was not touched, not in the least, she did not quite know why; but she freely acknowledged that she was more than amused.

"How charming of you!" she said. "But I have to thank you for coming as well. Now let us shake hands, or we shan't feel properly acquainted." Janet detected a half-tone of patronage in her voice, and fell into a rage with herself because of it. She looked at Elfrida sharply to note a possible resentment, but there was none. If she had looked a trifle more sharply she might have observed a subtler patronage in the little smile her visitor received this commonplace with; but, like the other, she was too much occupied in considering her personal effect. She had become suddenly desirous that it should be a good one.

Elfrida went on in the personal key. "I suppose you are very tired of hearing such things," she said, "but I owe you so much."

This was not quite justifiable, for Miss Cardiff was only a successful writer in the magazines, whose name was very familiar to other people who wrote in them, and had a pleasant association for the reading public. It was by no means fame; she would have been the first to laugh at the magniloquence of the word in any personal connection. For her father she would accept a measure of it, and only deplored that the lack of public interest in Persian made the measure small. She had never confessed to a soul how largely she herself was unacquainted with his books, and how considerably her knowledge of her father's specialty was covered by the opinion that Persian was a very decorative character. She could not let Elfrida suppose that she thought this anything but a politeness.

"Oh, thanks—impossible!" she cried gaily. "Indeed, I assure you it is months since I heard anything so agreeable," which was also a departure from the strictest verity.

"But truly! I'm afraid I am very clumsy," Elfrida added, with a pretty dignity, "but I should like to assure you of that."

"If you have allowed me to amuse you now and then for half an hour it has been very good of you," Janet returned, looking at Miss Bell with rather more curious interest than she thought it polite to show. It began to seem to her, however, that the conventional side of the occasion was not obvious from any point of view. "You are an American, aren't you?" she asked. "Mr. Kendal told me so. I suppose one oughtn't to say that one would like to be an American. But you have such a pull! I know I should like living there."

Elfrida gave herself the effect of considering the

matter earnestly. It flitted, really, over the surface of her mind, which was engaged in absorbing Janet and the room, and the situation.

"Perhaps it is better to be born in America than in—most places," she said, with a half glance at the prim square outside. "It gives you a point of view that is—splendid." In hesitating this way before her adjectives, she always made her listeners doubly attentive to what she had to say. "And having been deprived of so much that you 'have over here, we like it better, of course, when we get it, than you do. But nobody would live in constant deprivation. No, you wouldn't like living there. Except in New York, and, oh, I should say Santa Barbara, and New Orleans perhaps, the life over there is—infernal."

"You are like a shower-bath," said Janet to herself; but the shower-bath had no palpable effect upon her. "What have we that is so important that you haven't got?" she asked.

"Quantities of things." Elfrida hesitated, not absolutely sure of the wisdom of her example. Then she ventured it. "The picturesqueness of society—your duchesses and your women in the green-grocers' shops." It was not wise, she saw instantly.

"Really? It is so difficult to understand that duchesses are interesting—out of novels; and the green-grocers' wives are a good deal alike, too, aren't they?"

"It's the contrast; you see our duchesses were green-grocers' wives the day before yesterday, and our green-grocers' wives subscribe to the magazines. It's all mixed up, and there are no high lights anywhere. You move before us in a sort of panoramic pageant," Elfrida went on, determined to redeem her point, "with your Queen and Empress of India—she ought to be riding on an elephant, oughtn't she?—in front, and all your princes and nobles with their swords drawn to protect her. Then your Upper Classes and your Upper Middle Classes walking stiffly two and two; and then your Lower Middle Classes with large families, dropping their h's; and then your hideous people from the slums. And besides," she added, with prettily repressed enthusiasm, "there is the shadowy procession of all the people that have gone before, and we can see that you are a good deal like them, though they are more interesting still. It is very pictorial." She stopped suddenly and consciously, as if she had said too much, and Janet felt that she was suggestively apologized to.

"Doesn't the phenomenal squash make up for all that?" she asked. "It would to me. I'm dying to see the phenomenal squash, and the prodigious water-melon, and—"

"And the falls of Niagara?" Elfrida put in, with the faintest turning down of the corners of her mouth. "I'm afraid our wonders are chiefly natural, and largely vegetable, as you say."

"But they are wonders. Everything here has been measured so many times. Besides, haven't you got the elevated railway, and a statue of Liberty, and the "Jeanne d'Arc," and W. D. Howells! To say nothing of a whole string of poets—good gray poets that wear beards and laurels, and fanciful young ones that dance in garlands on the back pages of the *Century*. Oh, I know them all, the dear things! And I'm quite sure their ideas are indigenous to the soil."

Elfrida let her eyes tell her appreciation, and also the fact that she would take courage now, she was gaining confidence. "I'm glad you like them," she said. "Howells would do if he would stop writing about virtuous sewing-girls, and give us some real *romans psychologiques*. But he is too much afraid of soiling his hands, that monsieur; his *bêtes humaines* are always conventionalized, and generally come out at the end wearing the halo of the redeemed. He always reminds me of Cruikshank's

11

picture of the ghost being put out by the extinguisher in the 'Christmas Carol.' His genius is the ghost, and conventionality is the extinguisher. But it *is* genius, so it's a pity."

"It seems to me that Howells deals honestly with his materials," Janet said, instinctively stilling the jar of Elfrida's regardless note. She was so pretty, this new creature, and she had such original ways. Janet must let her talk about *romans psychologiques*, or worse things, if she wanted to. "To me he has a tremendous appearance of sincerity, psychological and other. But do you know, I don't think the English or American people are exactly calculated to reward the sort of vivisection you mean. The *bête* is too conscious of his moral fibre when he's respectable, and when he isn't respectable he doesn't commit picturesque crimes, he steals and boozes. I dare say he's bestial enough, but pure unrelieved filth can't be transmuted into literature, and as a people we're perfectly devoid of that extraordinary artistic nature that it makes such a foil for in the Latins. That is really the only excuse the naturalists have."

"Excuse!" Elfrida repeated, with a bewildered look. "You had Wainwright," she added hastily.

"*Nous nous en felicitons!* We've got him still—in Madame Tussaud's," cried Janet. "He poisoned for money in cold blood—not exactly an artistic vice! Oh, *he* won't do!"—she laughed triumphantly—"if he did write charming things about the Renaissance! Besides, he illustrates my case; among us he was a phenomenon, like the elephant-headed man. Phenomena are for the scientists. You don't mean to tell me that any literature that pretends to call itself artistic has a right to touch them."

By this time they had absolutely forgotten that up to twenty minutes ago they had never seen each other before. Already they had mutely and unconsciously begun to rejoice that they had come together; already each of them promised herself the exploration of the other's nature, with the preliminary idea that it would be a satisfying, at least an interesting process. The impulse made Elfrida almost natural, and Janet perceived this with quick self-congratulation. Already she had made up her mind that this manner was a pretty mask which it would be her business to remove.

"But—but you're not in it!" Elfrida returned. "Pardon me, but you're not *there*, you know. Art has no ideal but truth, and to conventionalize truth is to damn it. In the most commonplace material there is always truth, but here they conventionalize it out of all—"

"Oh," cried Janet, "we're a conventional people, I assure you, Miss Bell, and so are you, for how could you change your spots in a hundred years? The material here is conventional. Daudet couldn't have written of us. Our wicked women are too inglorious. Now Sapho—"

Miss Cardiff stopped at the ringing of the doorbell. "Oh," she said, "here is my father. You will let me give you a cup of tea now, won't you?" The maid was bringing in the tray. "I should like you to meet my father."

Lawrence Cardiff's grasp was on the door-handle almost as she spoke. Seeing Elfrida, he involuntarily put up his hand to settle the back of his coat collar—these little middle-aged ways were growing upon him—and shook hands with her as Janet introduced them, with that courtly impenetrable agreeableness that always provoked curiosity about him in strangers, and often led to his being taken for somebody more important than he was, usually somebody in politics. Elfrida saw that he was quite different from her conception of a university professor with a reputation in Persian and a clever daughter of twenty-four. He was straight and slender for one thing; he had gay inquiring eyes, and fair hair just beginning to show gray where the ends were brushed back; and Elfrida immediately became aware that his features were as modern and as mobile as possible. She had a moment of indecision and surprise—indecision as to the most effective way of presenting herself, and surprise that it should be necessary to decide upon a way. It had never occurred to her that a gentleman who had won scientific celebrity by digging about Arabic roots, and who had contributed a daughter like Janet to the popular magazines, could claim anything of her beyond a highly respectful consideration. In moments when she hoped to know the Cardiffs well she had pictured herself doing little graceful acts of politeness toward this paternal person—acts connected with his spectacles, his *Athenian*, his footstool. But apparently she had to meet a knight and not a pawn.

She was hardly aware of taking counsel with herself; and the way she abandoned her hesitations, and what Janet was inwardly calling her Burne-Jones-isms, had all the effect of an access of unconsciousness. Janet Cardiff watched it with delight. "But why," she asked herself in wonder, "should she have been so affected—if it was affectation—with *me?*" She would decide whether it was or was not afterward, she thought. Meanwhile she was glad her father had thought of saying something nice about the art criticism in the *Decade;* he was putting it so much better than she could, and it would do for both of them.

"You paint yourself, I fancy?" Mr. Cardiff was saying lightly. There was no answer for an instant, or perhaps three. Elfrida was looking down. Presently she raised her eyes, and they were larger than ever, and wet.

"No," she said, a little tensely. "I have tried"—"trr-hied," she pronounced it—"but—but I cannot."

Lawrence Cardiff looked at his teaspoon in a considering way, and Janet reflected, not without indignation, that this was the manner in which people who cared for them might be expected to speak of the dead. But Elfrida cut short the reflection by turning to her brightly. "When Mr. Cardiff came in," she said, "you were telling me why a Daudet could not write about the English. It was something about Sapho—"

Mr. Cardiff looked up curiously, and Janet, glancing in her father's direction, reddened. Did this strange young woman not realize that it was impossible to discuss beings like "Sapho" with one's father in the room? Apparently not, for she went on: "It seems to me it is the exception in that class, as in all classes, that rewards interest—"

That rewards interest! What might she not say next!

"Yes," interrupted Janet desperately, "but then my father came in and changed the subject of our conversation. Where are you living, Miss Bell?"

"Near Fleet Street," said Elfrida, rising. "I find the locality most interesting, when I can see it. I can patronize the Roman baths, and lunch at Dr. Johnson's pet tavern, and attend service in the church of the real Templars if I like. It is delightful. I did go to the Temple Church a fortnight ago," she added, "and I saw such a horrible thing that I am not sure that I will go again. There is a beautiful old Crusader lying there in stone, and on his feet a man who sat near had hung his silk hat. And nobody interfered. Why do you laugh?"

When she had fairly gone Lawrence and Janet Cardiff looked at each other and smiled. "Well!" cried Janet, "it's a find, isn't it, daddy?"

Her father shrugged his shoulders. His manner said that he was not pleased, but Janet found a tone in his voice that told her the impression of Elfrida had not been altogether distasteful.

"*Fin de siècle*," he said.

"Perhaps," Janet answered, looking out of the window, "a little *fin de siècle*."

"Did you notice," asked Lawrence Cardiff, "that she didn't tell you where she was living?"

"Didn't she? Neither she did. But we can easily find out from John Kendal."

CHAPTER XIV.

KENDAL hardly admitted to himself that his acquaintance with Elfrida had gone beyond the point of impartial observation. The proof of its impartiality, if he had thought of seeking it, would have appeared to him to lie in the fact that he found her, in her personality, her ideas, and her effects, to be damaged by London. The conventionality—Kendal's careless generalization preferred a broad term —of the place made her extreme in every way, and it had recently come to be a conclusion with him that English conventionality, in moderation, was not wholly to be smiled at. Returning to it, its protectiveness had impressed him strongly, and he had a comforting sense of the responsibility it imposed upon society. Paris and the Quartier stood out against it in his mind like something full of light and color and transient passion on the stage—something to be remembered with recurrent thrills of keen satisfaction and to be seen again. It had been more than this, he acknowledged, for he had brought out of it an element that lightened his life and vitalized his work, and gave an element of joyousness to his imagination—it was certain that he would go back there. And Miss Bell had been in it and of it—so much in it and of it that he felt impatient with her for permitting herself to be herself in any other environment. He asked himself why she could not see that she was crudely at variance with all color and atmosphere and law in her present one, and he speculated as to the propriety of telling her so, of advising her outright as to the expediency in her own interest, of being other than herself in London. That was what it came to, he reflected in deciding that he could not—if the girl's convictions and motives and aims were real; and he was beginning to think they were real. And although he had found himself at liberty to say to her things that were harder to hear, he felt a curious repugnance to giving her any inkling of what he thought about this. It would be a hideous thing to do, he concluded, an unforgivable thing, and an actual hurt. Kendal had for women the readiest consideration, and though one of the odd things he found in Elfrida was the slight degree to which she evoked it in him, he recoiled instinctively from any reasoned action which would distress her. But his sense of her inconsistency with British institutions—at least he fancied it was that—led him to discourage somewhat, in the lightest way, Miss Halifax's interested inquiries about her. The inquiries suggested dimly that eccentricity and obscurity might be overlooked in any one whose personality really had a value for Mr. Kendal, and made an attempt, which was heroic considering the delicacy of Miss Halifax's scruples, to measure his appreciation of Miss Bell as a writer —to Miss Halifax the word wore a halo—and as an individual. If she did not succeed it was partly because he had not himself quite decided whether Elfrida, in London, was delightful or intolerable, and partly because he had no desire to be complicated in social relations which, he told himself, must be either ludicrous or insincere. The Halifaxes were not in any sense literary; their proper pretensions to that sort of society were buried with Sir William, who had been editor of the *Brown Quarterly* in his day, and many other things. They had inherited his friends as they had inherited his manuscripts; and in spite of a grievous inability to edit either of them, they held to one legacy as fast as to the other. Kendal thought with a somewhat repelled amusement of any attempt of theirs to assimilate Elfrida. It was different with the Cardiffs; but even under their enthusiastic encouragement he was disinclined to be anything but discreet and cautious about Elfrida. In one way and another she was, at all events, a young lady of potentialities, he reflected, and with a view to their effect among one's friends it might be as well to understand them. He went so far as to say to himself that Janet was such a thoroughly nice girl as she was; and then he smiled inwardly at the thought of how angry she would be at the idea of his putting any prudish considerations on her account into the balance against an interesting acquaintance. He had, nevertheless, a distinct satisfaction in the fact that it was really circumstances, in the shape of the *Decade* article, that had brought them together, and that he could hardly charge himself with being more than an irresponsible agent in the matter.

Under the influence of such considerations Kendal did not write to Elfrida at the *Age* office asking her address, as he had immediately resolved to do when he discovered that she had gone away without telling him where he might find her. It seemed to him that he could not very well see her at her lodgings. And the pleasure of coming upon her suddenly as she closed the door of the *Age* behind her and stepped out into Fleet Street a fortnight later overcame him too quickly to permit him to reflect that he was yielding to an opposite impulse in asking her to dine with him at Baliero's, as they might have done in Paris. It was an unlooked-for opportunity, and it roused a desire which he had not lately been calculating upon—a desire to talk with her about all sorts of things, to feel the exhilaration of her artistic single-mindedness, to find out more about her, to guess at the meanings behind her eyes. If any privileged cynic had taken the chance to ask him whether he found her eyes expressive of purely abstract significance, Kendal would have answered affirmatively in all honesty. And he would have added a confession of his curiosity to discover what she was capable of, if she was capable of anything—which he considered legitimate enough. At the moment, however, he had no time to think of anything but an inducement, and he dashed through whole pickets of scruples to find one. "They give one such capital strawberry ices at Baliero's," he begged her to believe. His resolutions did not even reassert themselves when she refused. He was conscious only that it was a bore that she should refuse, and very inconsistent; hadn't she often dined with him at the Café Florian? His gratification was considerable when she added, "They smoke there, you know," and it became obvious, by whatever curious process of reasoning she arrived at it, that it was Baliero's restaurant she objected to, and not his society.

"Well," he urged, "there are plenty of places

where they don't smoke, though it didn't occur to me that—"

"Oh," she laughed, "but you must allow it to occur to you," and she put her finger on her lip. Considering their solitariness in the crowd, he thought, there was no reason why he should not say that he was under the impression she liked the smell of tobacco.

"There *are* other places," she went on. "There is a sweet little green-and-white place like a dairy in Oxford Street, that calls itself the 'Hyacinth,' which is sacred to ladies and to gentlemen properly chaperoned. If you would invite me to dine with you there I should like it very much."

"Anywhere," he said. He accepted her proposal to dine at the "Hyacinth" with the same unquestioning pleasure which he would have had in accepting her proposal to dine at the top of the Monument that evening; but he felt an under perplexity at its terms, which was vaguely disturbing. How could it possibly matter? Did she suppose that she advanced palpably nearer to the proprieties in dining with him in one place rather than the other? There was an unreasonableness about that which irritated him.

He felt it more distinctly when she proposed taking an omnibus instead of the cab he had signalled.

"Oh, of course, if you prefer it," he said; and there was almost a trace of injured feeling in his voice. It was so much easier to talk in a cab.

He lost his apprehensions presently, for it became obvious to him that this was only a mood, coming, as he said to himself devoutly, from the Lord knew what combination of circumstances—he would think that out afterward—but making Elfrida none the less agreeable while it lasted. Under its influence she kept away from all the matters she was fondest of discussing with that extraordinary candor and startling equity of hers, and talked to him with a pretty cleverness, about commonplaces of sorts arising out of the day's news, the shops, the weather. She treated them all with a gaiety that made her face a fascinating study while she talked, and pointed them, as it were, with all the little poises and expressions and reserves which are commonly a feminine result of considerable social training. Kendal, entering into her whim, inwardly compared her with an acknowledged successful girl of the season with whom he had sat out two dances the night before in Eaton Square, to the successful girl's disadvantage. Finding something lacking in that, he came upon a better analogy in a young married lady of the diplomatic circle, who had lately been dipping the third finger of her left hand into politics with the effect of considerably increasing her note. This struck him as satisfactory, and he enjoyed finding completion for his parallel wherever her words and gestures offered it. He took her at the wish she implied, and eddied with her around the pool which some counter-current of her nature had made for the hour in its stream, pleasantly enough. He made one attempt, as Elfrida unbuttoned her gloves at their little table at the "Hyacinth," to get her to talk about her work for the *Age*.

"Please, *please* don't mention that," she said. "It is too revolting. You don't know how it makes me suffer."

A moment later she returned to it of her own accord, however. "It is absurd to try to exact pledges from people," she said, "but I should really be happier—*much* happier—if you would promise me something."

"'By Heaven, I will promise *any* thing!'" Kendal quoted, laughing, from a poet much in vogue.

"Only this—I hope I am not selfish—" she hesitated; "but I think—yes, I think I must be selfish here. It is that you will never read the *Age*."

"I never do," leapt to his lips, but he stopped it in time. "And why?" he asked instead.

"Ah, you know why! It is because you might recognize my work in it—by accident you might—

and that would be so painful to me. It is *not* my best—please believe it is not my best!"

"On one condition I promise," he said: "that when you do your best you will tell me where to find it."

She looked at him gravely and considered. As she did so it seemed to Kendal that she was regarding his whole moral, mental, and material nature. He could almost see it reflected in the glass of her great dark eyes. "Certainly, yes. That is fair—if you really and truly care to see it. And I don't know," she added, looking up at him from her soup, "that it matters whether you do or not, so long as you carefully and accurately pretend that you do. When my best, my real best, sees the light of common—"

"Type," he suggested.

"Type," she repeated unsmilingly, "I shall be so insatiate for criticism—I ought to say praise—that I shall even go so far as to send you a marked copy, *very plainly* marked, with blue pencil. Already," she smiled with a charming effect of assertiveness, "I have bought the blue pencil."

"Will it come soon?" Kendal asked seriously.

"*Cher ami*," Elfrida said, drawing her handsome brows together a little, "it will come sooner than you expect. That is what I want," she went on deliberately, "more than anything else in the whole world, to do things—*good* things, you understand—and to have them appreciated and paid for in the admiration of people who feel and see and know. For me life has nothing else, except the things that other people do, better and worse than mine."

"Better and worse than yours," Kendal repeated. "Can't you think of them apart?"

"No, I can't," Elfrida interrupted; "I've tried, and I can *not*. I know it's a weakness—at least I'm half persuaded that it is—but I must have the personal standard in everything."

"But you are a hero-worshipper; often I have seen you at it."

"Yes," she said cynically, while the white-capped maid who handed Kendal asparagus stared at her with a curiosity few of the Hyacinth's lady diners inspired, "and when I look into that I find it is because of a secret consciousness that tells me that I, in the hero's place, should have done just the same thing. Or else it is because of the gratification my vanity finds in my sympathy with his work, whatever it is. Oh, it is no special virtue, my kind of hero-worship." The girl looked across at Kendal and laughed a bright, frank laugh, in which was no discontent with what she had been telling him.

"You are candid," Kendal said.

"Oh yes, I'm candid. I don't mind lying for a noble end, but it isn't a noble end to deceive one's self."

"'Oh, purblind race of miserable men—'" Kendal began lightly, but she stopped him.

"Don't!" she cried. "Nothing spoils conversation like quotations. Besides, that's such a trite one; I learned it at school."

But Kendal's offence was clearly in his manner. It seemed to Elfrida that he would never sincerely consider what she had to say about herself. She went on softly, holding him with her eyes: "You may find me a simple creature—"

"*A propos*," laughed Kendal easily, "what is this particular noble end?"

"Bah!" she said, "you are right. It was a lie, and it had no end at all. I am complex enough, I dare say. But this is true, that my egotism is like a little flame within me. All the best things feed it, and it is so clear that I see everything in its light. To me it is most dear and valuable, it simplifies things so. I assure you I wouldn't be one of the sloppy, unselfish people the world is full of for anything."

"As a source of gratification isn't it rather limited?" Kendal asked. He was thinking of the extra drop of nervous fluid in Americans that he had been reading about in the afternoon, and wondering if it often had this development.

"I don't quite know what you mean," Elfrida returned. "It isn't a source of gratification, it's a channel. And it intensifies everything so that I don't care how little comes that way. If there's anything of me left when I die it will be that little fierce flame. And when I do the tiniest thing, write the shortest sentence that rings *true*, see a beauty or a joy which the common herd pass by, I have my whole life in the flame, and it becomes my soul—I'm sure I have no other!

"When you say that there is no real pleasure in the world that does not come through art," Elfrida went on again, widening her eyes seriously, "don't you feel as if you were uttering something religious—part of a creed—as the Mussulman feels when he says there is no God but one God, and Mohammed is his prophet? I do."

"I never say it," Kendal returned, with a smile. "Does that make me out a Philistine, or a Hindu, or what?"

"*You* a Philistine!" Elfrida cried, as they rose from the little table. "You are saying a thing that is absolutely wicked."

Her quasi-conventional mood had vanished completely, and as they drove together in a hansom through the mysterious movement of the lamp-lit London streets, toward her lodgings, she plunged enjoyingly into certain theories of her religion, which embraced Arnold and Aristotle and did not exclude Mr. Whistler, and made wide, ineffectual, and presumptuous grasps to include all beauty and all faith. She threw handfuls of the foam of these things at Kendal, who watched them vanish into the air with pleasure, and asked if he might smoke. At which she reflected, deciding that for the present he might not, but when they reached her lodgings she would permit him to renew his acquaintance with Buddha, and give him a cigarette.

During the hour they smoked and talked together Elfrida was wholly delightful, and only one thing occurred to mar the enjoyment of the evening as Kendal remembered it. That was Mr. Golightly Ticke, who came up and smoked too, and seemed to have an extraordinary familiarity, for such an utterly impossible person, with Miss Bell's literary engagements. On his way home Kendal reflected that it was doubtless a question of time; she would take to the customs of civilization by degrees, and the sooner the better.

CHAPTER XV.

SHORTLY afterward Elfrida read Mr. Pater's "Marius," with what she herself called, somewhat extravagantly, a "hungry and hopeless" delight. I cannot say that this Oxonian's tender classical recreation had any critical effect upon her; she probably found it much too limpid and untroubled to move her in the least. I mention it by way of saying that Lawrence Cardiff lent it to her, with a smile of half-indulgent, half-contemptuous assent to some of her ideas, which was altered, when she returned the volumes, by the active necessity of defending his own. Elfrida had been accepted at the Cardiffs, with the ready tolerance which they had for types that were remarkable to them, and not entirely disagreeable; though Janet was always telling her father that it was impossible that Elfrida should be a type—she was an exception of the most exceptionable sort. "I'll admit her to be abnormal, if you like," Cardiff would return, "but only from an insular point of view. I dare say they grow that way in Illinois." But that was in the early stages of their acquaintance with Miss Bell, which ripened with unprecedented rapidity for an acquaintance in Kensington Square. It was before Janet had taken to walking across the gardens with Elfrida in the half-hour between tea-time and dressing for dinner, when the two young women, sometimes under dripping umbrellas, would let the right omnibus follow the wrong one toward Fleet Street twice and thrice in their disinclination to postpone what they had to say to each other. It was also before Elfrida's invasion of the library and fee-simple of the books, and before she had said there many things that were original, some that were impertinent, and a few that were true. The Cardiffs discussed her less freely as the weeks went on—a sure sign that she was becoming better liked, accepted less as a phenomenon, and more as a friend. There grew up in Janet the beginnings of the strong affection which she felt for a very few people, an affection which invariably mingled itself with a lively desire to bestir herself on their account, to be fully informed as to their circumstances, and above all to possess relations of absolute directness with them. She had an imperious successful strain which insisted upon all this. She was a capable creature of much perception for twenty-four, and she had a sense of injury when for any reason she was not allowed to use her faculties for the benefit of any one she liked in a way which excited the desire to do it. Janet had to reproach herself, when she thought of it, that this sort of liking seldom came by entirely approved channels, and hardly ever found an object in her visiting-list. Its first and almost its only essential, to speak boldly, was an artistic susceptibility with some sort of relation to her own, which her visiting-list did not often supply, though it might have been said to overflow with more widely recognized virtues. For that Miss Cardiff was known to be willing to sacrifice the Thirty-nine Articles, respectable antecedents, the possession of a dress-coat. Her willingness was the more widely known because in the circle which fate had drawn around her—ironically, she sometimes thought—it was not usual to sacrifice these things. As for Janet's own artistic susceptibility, it was a very private atmosphere of her soul. She breathed it, one might say, only occasionally, and with a kind of delicious shame. She was incapable of sharing her caught-up felicity there with any one, but it was indispensable that she should see it sometimes in the eyes of others less contained, less conscious, whose sense of humor might be more slender perhaps. Her own nature was practical and managing in its ordinary aspect, and she had a degree of tact that was always interfering with her love of honesty. Having established a friendship by the arbitrary law of sympathy, it must be admitted that she had an instinctive way of trying to strengthen it by voluntary benefits, for affection was a great need with her.

It was only about this time and very gradually that she began to realize how much more she cared for John Kendal than for other people. Since it seemed to be obvious that Kendal gave her only a share of the affectionate interest he had for humanity at large, the realization was not wholly agreeable, and Janet doubtless found Elfrida, on this account, even a more valuable distraction than she otherwise would. One of the matters Miss Bell was in the habit of discussing with some vivacity was the sexlessness of artistic sympathy. Upon this subject Janet found her quite inspired. She made a valiant effort to illumine her thoughts of Kendal by the light Elfrida threw upon such matters, and although she had to confess that the future was still hid in embarrassed darkness, she did manage to construct a theory by which it was possible to grope along for the present. She also cherished a hope that this trouble would leave her, as a fever abates in the night, that she would awake some morning, if she only had patience, strong and well. In other things Miss Cardiff was sometimes jarred rather than shocked by the American girl's mental attitudes, which, she began to find, were not so posed as her physical ones. Elfrida often left her repelled and dissenting. The dissent she showed vigorously; the repulsion she concealed, sore with herself because of the concealment. But she could not lose Elfrida, she told herself; and besides, it was only a matter of a little tolerance—time and life would change her, tone her inner self down into the something altogether exquisite and perfect that she was, to look at, now.

Elfrida called the Cardiffs' house the oasis of Kensington, and valued her privileges there more than she valued anything else in the circumstances about her, except, perhaps, the privilege she had enjoyed in making the single contribution to the *Decade* of which we know. That was an event lustrous in her memory, the more lustrous because it remained solitary; and when the editor's check made its tardy appearance she longed to keep it as a glorious archive—glorious, that is to say, in suggestion, if not particularly impressive intrinsically. In the end she fought the temptation of giving herself a dinner a day for a fortnight out of it, and bought a slender gold bangle with the money, which she slipped upon her wrist with a resolution to keep it there always. It must be believed that her personal decoration did not enter materially into this design; the bangle was an emblem of one success and an earnest of others. She wore it as she might have worn a medal, except that a medal was a public voice, and the little gold hoop spoke only to her.

After the triumph that the bangle signified Elfrida felt most satisfaction in what was constantly present to her mind as her conquest of the Cardiffs. She measured its importance by their value. Her admiration for Janet's work in the beginning had been as sincere as her emulation of its degree of excellence had been passionate, and neither feeling had diminished with their intimacy. In Lawrence Cardiff she felt vaguely the qualities that made him a marked man among his fellows, his intellectual breadth and keenness, his poise of brain, if one might call it so, and the *habileté* with which, without permitting it to be part of his character, he sometimes allowed himself to charm even people of whom he disapproved. These things were indeterminately present to her, and led her often to speculate as to how it was that Mr. Cardiff's work expressed him so little. It seemed to her that the one purpose of a personality like his was its expression—otherwise one might as well be of the ruck.

"You write with your intellectual faculties," she said to him once; "your soul is curiously dumb." But that was later.

The plane of Elfrida's relations with Janet altered gradually, one might say, from the inclined, with Elfrida on her knees at the lower end, to the horizontal. It changed insensibly enough, through the freemasonry of confessed and unconfessed ideals, through growing attraction, through the feeling they shared, though only Janet voiced it, that there was nothing but the opportunities and the experience of four years between them, that in the end Elfrida would do better, stronger, more original work than she. Elfrida was so much more original a person, Janet declared to herself, so—and when she hesitated for this word she usually said "enigmatical." The answer to the enigma, Janet was sure, would be written large in publishers' advertisements one day. In the meantime, it was a vast satisfaction to Janet to be, as it were, behind the enigma, to consider it with the privileges of intimacy. These young women felt their friendship deeply, in their several ways. It held for them all sacredness and honor and obligation. For Elfrida it had an intrinsic beauty and interest, like a curio —she had half a dozen such curios in the museum of her friends—and for Janet it added something to existence that was not there before, more delightful and important than a mere opportunity of expansion. The time came speedily when it would have been a positive pain to either of them to hear the other discussed, however favorably.

CHAPTER XVI.

LADY HALIFAX and her daughter had met Miss Bell several times at the Cardiffs', in a casual way, before it occurred to either of them to take any sort of advantage of the acquaintance. The younger lady had a shivering and frightened delight in occasionally wading ankle-deep in unconventionality, but she had lively recollections, in connection with the Cardiffs, of having been very nearly taken off her feet. They had since decided that it was more discreet to ignore Janet's enthusiasms, which were sometimes quite impossible in their verdict, and always improbable. The literary ladies and gentlemen whom the ghost of the departed Sir William brought more or less unwillingly to Lady Halifax's drawing-rooms were all of unexceptionable *cachet;* the Halifaxes were constantly seeing paragraphs about them in the "Literary Gossip" department of the *Athenian*, mentioning their state of health, their retirement from scientific appointments, or the fact that their most recent work of fiction had reached its fourth edition. Lady Halifax always read the *Athenian*, even the publishers' announcements; she liked to keep "in touch," she said, with the literary activities of the day, and it gave her a special gratification to notice the prosperity of her writing friends indicated in tall figures. Miss Halifax read it too, but she liked the "Art Notes" best; it was a matter of complaint with her that the house was not more open to artists—new, original artists like John Kendal. In answer to this Lady Halifax had a habit of stating that she did not see what more they could possibly want than the president of the Royal Academy and the one or two others that came already. As for John Kendal, he was certainly new and original, but he was respectable notwithstanding; they could be certain that he was not putting his originality on—with a hearth-brush, for the sake of advertisement. Lady Halifax was not so sure of Elfrida's originality, of which she had been given a glimpse or two at first, and which the girl's intimacy with the Cardiffs would have presupposed in any case. But presently, and somewhat to Lady Halifax's perplexity, Miss Bell's originality disappeared. It seemed to melt into the azure of perfect good-breeding, flecked by little clouds of gay sayings and politenesses, whenever chance brought her under Lady Halifax's observation. A not unreasonable solution of the problem might have been found in

Elfrida's instinctive objection to casting her pearls where they are proverbially unappreciated, and the necessity in her nature of pleasing herself by one form of agreeable behavior if not by another. Lady Halifax, however, ascribed it to the improving influence of insular institutions, and finally concluded that it ought to be followed up.

Elfrida wore amber and white the evening on which Lady Halifax followed it up—a Parisian modification of a design carried out originally by the Sparta dressmaker, with a degree of hysteria, under Miss Bell's direction. She wore it with a touch of unusual color in her cheeks and an added light in her dark eyes that gave a winsomeness to her beauty which it had not always. A cunningly bound spray of yellow-stamened lilies followed the curving line of her low-necked dress, ending in a cluster in her bosom; the glossy little leaves of the smilax the florist had wreathed in with them stood sharply against the whiteness of her neck. Her hair was massed at the back of her head simply and girlishly enough, and its fluffiness about her forehead made a sweet shadow above her eyes. She had a little fever of expectation, Janet had talked so much about this reception. Janet had told her that the real thing, the real English literary thing in numberless volumes, would be on view at Lady Halifax's. Miss

Cardiff had mentioned this in their discussion of the Arcadia Club, at which institution she had scoffed so unbearably that Elfrida, while she cherished the memory of Georgiadi, had not mentioned it since. Perhaps, after all, she reflected, Janet was just a trifle blind where people were not hall-marked. It did not occur to her to consider how far she herself illustrated this theory.

But as she went down Mrs. Jordan's narrow flights of stairs covered with worn oil-cloth, she kissed her own soft arm for pure pleasure.

"You are ravishing to-night," she told herself.

Golightly Ticke's door was open, and he was standing in it, picturesquely smoking a cigarette with the candle burning behind him—"Just to see you pass," he said.

Elfrida paused and threw back her cloak. "How is it?" she asked, posing for him with its folds gathered in either hand.

Ticke scanned her with leisurely appreciation. "It is exquisite," he articulated.

Elfrida gave him a look that might have intoxicated nerves less accustomed to dramatic effects.

"Then whistle me a cab," she said.

Mr. Ticke whistled her a cab and put her into it. There was the least pressure of his long fingers as he took her hand, and Elfrida forbade herself to resent it. She felt her own beauty so much that night that she could not complain of an enthusiasm for it in such a *belle âme* as Golightly.

They went up to the drawing-room together, Elfrida and the Cardiffs, and Lady Halifax immediately introduced to Miss Bell a hollow-cheeked gentleman with a long gray beard and bushy eyebrows as a fellow-countryman. "You can compare your impressions of Hyde Park and St. Paul's," said Lady Halifax, "but *don't* call us 'Britishers.' It really isn't pretty of you."

Elfrida discovered that the bearded gentleman was principal of a college in Florida, and corresponded regularly at one time with the late Sir William. "It is to that," said he ornately, "that I owe the honor of joining this brilliant company to-night." He went on to state that he was over there principally on account of his health—acute dyspepsia he had, it seemed he'd got out of running order generally, regularly off the track. "But I've just about concluded," he continued, with a pathetic twinkle under his bushy brows, "that I might have a worse reason for going back. What do you think of the meals in Victoria's country, Miss Bell? It seems to me sometimes that I'd give the whole British Museum for a piece of Johnny-cake."

Elfrida reflected that this was not precisely

what she expected to experience, and presently the hollow-cheeked Floridian was again at Lady Halifax's elbow for disposal, while the young lady whose appearance and nationality had given him so much room for hope smilingly drifted away from him. The Cardiffs were talking to a rosy and smooth-faced round-waistcoated gentleman just returned from Siberia about the unfortunate combination of accidents by which he lost the mail train twice in three days, and Janet had just shaken hands with a short and cheerful-looking lady astrologist.

"Behind that large person in the heliotrope brocade—she's the wife of the *Daily Mercury*—there's a small sofa," Janet said in an undertone. "I don't think she'll occupy it, the brocade looks so much better standing—no, there she goes! Let us sit down." As they crossed the room Janet added: "In another minute we should have been shut up in a Russian prison. Daddy's incarcerated already. And the man told all he knew about them in the public prints a month ago." They sat down luxuriously together, and made ready, in their palm-shaded corner, to wreak the whole of their irresponsible youth upon Lady Halifax's often venerable and always considerable guests. The warm atmosphere of the room had the perceptible charge of personalities. People in almost every part of it were trying to look unconscious as they pointed out other people.

"Tell me about everybody—everybody," said Elfrida.

"H'm! I don't see anybody, that *is* anybody, at this moment. Oh, there's Sir Bradford Barker. Regard him well, for a brave soul is Sir Bradford, Frida mine."

"A soldier? At this end of the century one can't feel an enthusiasm for killing."

"Not in the least. A member of Parliament who writes verses and won't be intimidated by Punch into not publishing them. And the man he is talking to has just done a history of the Semitic nations. He took me down to dinner last night, and we talked in the most intelligent manner about the various ways of preparing crabs. He liked them in five styles; I wouldn't subscribe to more than three. That little man with the orchid that daddy has just seized is the author of the last of the 'Rulers of India' series—Sir Somebody Something, K.C.S.I. My unconscionable humbug of a parent probably wants to get something approaching a fact out of him. Daddy's writing a thing for one of the reviews on the elective principle for India this week. He says he's the only writer on Indian subjects who isn't disqualified by ever having been there, and is consequently quite free of prejudice."

"Ah!" said Elfrida, "how *banal!* I thought you said there would be something real here—somebody in whose garment's hem there would be virtue."

"And I suggest the dress-coat of the historian of the Semitic nations!" Janet laughed. "Well, if nearly all our poets are dead and our novelists in the colonies, I can't help it, can I? Here is Mr. Kendal, at all events."

Kendal came up, with his perfect manners, and immediately it seemed to Elfrida that their little group became distinct from the rest, more important, more worthy of observation. Kendal never added anything to the unities of their conversation when he joined these two; he seemed rather to break up what they had to say to each other and attract it to himself. He always gave an accent to the life and energy of their talk; but he made them both self-conscious and watchful—seemed to put them, as it were, upon their guard against one another, in a way which Janet found vaguely distressing. It was invariably as if Kendal turned their intercourse into a joust by his mere presence as spectator; as if—Janet put it plainly to herself, reddening—they mutely asked him to bestow the wreath on one of them. She almost made up her mind to ask Elfrida where their understanding went to when John Kendal came up, but she had not found it possible yet. There was an embarrassing chance that Elfrida did not feel their change of attitude, which would entail nameless surmises.

"You ought to be at work," Janet said severely to Kendal, "back at Barbizon or in the fields somewhere. It won't be always June."

"Ah, would you banish him!" Elfrida exclaimed daintily. "Surely Hyde Park is rustic enough—in June."

Kendal smiled into her face. "It combines all the charm of the country," he began.

"And the chic of the town," Elfrida finished for him gaily. "I know—I've seen the Boot Show."

"Extremely frivolous," Janet commented.

"Ah, now we are condemned!" Elfrida answered, and for an instant it almost seemed as if it were so.

"Daddy wants you to go and paint straggling gray stone villages in Scotland now—straggling, climbing gray stone villages with only a bit of blue at the end of the 'Dead Wynd,' where it turns into the churchyard gate."

"How charming!" Elfrida exclaimed.

"I suppose he has been saturating himself with Barrie," Kendal said. "If I could reproduce Barrie on canvas, I'd go, like a shot. By the way, Miss

Bell, there's somebody you are interested in—do you see a middle-aged man, rather bald, thick-set, coming this way?—George Jasper."

"Really!" Elfrida exclaimed, jumping to her feet. "Oh, *thank* you! The most consummate artist in human nature that the time has given!" she added, with intensity. "There can be no question. Oh, I am *so* happy to have seen him!"

"I'm not altogether sure," Kendal began, and then he stopped, looking at Janet in astonished question. Elfrida had taken half a dozen steps into the middle of the room, steps so instinct with effect that already as many heads were turned to look at her. Her eyes were large with excitement, her cheeks flushed, and she bent her head a little, almost as if to see nothing that might dissuade her from her purpose. The author of "The Alien," "A Moral Catastrophe," "Her Disciple," and a number of other volumes which cause envy and heart-burnings among publishers, in the course of his somewhat short-sighted progress across the room, paused with a confused effort to remember who this pretty girl might be who wanted to speak to him.

Elfrida said, "Pardon me!" and Mr. Jasper instantly perceived that there could be no question of that, with her face. She was holding out her hand, and he took it with absolute mystification.

Elfrida had turned very pale, and a dozen people were listening. "Give me the right to say I have done this!" she said, looking at him with shy bravery in her beautiful eyes. She half sank on one knee and lifted the hand that wrote "A Moral Catastrophe" to her lips.

Mr. Jasper repossessed himself of it rather too hastily for dignity, and inwardly he expressed his feelings by a puzzled oath. Outwardly he looked somewhat ashamed of having inspired this unknown young lady's enthusiasm, but he did his confused best, on the spur of the moment, to carry off the situation as one of the contingencies to which the semi-public life of a popular novelist is always subject.

"Really, you are—much too good. I can't imagine —if the case had been reversed—"

Mr. Jasper found himself, accustomed as he was to the exigencies of London drawing-rooms, horribly in want of words. And in the bow with which he further defined his discomfort he added to it by dropping the bit of stephanotis which he wore in his buttonhole.

Elfrida sprang to pick it up. "Oh," she cried, "it is broken at the stem; see, you cannot wear it any more. May I keep it?"

A deadly silence had been widening around them,

and now the daughter of the historian of the Semitic races broke it by twittering into a laugh behind her fan. Janet met Kendal's eyes instinctively; he was burning red, and his manner was eloquent of his helplessness. Angry with herself for having waited so long, Janet joined Elfrida just as the twitter made itself heard, and Mr. Jasper's face began to stiffen with indignation.

"Ah, Miss Cardiff," he said with relief, "how do you do! The rooms are rather warm, don't you think?"

"I want to introduce you to my Am—my very great friend, Miss Bell, Mr. Jasper," Janet said quickly, as the buzz of conversation began again about them.

Elfrida turned to her reproachfully. "If I had known it was at all possible that you would do *that*," she said, "I might have—waited. But I did not know."

People were still looking at them with curious attentiveness; they were awkwardly solitary. Kendal in his corner was asking himself how she could have struck such a false note—and of all people Jasper, whose polished work held no trace of his personality, whose pleasure it was to have no public entity whatever. As Jasper moved off almost immediately, Kendal saw his tacit discomfort in the set of his shoulders, and so sure was he of Elfrida's embarrassment that he himself slipped away to avoid adding to it.

"It was all wrong and ridiculous, and she was mad to do it," thought Janet as she drove home with her father; "but why need John Kendal have blushed for her?"

CHAPTER XVII.

"I AM sure you are enjoying it," said Elfrida.

"Yes," Miss Kimpsey returned. "It's a great treat—it's a *very* great treat. Everything surpasses my expectations, everything is older and blacker and more interesting than I looked for. And I must say we're getting over a great deal in the time. Yesterday afternoon we did the entire Tower. It *did* give one an idea. But of course you know every stone in it by now!"

"I'm afraid I've not seen it," Elfrida confessed gravely. "I know it's shocking of me."

"You haven't visited the Tower! Doesn't that show how benumbing opportunity is to the energies! Now I dare say that I," Miss Kimpsey went on with gratification, "coming over with a party of tourists from our State, all bound to get London and the cathedral towns and the lakes and Scotland and Paris and Switzerland into the summer vacation—I presume I may have seen more of the London sights than you have, Miss Bell." As Miss Kimpsey spoke she realized that she had had no intention of calling Elfrida "Miss Bell" when she saw her again, and wondered why she did it. "But you ought to be fond of sight-seeing, too," she added, "with your artistic nature."

Elfrida seemed to restrain a smile. "I don't know that I am," she said. "I'm sorry that you didn't leave my mother so well as she ought to be. She hasn't mentioned it in her letters." In the course of time Miss Bell's correspondence with her parents had duly re-established itself.

"She *wouldn't*, Elf—Miss Bell. She was afraid of suggesting the obligation to come home to you. She said with your artistic conscience you couldn't come, and it would only be inflicting unnecessary pain upon you. But her bronchitis was no light matter last February. She was real sick."

"My mother is always so considerate," Elfrida answered, reddening, with composed lips. "She is better now, I think you said."

"Oh yes, she's some better. I heard from her last week, and she says she doesn't know how to wait to see me back. That's on your account, of course. Well, I can tell her you appear comfortable," Miss Kimpsey looked around, "if I *can't* tell her exactly when you'll be home."

"That is so doubtful, just now—"

"They're introducing drawing from casts in the

High School," Miss Kimpsey went on, with a note of urgency in her little twanging voice, "and Mrs. Bell told me I might just mention it to you. She thinks you could easily get taken on to teach it. I just dropped round to one or two of the principal trustees the day before I left, and they said you had only to apply. It's seven hundred dollars a year."

Elfrida's eyebrows contracted. "Thanks very much! It was extremely kind—to go to so much trouble. But I have decided that I am not meant to be an artist, Miss Kimpsey," she said, with a self-contained smile. "I think my mother knows that. I—I don't much like talking about it. Do you find London confusing? I was dreadfully puzzled at first."

"I *would* if I were alone. I'd engage a special policeman—the policemen *are* polite, aren't they? But we keep the party together, you see, to economize time, so none of us get lost. We all went down Cheapside this morning and bought umbrellas—two and three apiece. This is the most reasonable place for umbrellas. But isn't it ridiculous to pay for apples by the *pound?* And then they're not worth eating. This room does smell of tobacco. I suppose the gentleman in the apartment below smokes a great deal."

"I think he does. I'm so sorry. Let me open another window."

"Oh, don't mind *me!* I don't object to tobacco, except on board ship. But it must be bad to sleep in."

"Perhaps," said Elfrida sweetly. "And have you no more news from home for me, Miss Kimpsey?"

"I don't know as I have. You've heard of the Rev. Mr. Snider's second marriage to Mrs. Abraham Peeley, of course. There's a great deal of feeling about it in Sparta—the first Mrs. Snider was so popular, you know—and it isn't a full year. People say it isn't the *marriage* they object to under such circumstances, it's—all that goes before," said Miss Kimpsey, with decorous repression, and Elfrida burst into a peal of laughter. "Really," she sobbed, "it's too delicious. Poor Mr. and Mrs. Snider! Do you think people woo with improper warmth—at that age, Miss Kimpsey?"

"I don't know anything about it," Miss Kimpsey declared, with literal truth. "I suppose such things justify themselves somehow, especially when it's a clergyman. And of course you know about your mother's idea of coming over here to settle?"

"No!" said Elfrida, arrested. "She hasn't mentioned it. Do they talk of it seriously?"

"I don't know about *seriously*. Mr. Bell doesn't seem as if he could make up his mind. He's so fond of Sparta, you know. But Mrs. Bell is just wild to come. She thinks, of course, of having you to live with them again; and then she says that on their present income—you will excuse my referring to your parents' reduced circumstances, Miss Bell?"

"Please go on."

"Your mother considers that Mr. Bell's means would go further in England than in America. She asked me to make inquiries; and I must say, judging from the price of umbrellas and woolen goods, I think they would."

Elfrida was silent for a moment, looking steadfastly at the possibility Miss Kimpsey had developed. "What a complication!" she said, half to herself; and then, observing Miss Kimpsey's look of astonishment: "I had no idea of that," she repeated; "I wonder that they have not mentioned it."

"Well then!" said Miss Kimpsey, with sudden compunction, "I presume they wanted to surprise you. And I've gone and spoiled it!"

"To surprise me!" Elfrida repeated in her absorption. "Oh yes; very likely!" Inwardly she saw her garret, the garret that so exhaled her, where she had tasted success and knew a happiness that never altogether failed, vanish into a snug cottage in Hampstead or Surbiton. She saw the ruin of her independence, of her delicious solitariness, of the life that began and ended in her sense of the strange and the beautiful and the grotesque in a world of curious slaveries, of which it suited her to be an alien spectator, amused and free. She foresaw long conflicts and discussions, pryings which she could not resent, justifications which would be forced upon her, obligations which she must not refuse. More intolerable still, she saw herself in the rôle of a family idol, the household happiness hinging on her moods, the question of her health, her work, her pleasure being eternally the chief one. Miss Kimpsey talked on about other things—Windsor Castle, the Abbey, the Queen's stables; and Elfrida made occasional replies, politely vague. She was mechanically twisting the little gold hoop on her wrist, and thinking of the artistic sufferings of a family idol. Obviously the only thing was to destroy the prospective shrine.

"We don't find board as cheap as we expected," Miss Kimpsey was saying.

"Living, that is food, is very expensive," Elfrida replied quickly; "a good beefsteak, for instance, costs three francs—I mean two and fivepence, a pound."

"I *can't* think in shillings!" Miss Kimpsey interposed plaintively.

"And about this idea my people have of coming

over here—I've been living in London four months now, and I can't quite see your grounds for thinking it cheaper than Sparta, Miss Kimpsey."

"Of course you *have* had time to judge of it."

"Yes. On the whole I think they would find it more expensive and much less satisfactory. They would miss their friends, and their place in the little world over there. My mother, I know, attaches a good deal of importance to that. They would have to live very modestly in a suburb, and all the nice suburbs have their social relations in town. They wouldn't take the slightest interest in English institutions; my father is too good a citizen to make a good subject, and they would find a great many English ideas very—trying. The only Americans who are happy in England are the millionaires," Elfrida answered. "I mean the millionaires who are not too sensitive."

"Well now, you've got as sensitive a nature as I know, Miss Bell, and you don't appear to be miserable over here."

"I!" Elfrida frowned just perceptibly. This little creature who once corrected the punctuation of her essays, and gave her bad marks for spelling, was too intolerably personal. "We won't consider my case, if you please. Perhaps I'm not a good American."

"Mrs. Bell seems to think she would enjoy the atmosphere of the past so much in London."

"It's a fatal atmosphere for asthma. Please impress that upon my people, Miss Kimpsey. There would be no justification in letting my mother believe she could be comfortable here. She must come and experience the atmosphere of the past, as you are doing, on a visit. As soon as it can be afforded I hope they will do that."

Since the day of her engagement with the *Illustrated Age* Elfrida had been writing long, affectionate, and prettily worded letters to her mother by every American mail. They were models of sweet elegance, those letters; they abounded in dainty bits of description and gay comment, and they reflected as little of the real life of the girl who wrote them as it is possible to conceive. In this way they were quite remarkable, and in their charming discrimination of topics. It was as if Elfrida dictated that a certain relation should exist between herself and her parents. It should acknowledge all the traditions, but it should not be too intimate. They had no such claim upon her, no such closeness to her, as Nádie Palicsky, for instance, had.

When Miss Kimpsey went away that afternoon, trying to realize the intrinsic reward of virtue—she had been obliged to give up the National Gallery to make this visit—Elfrida remembered that the American mail went out next day, and spent a longer time than usual over her weekly letter. In its course she mentioned with some amusement the absurd idea Miss Kimpsey had managed to absorb of their coming to London to live, and touched in the lightest possible way upon the considerations that made such a project impossible. But the greater part of the letter was taken up with a pleased forecast of the time—could it possibly be next summer?—when Mr. and Mrs. Bell would cross the Atlantic on a holiday trip. "I will be quite an affluent person by then," Elfrida wrote, "and I will be able to devote the whole of my magnificent leisure to entertaining you."

She turned from the sealing of this to answer a note from Lawrence Cardiff. He wrote to her, on odds and ends of matters, almost as often as Janet did now. He wrote as often, indeed, as he could, and always with an amused, uncertain expectancy of what the consciously directed little square envelopes which brought back the reply would contain. It was becoming obvious to him that they brought something a little different, in expression or feeling or suggestion, from the notes that came for Janet, which Janet often read out for their common benefit. He was unable to define the difference, but he was aware that it gave him pleasure, especially as he could not find that it was in any way connected with the respectful consideration that Elfrida might have thought due to his forty-seven years. If Mr. Cardiff had gone so far as to soliloquize upon the subject he would have said to himself, "In my trade a man gets too much of that." I do not know that he did, but the subtle gratification this difference gave him was quite strong enough, at all events, to lead to the reflection. The perception of it was growing so vivid that he instinctively read his notes in silence, paraphrasing them for Janet if she happened to be there. They had, as it were, a bloom and a freshness, a mere perfume of personality that would infallibly vanish in the communicating, but that left him, as often as not, when he slipped the note back into the envelope with a half smile on his lips.

Janet was conscious of the smile and of the paraphrasing. In reprisal—though she would not have admitted it was that—she kept her own missives from Elfrida to herself whenever it occurred to her to check the generous impulse of sharing the pleasure they gave her, which was not often, after all. It was the seldomer because she could not help feeling that her father was thoroughly aware of her action, and fancying that he speculated upon the reason of it. It was unendurable that daddy should speculate about the reason of anything she did in connection with Frida, or with any other young lady. Her conduct was perfectly simple; there was no reason whatever why it should not be perfectly simple.

When Miss Kimpsey arrived at Euston Station next day, with all her company, to take the train for Scotland, she found Elfrida waiting for her, a picturesque figure in the hurrying crowd, with her hair blown about her face with the gusts of wind and rain, and her wide dark eyes looking quietly about her. She had a bunch of azaleas in her hand, and as Miss Kimpsey was saying with gratification that Elfrida's coming down to see her off was a thing she did *not* expect, Miss Bell offered her these

"They will be pleasant in the train perhaps," said she. "And do you think you could find room for this in one of your boxes? It isn't very bulky—a trifle I should like so much to send to my mother, Miss Kimpsey. It might go by post, I know, but the pleasure will be much greater to her if you could take it."

In due course Mrs. Bell received the packet. It contained a delicate lace head-dress, which cost Elfrida the full pay and emoluments of a fortnight.

Mrs. Bell wore it at all social gatherings of any importance in Sparta the following winter, and often reflected with considerable pleasure upon the taste and unselfishness that so obviously accompanied the gift.

CHAPTER XVIII.

IF John Kendal had been an on-looker at the little episode of Lady Halifax's drawing-room in Paris six months earlier it would have filled him with the purest amusement. He would have added the circumstance to his conception of the type of young woman who enacted it, and turned away without stopping to consider whether it flattered her or not. His comprehension of human nature was too catholic very readily to permit him impressions either of wonder or contempt—it would have been a matter of registration and a smile. Realizing this, Kendal was the more at a loss to explain to himself the feeling of irritation which the recollection of the scene persistently aroused in him, in spite of a pronounced disposition, of which he could not help being aware, not to register it but to ignore it. His memory refused to be a party to his intention, and the tableau recurred to him with a persistence which he found distinctly disagreeable. Upon every social occasion which brought young ladies of beauty and middle-aged gentlemen of impressive eminence into conversational contact he saw the thing in imagination done again. In the end it suggested itself to him as paintable—the astonished drawing-room, the graceful half-kneeling girl with the bent head, the other dismayed and uncomprehending figure yielding a doubtful hand, his discomfort indicated in the very lines of his waistcoat. "*A Fin de Siècle Tribute*," Kendal named it. He dismissed the idea as absurd, and then reconsidered it as a means of disposing of the incident finally. He knew it could be very effectually put away in canvas. He assured himself again that he could not entertain the idea of painting it seriously, and that this was because of the inevitable tendency which the subject would have toward caricature. Kendal had an indignant contempt for such a tendency, and the liberty which men who used it took with their art. He had never descended to the flouting of his own aims which it implied. He threw himself into his pictures without reserve; it was the best of him that he painted, the strongest he could do, and all he could do; he was sincere enough to take it always seriously. The possibility of caricature seemed to him to account admirably for his reluctance to paint "*A Fin de Siècle Tribute*," —it was a matter of conscience. He found that the desire to paint it would not go, however; it took daily more complete possession of him, and fought his scruples with a strong hand. It was a fortnight after, and he had not seen Elfrida in the meantime, when they were finally defeated by the argument that a sketch would show whether caricature were necessarily inherent or not. He would make a sketch purely for his own satisfaction. Under the circumstances Kendal realized perfectly that it could never be for exhibition, and indeed he felt a singular shrinking from the idea that any one should see it. Finally, he gave a whole day to the thing, and made an admirable sketch.

After that Kendal felt free to make the most of his opportunities of seeing Elfrida—his irritation with her subsided, her blunder had been settled to his satisfaction. He had an obscure idea of having inflicted discipline upon her in giving the incident form and color upon canvas, in arresting its grotesqueness and sounding its true *motif* with a pictorial tongue. It was his conception of the girl that he punished, and he let his fascinated speculation go out to her afterward at a redoubled rate. She brought him sometimes to the verge of approval, to the edge of liking; and when he found that he could not take the further step he told himself impatiently that it was not a case for anything so ordinary as approval, or anything so personal as liking; it was a matter of observation, enjoyment, stimulus. He availed himself of these abstractions with a candor that was the more open for not being complicated with any less hardy motive. He had long ago decided that relations of sentiment with Elfrida would require a temperament quite different from that of any man he knew. It was entirely otherwise with Janet Cardiff, and Kendal smiled as he thought of the feminine variation the two girls illustrated. He had a distinct recollection of one crisp October afternoon before he went to Paris, as they walked home together under the brown curling leaves and passed the Serpentine, when he had found that the old charm of Janet's gray eyes was changing to a new one. He remembered the pleasure he had felt in dallying with the thought of making them lustrous, one day, with tenderness for himself. It had paled since then, there had been so many other things; but still they were dear, honest eyes—and Kendal never brought his reverie to a conclusion under any circumstances whatever.

CHAPTER XIX.

I HAVE mentioned that Miss Bell had looked considerations of sentiment very full in the face at an age when she might have been expected to be blushing and quivering before them, with downcast countenance. She had arrived at conclusions about them —conclusions of philosophic contumely, indifference, and some contempt. She had since frequently talked about them to Janet Cardiff with curious disregard of time and circumstance, mentioning her opinion in a Strand omnibus, for instance, that the only dignity attaching to love as between a man and a woman was that of an artistic idea. Janet had found Elfrida possessed of so savage a literalism in this regard that it was only in the most hardily adventurous of the moods of investigation her friend inspired that she cared to combat her here. It was not, Janet told herself, that she was afraid to face the truth in any degree of nakedness; but she rose in hot inward rebellion against Elfrida's borrowed psychological cynicisms—they were not the truth, Tolstoi had not all the facts, perhaps from pure Muscovite inability to comprehend them all. The spirituality of love might be a western product—she was half inclined to think it was; but at all events it existed, and it was wanton to leave out of consideration a thing that made all the difference. Moreover, if these things ought to be probed—and Janet was not of serious opinion that they ought to be—for her part she preferred to obtain advices thereon from between admissible and respectable bookcovers. It hurt her to hear them drop from Elfrida's lips—lips so plainly meant for all tenderness. Janet had an instinct of helpless anger when she heard them; the woman in her rose in protest, less on behalf of her sex than on behalf of Elfrida herself, who seemed so blind, so willing to revile, so anxious to reject. "Do you really hope you will marry?" Elfrida had asked her once; and Janet had answered candidly, "Of course I do, and I want to die a grandmother too." "*Vraiment!*" exclaimed Miss Bell ironically, with a little shudder of disgust, "I hope you may!"

That was in the very beginning of their friendship, however, and so vital a subject could not remain outside the relations which established themselves more and more intimately between them as the days went on. Janet began to find herself constantly in the presence of a temptation to bring the matter home to Elfrida personally in one way or another, as young women commonly do with other young women who are obstinately unorthodox in these things—to say to her in effect, "Your turn will come when *he* comes! These pseudo-philosophies will vanish when *he* looks at them, like snow in spring. You will succumb—you will succumb!" But she never did. Something in Elfrida's attitude forbade it. Her opinions were not vagaries, and she held them, so far as they had a personal application, haughtily. Janet felt and disliked the tacit limitation, and preferred to avoid the clash of their opinions when she could. Besides, her own ideas upon the subject had latterly retired irretrievably from the light of discussion. She had one day found it necessary to lock the door of her soul upon them; in the new knowledge that had taken sweet possession of her she recognized that they were no longer theoretical, that they must be put away. She challenged herself to sit in a jury upon Love, and found herself disqualified.

The discovery had no remarkable effect upon Janet. She sometimes wasted an hour, pen in hand, in inconsequent reverie, and worked till midnight to make up; and she took a great liking for impersonal conversations with Miss Halifax about Kendal's pictures, methods and meanings. She found dining in Royal Geographical circles less of a bore than usual, and deliberately laid herself out to talk well. She looked in the glass sometimes at a little vertical line that seemed to be coming at the corners of her mouth, and wondered whether at twenty-four one might expect the first indication of approaching old-maidenhood. When she was paler than usual she reflected that the season was taking a good deal out of her. She was bravely and rigidly commonplace with Kendal, who told her that she ought to drop it and go out of town—she was not looking well. She drew closer to her father, and at the same time armed her secret against him at all points. Janet would have had any one know rather than he. She felt that it implied almost a breach of faith, of comradeship, to say nothing of the complication of her dignity, which she wanted upheld in his eyes before all others. In reality she made him more the sovereign of her affections and the censor of her relations than nature designed Lawrence Cardiff to be in the parental connection. It gave him great pleasure that he could make his daughter a friend, and accord her the independence of a friend; it was a satisfaction to him that she was not obtrusively filial. Her feeling for Kendal, under the circumstances, would have hurt him if he had known of it, but only through his sympathy and his affection—he was unacquainted with the jealousy of a father. But in Janet's eyes they made their little world together, indispensable to each other as its imaginary hemispheres. She had a quiet pain, in the infrequent moments when she allowed herself the full realization of her love for Kendal, in the knowledge that she, of her own motion, had disturbed its unities and its ascendancies.

Since that evening at Lady Halifax's, when Janet saw John Kendal reddening so unaccountably, she had felt singularly more tolerant of Elfrida's theories. She combated them as vigorously as ever, but she lost her dislike to discussing them. As it became more and more obvious that Kendal found in Elfrida a reward for the considerable amount of time he spent in her society, so Janet arrived at the point of encouraging her heresies, especially with their personal application. She took secret comfort in them; she hoped they would not change, and she was too honest to disguise to herself the reason. If Elfrida cared for him, Janet assured herself, the case would be entirely different—she would stamp out her own feeling without mercy, to the tiniest spark. She would be glad, in time, to have crushed it for Elfrida, though it did seem that it would be more easily done for a stranger, somebody she wouldn't have to know afterward. But if Elfrida didn't care, as a matter of principle Janet was unable to see the least harm in making her say so as often as possible. They were talking together in Mr. Cardiff's library late one June afternoon, when it seemed to Janet that the crisis came, that she could never again speak of such matters to Elfrida without betraying herself. Things were growing dim about the room, the trees stood in dusky groups in the square outside. There was the white glimmer of the tea-things between them, and just light enough to define the shadows round the other girl's face, and write upon it the difference it bore, in Janet's eyes, to every other face.

"Oh!" Elfrida was saying, "it does make life more interesting, I admit—up to a certain point. And I suppose it's to be condoned from the point of view of the species. Whoever started us, and wants us to go on, excuses marriage, I suppose. And of course the men are not affected by it. But for women, it is degrading—horrible. Especially for women like you and me, to whom life may mean something else. Fancy being the author of babies when one could be the author of books! *Don't* tell me you'd rather!"

"I!" said Janet. "Oh, I'm out of it. But I approve the principle."

"Besides, the commonplaceness, the eternal routine, the being tied together, the—the domestic virtues! It must be death, absolute death, to any fineness of nature. No," Elfrida went on decisively, "people with anything in them that is worth saving may love as much as they feel disposed, but they ought to keep their freedom. And some of them do nowadays."

"Do you mean," said Janet slowly, "that they dispense with the ceremony?"

"They dispense with the condition. They—they don't go so far."

"I thought you didn't believe in Platonics," Janet answered, with wilful misunderstanding.

"You know I don't believe in them. Any more," Elfrida added lightly, "than I believe in this exaltation you impute to the race of a passion it shares with—with the mollusks. It's pure self-flattery."

There was a moment's silence. Elfrida clasped her hands behind her head and turned her face toward the window so that all the light that came through softly gathered in it. Janet felt the girl's beauty as if it were a burden, pressing with literal physical weight upon her heart. She made a futile effort to lift it with words. "Frida," she said, "you are beautiful to—to hurt to-night. Why has nobody ever painted a creature like you?"

It was as if she touched an inner spring of the girl's nature, touched it electrically. Elfrida leaned forward consciously with shining eyes. "Truly am I, Janetta? Ah—to-night! Well, yes, perhaps tonight, I am. It is an effect of chiaroscuro. But what about always—what about generally, Janetta? I have such horrid doubts. If it weren't for my nose I should be satisfied—yes, I think I should be satisfied. But I *can't* deceive myself about my nose, Janetta; it's thick!"

"It isn't a particularly spiritually-minded nose," Janet laughed. "But console yourself, it's thoughtful."

Elfrida put her elbows on her knees and framed her face with the palms of her hands. "If I am beautiful to-night you ought to love me. Do you love me, Janetta? Really *love* me? Could you imagine," she went on, with a whimsical spoiled shake of her head, "any one else doing it?"

Janet's fingers closed tightly on the arm of her chair. Was it coming already, then?

"Yes," she said slowly, "I could imagine it well."

"More than one?" Elfrida insisted prettily. "More than two or three? A dozen, perhaps?"

"Quite a dozen," Janet smiled. "Is that to be the limit of your heartless proceedings?"

"I don't know how soon one would grow tired of it. Maybe in three or four years. But for now—it is very amusing."

"Playing with fire?"

"Bah!" Elfrida returned, going back to her other mood. "I'm not inflammable. But to that extent, if you like, I value what you and the poets are pleased to call love. It's part of the game; one might as well play it all. It's splendid to win—anything. It's a kind of success."

"Oh, I know," she went on after an instant. "I have done it before—I shall do it again, often! It is worth doing—to sit within three feet of a human being who would give all he possesses just to touch your hand—and to tacitly dare him to do it."

"Stop, Elfrida!"

"Shan't stop, my dear. Not only to be able to check any such demonstration yourself, with a movement, a glance, a turn of your head, but without even a sign, to make your would-be adorer check it himself! And to feel as still and calm and superior to it all! Is that nothing to you?"

"It's less than nothing. It's hideous!"

"I consider it a compensation vested in the few for the wrongs of the many," Elfrida replied gaily. "And I mean to store up all the compensation in my proper person that I can."

"I believe you have had more than your share already," Janet cried.

"Oh no! a little, only a little. Hardly anything here—people fall in love in England in such a mathematical way. But there is a callow artist on the *Age*, and Golightly Ticke has become quite mad lately, and Solomon—I mean Mr. Rattray—will propose next week—he thinks I won't dare to refuse the sub-editor. How I shall laugh at him! Afterward, if he gives me any trouble, I shall threaten to write up the interview for the *Pictorial News*. On the whole though, I dare say I'd better not suggest such a thing; he would want it for the *Age*. He is equal to any personal sacrifice for the *Age*."

"Is that all?" asked Janet, turning away her head.

"You are thinking of John Kendal! Ah, there it becomes exciting. From what you see, Janetta *mia*, what should you *think?* Myself, I don't quite know. Don't you find him rather—a good deal—interested?"

Janet had an impulse of thankfulness for the growing darkness. "I—I see him so seldom!" she said. Oh, it was the last time, the very last time, that she would ever let Elfrida talk like this.

"Well, I think so," Elfrida went on coolly. "He fancies he finds me curious, original, a type—just now. I dare say he thinks he takes an anthropological pleasure in my society! But in the beginning it is all the same thing, my dear, and in the end it will be all the same thing. This delicious Loti," and she picked up "Aziàdé"—"what an anthropologist he is—with a feminine bias!"

Janet was tongue-tied. She struggled with herself for an instant, and then, "I *wish* you'd stay and dine," she said desperately.

"How thoughtless of me!" Elfrida replied, jumping up. "You ought to be dressing, dear. No, I can't; I've got to sup with some ladies of the Alhambra to-night—it will make such lovely copy. But I'll go now, this very instant."

Half-way downstairs Janet, in a passion of helpless tears, heard Elfrida's footsteps pause and turn. She stepped swiftly into her own room and locked the door. The footsteps came tripping back into the library, and then a tap sounded on Janet's door. Outside Elfrida's voice said plaintively, "I had to come back. Do you love me—are you quite sure you love me?"

"You humbug!" Janet called from within, steadying her voice with an effort, "I'm not at all sure. I'll tell you to-morrow!"

"But you do!" cried Elfrida, departing. "I know you do."

CHAPTER XX.

July thickened down upon London. The society papers announced that with the exception of the few unfortunate gentlemen who were compelled to stay and look after their constituents' interests at Westminster, "everybody" had gone out of town, and filled up yawning columns with detailed information as to everybody's destination. To an inexperienced eye, with the point of view of the top of an Uxbridge Road omnibus for instance, it might not appear that London had diminished more than to the extent of a few powdered footmen on carriage boxes; but the census of the London world is after all not to be taken from the top of an Uxbridge Road omnibus. London teemed emptily, the tall houses in the narrow lanes of Mayfair slept standing, the sunlight filtered through a depressing haze and stood still in the streets for hours together. In the Park the policemen wooed the nursery-maids free from the embarrassing smiling scrutiny of people to whom this serious preoccupation is a diversion. The main thoroughfares were full of "summer sales," St. Paul's echoed to admiring Transatlantic criticism, and the Bloomsbury boarding-houses to voluble Transatlantic complaint.

The Halifaxes were at Brighton, Lady Halifax giving musical teas, Miss Halifax painting marine views in a little book. Miss Halifax called them "impressions," and always distributed them at the musical teas. The Cardiffs had gone to Scotland for golf, and later on for grouse. Janet was almost as expert on the links as her father, and was on very familiar terms with a certain Highland moor and one Donald Macleod. They had laid every compulsion upon Elfrida to go with them, in vain; the girl's sensitiveness on the point of money obligations was intense, and Janet failed to measure it accurately when she allowed herself to feel hurt that their relations did not preclude the necessity for taking any thought as to who paid. Elfrida staid, however, in her by-way of Fleet Street, and did a little bit of excellent work for the *Illustrated Age* every day. If it had not been for the editor-in-chief, Rattray would have extended her scope on the paper; but the editor-in-chief said no, Miss Bell was dangerous, there was no telling what she might be up to if they gave her the reins. She went very well, but she was all the better for the severest kind of a bit. So Miss Bell wrote about colonial exhibitions and popular spectacles, and country outings for babies of the slums, and longed for a fairer field. As midsummer came on there arrived a dearth in these objects of orthodox interest, and Rattray told her she might submit "anything on the nail" that occurred to her, in addition to such work as the office could give her to do. Then, in spite of the vigilance of the editor-in-chief, an odd unconventional bit of writing crept now and then into the *Age*—an interview with some eccentric notability with the piquancy of a page from Gyp, a bit of pathos picked out of the common streets, a fragment of character-drawing which smiled visibly and talked audibly. Elfrida in her garret drew a joy from these things. She cut them out and read them over and over again, and put them sacredly away, with Nádie's letters and a manuscript poem of a certain Bruynotin's, and a scrawl from one Hakkoff, with a vigorous sketch of herself, from memory, in pen and ink in the corner of the page, in the little eastern-smelling wooden box which seemed to her to represent the core of her existence. They quickened her pulse, they gave her a curious uplifted happiness that took absolutely no account of any other circumstance.

There were days when Mrs. Jordan had real twinges of conscience about the quality of Miss

Bell's steak. "But there," Mrs. Jordan would soothe herself, "I might bring her the best sulline, and she wouldn't know no diffrence." In other practical respects the girl was equally indifferent. Her clothes were shabby, and she did not seem to think of replacing them; Mrs. Jordan made preposterous charges for candles, and she paid them without question. She tipped people who did little services for her with a kind of royal delicacy; the girl who scrubbed the landings worshipped her, and the boy who came every day for her copy once brought her a resplendent "button-hole" consisting of two pink rosebuds and a scarlet geranium, tendering it with a shy lie to the effect that he had found it in the street. She went alone now and again to the opera, taking an obscure place, and she lived a good deal among the foreign art exhibitions of Bond Street. Once she bought an etching and brought it home under her arm. That kept her poor for a month, though she would have been less aware of it if she had not, before the month was out, wanted to buy another. A great Parisian actress had made her yearly visit to London in June, and Elfrida, conjuring with the name of the *Illustrated Age*, won an appointment from her. The artiste staid only a fortnight—she declared that one half of an English audience came to see her because it was proper and the other because it was sinful, and she found it insupportable—and in that time she asked Elfrida three times to pay her morning visits, when she appeared in her dressing-gown, little unconventional visits *"pour bavarder."* When Miss Bell lacked entertainment during the weeks that followed she thought of these visits, and little smiles chased each other round the corners of her mouth.

She wrote to Janet when she was in the mood—delicious scraps of letters, broad-margined, fantastic, each, so far as charm went, a little literary gem disguised in wilfulness, in a picture, in a diamond-cut cynicism that shone sharper and clearer for the dainty affectation of its setting. When she was not in the mood she did not write at all. With an instinctive recognition of the demands of any relation such as she felt her friendship with Janet Cardiff to be, she simply refrained from imposing upon her anything that savored of dullness or commonplaceness. So that sometimes she wrote three or four times in a week and sometimes not at all for a fortnight, sometimes covered pages and sometimes sent three lines and a row of asterisks. There was a fancifulness in the hour as well, that usually made itself felt all through the letter—it was rainy twilight in her garret, or a gray wideness was creeping up behind St. Paul's, which meant that it was morning. To what she herself was actually doing, or to any material fact about her, they made the very slightest reference. Janet, in Scotland, perceived half of this, and felt aggrieved on the score of the other half. She wished, more often than she said she did, that Elfrida were a little more human, that she had a more appreciative understanding of the warm value of common every-day matters between people who were interested in one another. The subtle imprisoned soul in Elfrida's letters always spoke to hers, but Janet never received so artistic a missive of three lines that she did not wish it were longer, and she had no fund of confidence to draw on to meet her friend's incomprehensible spaces of silence. To cover her real soreness she scolded, chaffed brusquely, affected lofty sarcasms.

"Twelve days ago," she wrote, "you mentioned casually that you were threatened with pneumonia; your communication of to-day you devote to proving that Hector Malot is a carpenter. I agree with you with reservations, but the sequence worries me. In the meantime have you had the pneumonia?"

Her own letters were long and gossipping, full of the scent of the heather and the eccentricities of Donald Macleod; and she wrote them regularly twice a week, using rainy afternoons for the purpose and every inch of the paper at her disposal.

Elfrida put a very few of them into the wooden box, just as she would have embalmed, if she could, a very few of the half-hours they had spent together.

CHAPTER XXI.

JOHN KENDAL had turned the key upon his dusty work-room in Bryanston Street among the first of those who, according to the papers, depopulated London in July. He had an old engagement to keep, which took him, with Carew of the *Dial* and Limley of the Civil Service, to explore and fish in the Norwegian fjords. The project matured suddenly, and he left town without seeing anybody—a necessity which disturbed him a number of times on the voyage. He wrote a hasty line to Janet, returning a borrowed book, and sent a trivial message to Elfrida, whom he knew to be spending a few days in Kensington Square at the time. Janet delivered it with an intensity of quiet pleasure which she showed extraordinary skill in concealing. "May I ask you to say to Miss Bell—" seemed to her to be eloquent of many things. She looked at Elfrida with inquiry, in spite of herself, when she gave the message, but Elfrida received it with a nod and a smile of perfect indifference.

"It is because she does not care—does not care *an iota*," Janet told herself; and all that day it seemed to her that Elfrida's personality was inexhaustibly delightful.

Afterward, however, one or two letters found their way into the sandal-wood box, bearing the Norwegian postmark. They came seldomer than Elfrida expected. "*Enfin!*" she said when the first arrived, and she felt her pulse beat a little faster as she opened it. She read it eagerly, with serious lips, thinking how fine he was, and with what exquisite force he brought himself to her as he wrote. "I must be a very exceptional person," she said in her reverie afterward, "to have such things written to me. I must—I *must!*" Then as she put the letter away she reflected that she couldn't amuse herself with Kendal without treachery to their artistic relationship; there would be somehow an outrage in it. And she would not amuse herself with him; she would sacrifice that, and be quite frank and simple always. So that when *it* came to pass—here Elfrida retired into a lower depth of consciousness—there would be only a little pity and a little pain, and no reproach or regret. There was a delay in the arrival of the next letter which Elfrida felt to be unaccountable, a delay of nearly three weeks. She took it with an odd rush of feeling from the hand of the housemaid who brought it up, and locked herself in alone with it.

A few days later, driving through Bryanston Street in a hansom, Elfrida saw the windows of Kendal's studio wide open. She leaned forward to realize it with a little tumult of excitement at the possibility it indicated, half turned to bid the cabman stop, and rolled on undecided. Presently she spoke to him.

"Please go back to number sixty-three," she said, "I want to get out there," and in a moment or two she was tripping lightly up the stairs.

Kendal, in his shirt-sleeves, with his back to the door, was bending over a palette that clung obstinately to the hardened round dabs of color he had left upon it six weeks before. He threw it down at Elfrida's step, and turned with a sudden light of pleasure in his face to see her framed in the doorway, looking at him with an odd shyness and silence. "You spirit!" he cried, "how did you know I had come back?" and he held her hand for just an appreciable instant, regarding her with simple delight. Her tinge of embarrassment became her sweetly, and the pleasure in his eyes made her almost instantly aware of this.

"I didn't know," she said, with a smile that shared his feeling. "I saw the windows open, and

I thought the woman downstairs might be messing about here. They can do such incalculable damage when they really set their minds to it, these *concierge* people. So I—I came up to interfere. But it is you!" She looked at him with wide, happy eyes which sent the satisfaction she found in saying that to his inmost consciousness.

"That was extremely good of you," he said, and in spite of himself a certain emphasis crept into the commonplace. "I hardly realize myself that I am here. It might very well be the Skaagerak outside."

"Does the sea in Norway sound like that?" Elfrida asked, as the roar of London came across muffled from Piccadilly. She made a little theatrical movement of her head to listen, and Kendal's appreciation of it was so evident that she failed to notice exactly what he answered. "You have come back sooner than you intended?"

"By a month."

"Why?" she asked. Her eyes made a soft bravado, but that was lost. He did not guess for a moment that she believed she knew why he had come.

"It was necessary," he answered, with remembered gravity, "in connection with the death of— of a relative, a granduncle of mine. The old fellow went off suddenly last week, and they telegraphed for me. I believe he wanted to see me, poor old chap, but of course it was too late."

"Oh!" said Elfrida gently, "that is very sad. Was it a granduncle you were—fond of?"

Kendal could not restrain a smile at her earnestness.

"I was, in a way. He was a good old fellow, and he lived to a great age—over ninety. He has left me all the duties and responsibilities of his estate," Kendal went on, with sudden gloom. "The Lord only knows what I'll do with them."

"That makes it sadder," said the girl.

"I should think it did," Kendal replied; and then their eyes met, and they laughed the healthy instinctive laugh of youth when it is asked to mourn fatuously, which is always a little cruel.

"I hope," said Elfrida quickly, "that he has not saddled you with a title. An estate is bad enough, but with a title added it would ruin you. You would never do any more good work, I am sure—sure. People would get at you—you would take to rearing farm creatures from a sense of duty—you might go into Parliament. Tell me there is no title!"

"How do you know all that?" Kendal exclaimed, laughing. "But there is no title—never has been."

Elfrida drew a long sigh of relief, and held him with her eyes as if he had just been snatched away from some impending danger. "So now you are—what do you say in this country?—a landed proprietor. You belong to the country gentry. In America I used to read about the country gentry in *London Society*—all the contributors and all the subscribers to *London Society* used to be country gentry, I believe, from what I remember. They were always riding to hounds, and having big Christmas parties, and telling ghost stories about the family diamonds."

"All very proper," Kendal protested against the irony of her tone.

"Oh, if one would be quite *sure* that it will not make any difference," Elfrida went on, clasping her knee with her shapely gloved hands. "I should like—I should like to beg you to make me a promise that you will never give up your work—your splendid work!" She hesitated, and looked at him almost with supplication. "But then why should you make such a promise to *me!*"

They were sitting opposite one another in the dusty confusion of the room, and when she said this Kendal got up and walked over to her, without knowing exactly why.

"If I made such a promise," he said, looking down at her, "it would be more binding given to you than to anybody else—more binding and more sacred."

If she had exacted it he would have promised then and there, and he had some vague notion of sealing the vow with his lips upon her hand, and of arranging—this was more indefinite still—that she should always insist, in her sweet personal way, upon its fulfilment. But Elfrida felt the intensity in his voice with a kind of fear, not of the situation—she had a nervous delight in the situation—but of herself. She had a sudden terror in his coming so close to her, in his changed voice, and its sharpness lay in her recognition of it. Why should she be frightened? She jumped up gaily with the question still throbbing in her throat.

"No," she cried, "you shall not promise me. I'll form a solemn committee of your friends—your *real* friends—and we'll come some day and exact an oath from you, individually and collectively. That will be *much* more impressive. I must go now," she went on reproachfully, "and you have shown me nothing that you've brought back with you. Is there anything here?" In her anxiety to put space between them she had walked to the furthest and untidiest corner of the room, where half a dozen canvases leaned with their faces to the wall.

Kendal watched her tilt them forward one after another with a kind of sick impotence.

"Absolutely nothing!" he cried.

But it was too late—she had paused in her running commentary on the pictures, she was standing looking, absolutely silent, at the last but one. She had come upon it—she had found it—his sketch of the scene in Lady Halifax's drawing-room.

"Oh yes, there is something!" she said at last, carefully drawing it out and holding it at arm's length. "Something that is quite new to me. Do you mind if I put it in a better light?" Her voice had wonderfully changed; it expressed a curious interest and self-control. In effect that was all she felt for the moment; she had a dull consciousness of a blow, but did not yet quite understand being struck. She was gathering herself together as she looked, growing conscious of her hurt and of her resentment. Kendal was silent, cursing himself inwardly for not having destroyed the thing the day after he had let himself do it.

"Yes," she said, placing it on an easel at an oblique angle with the north window of the room, "it is better so."

She stepped back a few paces to look at it, and stood immovable, searching every detail. "It does you credit," she said slowly; "immense credit. Oh, it is very clever!"

"Forgive me," Kendal said, taking a step toward her. "I am afraid it doesn't. But I never intended you to see it."

"Is it an order?" she asked calmly. "Ah, but that would not have been fair—not to show it to me first!"

Kendal crimsoned. "I beg," he said earnestly, "that you will not think such a thing possible. I intended to destroy it—I don't know why I have not destroyed it!"

"But why? It is so good, so charming, so—so *true!* You did it for your own amusement, then! But that was very selfish."

For answer Kendal caught up a tube of Indian red, squeezed it on the crusted palette, loaded a brush with it, and dashed it across the sketch. It was a feeble piece of bravado, and he felt it, but he must convince her in some way that the thing was worthless to him.

"Ah," she said, "that is a pity!" and she walked to the door. She must get away, quite away, and quickly, to realize this thing, and find out exactly what it meant to her. And yet, three steps down the stairs she turned and came back again. John

Kendal stood where she had left him, staring at the sketch on the easel.

"I have come back to thank you," Elfrida said quickly, "for showing me what a fool I made of myself," and she was gone.

An hour later Kendal had not ceased to belabor himself; but the contemplation of the sketch—he had not looked at it for two months—brought him to the conclusion that perhaps, after all, it might have some salutary effect. He found himself so curiously sore about it though, so thoroughly inclined to brand himself a traitor and a person without obligation, that he went back to Norway the following week—a course which left a number of worthy people in the neighborhood of Bigton, Devonshire, very indignant indeed.

CHAPTER XXII.

"Daddy," Janet said to her father a few days after their return to town, "I've been thinking that we might—that you might—be of use in helping Frida to place something somewhere else than in that eternal picture paper."

"For instance?"

"Oh, in *Peterson's,* or the *London Magazine,* or *Piccadilly.*"

It was in the library after dinner, and Lawrence Cardiff was smoking. He took the slender stem of his pipe from his lips and pressed down the tobacco in the bowl with a caressing thumb, looking appreciatively, as he did it, at the mocking buffoon's face that was carved on it.

"It seems to me that you are the influential person in those quarters," he said, with the smile that Janet privately thought the most delightfully sympathetic she knew.

"Oh, I'm not really!" the girl answered quickly; "and besides—" she hesitated, to pick words that would hurt her as little as possible—"besides, Frida wouldn't care about my doing it."

"Why?"

"I don't know quite why. But she wouldn't—it's of no use. I don't think she likes having things done for her by people anything like her own age, and —and standing."

Cardiff smiled inwardly at this small insincerity. Janet's relation with Elfrida was a growing pleasure to him. He found himself doing little things to enhance it, and fancying himself in some way connected with its initiation.

"But I'm almost certain she would let you do it," his daughter urged.

"*In loco parentis*," Cardiff smiled, and immediately found that the words left an unpleasant taste in his mouth. "But I'm not at all sure that she could do anything they would take."

"My dear daddy!" cried Janet resentfully. "Wait till she tries! You said yourself that some of those scraps she sent us in Scotland were delicious."

"So they were. She has a curious, prismatic kind of mind—"

"Soul, daddy."

"Soul, if you like. It reflects quite wonderfully, the angles at which it finds itself with the world are so unusual. But I doubt her power, you know, of construction or cohesion, or anything of that kind."

"I don't," Janet returned confidently. "But talk

to her about it, daddy; get her to show you what she's done—I never see a line till it's in print. And—I don't know anything about it, you know. Above all things, don't let her guess that I suggested it."

"I'll see what can be done," Mr. Cardiff returned, "though I profess myself faithless. Elfrida wasn't designed to please the public of the magazines—in England."

When Janet reflected afterward upon what had struck her as being odd about this remark of her father's, she found it was Elfrida's name. It seemed to have escaped him; he had never referred to her in that way before—which was a wonder, Janet assured herself, considering how constantly he heard it from her lips.

"How does the novel come on?" Mr. Cardiff asked before she went to bed that night. "When am I to be allowed to see the proofs?"

"I finished the nineteenth chapter yesterday," Janet answered, flushing. "It will only run to about twenty-three. It's a very little one, daddy."

"Still nobody in the secret but Lash and Black?"

"Not a soul. I hope they're the right people," Janet said anxiously. "I haven't even told Elfrida," she added. "I want to surprise her with an early copy. She'll like it, I think. I like it pretty well myself. It has an effective leading idea."

Her father laughed, and threw her a line of Horace which she did not understand. "Don't let it take too much time from your other work," he warned her. "It's sure, you know, to be an arrant imitation of somebody, while in your other things you have never been anybody but yourself." He looked at her in a way that disarmed his words, and went back to his *Revue Bleue*.

"Dear old thing! You want to prepare me for anything, don't you? I wonder whom I've imitated! Hardy, I think, most of all—but then it's such a ludicrously far-away imitation! If there's nothing in the thing but *that*, it deserves to fall as flat as flat. But there is, daddy!"

Cardiff laid down his journal again at the appealing note.

"No!" she cried, "I won't bore you with it now; wait till the proofs come. Good-night!" She kissed him lightly on the cheek. "About Elfrida," she added, still bending over him. "You'll be *very* careful, won't you, daddy dear—not to hurt her feelings in any way, I mean?"

After she had gone, Lawrence Cardiff laid down the *Revue* again and smoked meditatively for half an hour. During that time he revolved at least five subjects which he thought Elfrida, with proper supervision, might treat effectively. But the supervision would be very necessary.

A fortnight later Mr. Cardiff sat in the same chair, smoking the same pipe, and alternately frowned and smiled upon the result of that evening's meditation. It had reached him by post in the afternoon without an accompanying word; the exquisite self-conscious manuscript seemed to breathe a subdued defiance at him, with the merest ghost of a perfume that Cardiff liked better. Once or twice he held the pages closer to his face to catch it more perfectly.

Janet had not mentioned the matter to him again; indeed, she had hardly thought of it. Her whole nature was absorbed in her fight with herself, in the struggle for self-control, which had ceased to come to the surface of her life at intervals, and had now become constant and supreme with her. Kendal had made it harder for her lately by continually talking of Elfrida. He brought his interest in her to Janet to discuss as he naturally brought everything that touched him to her, and Janet, believing it to be a lover's pleasure, could not forbid him. When he criticised Elfrida, Janet fancied it was to hear her warm defence, which grew oddly reckless in her anxiety to hide the bitterness that tinged it.

"Otherwise," she permitted herself to reflect, "he is curiously just in his analysis of her—for a man," and hated the thought for its touch of disloyalty.

Knowing Elfrida as she thought she knew her, Kendal's talk wounded her once for herself and twice for him. He was going on blindly, confidently, trusting, Janet thought bitterly, to his own sweetness of nature, to his comeliness and the fineness of his sympathies—who had ever refused him anything yet? And only to his hurt, to his repulse—from the point of view of sentiment, to his ruin. For it did not seem possible to Janet that a hopeless passion for a being like Elfrida Bell could result in anything but collapse. Whenever he came to Kensington Square, and he came often, she went down to meet him with a quaking heart, and sought his face nervously for the haggard, broken look which should mean that he had asked Elfrida to marry him and been artistically refused. Always she looked in vain; indeed, Kendal's spirits were so uniformly like a schoolboy's that once or twice she asked herself, with sudden terror, whether Elfrida had deceived her—whether it might not be otherwise between them, recognizing then, with infinite humiliation, how much worse that would be. She took to working extravagantly hard, and Elfrida noticed with distinct pleasure how much warmer her manner had grown, and in how many pretty ways she showed her enthusiasm. Janet was such a conquest! Once when Kendal seemed to Janet on the point of asking her what she thought of his chances, she went to a florist's in the High, and sent Elfrida a pot of snowy chrysanthemums, after which she allowed herself to refrain from seeing her for a week. Her talk with her father about helping Elfrida to place her work with the magazines had been one of the constant impulses by which she tried to compensate her friend, as it were, for the amount of suffering that young woman was inflicting upon her—she would have found a difficulty in explaining it more intelligibly than that.

As he settled together the pages of Miss Bell's article on "The Nemesis of Romanticism" and laid them on the table, Lawrence Cardiff thought of it with sincere regret.

"It is hopeless—hopeless," he said to himself. "It must be rewritten from end to end. I suppose she must do it herself," he added, with a smile that he drew from some memory of her, and he pulled writing materials toward him to tell her so. Re-reading his brief note, he frowned, hesitated, and tore it up. The next followed it into the waste-paper basket. The third gave Elfrida gently to understand that in Mr. Cardiff's opinion the article was a little unbalanced—she would remember her demand that he should be absolutely frank. She had made some delightful points, but there was a lack of plan and symmetry. If she would give him the opportunity he would be very happy to go over it with her, and possibly she would make a few changes. More than this Cardiff could not induce himself to say. And he would await her answer before sending the article back to her.

It came next day, and in response to it Mr. Cardiff found himself walking, with singular lightness of step, toward Fleet Street in the afternoon with Elfrida's manuscript in his pocket. Buddha smiled more inscrutably than ever as they went over it together, while the water hissed in the samovar in the corner, and little blue flames chased themselves in and out of the anthracite in the grate, and the queer Orientalism of the little room made its picturesque appeal to Cardiff's senses. He had never been there before.

From beginning to end they went over the manuscript, he criticising and suggesting, she gravely listening, and insatiately spurring him on.

"You may say anything," she declared. "The sharper it is the better, you know, for me. Please don't be polite—be savage!" and he did his best to comply.

She would not always be convinced; he had to

leave some points unvanquished; but in the main she agreed and was grateful. She would remodel the article, she told him, and she would remember all that he had said. Cardiff found her recognition of the trouble he had taken delightful; it was nothing, he declared; he hoped very particularly that she would let him be of use, if possible, often again. He felt an inexplicable jar when she suddenly said, "Did you ever do anything—of this sort—for Janet?" and he was obliged to reply that he never did—her look of disappointment was so keen. "She thought," he reflected, "that I hoisted Janet into literature, and could be utilized again perhaps," in which he did her injustice. But he lingered over his tea, and when he took her hand to bid her good-by he looked down at her and said, "Was I very brutal?" in a way which amused her for quite half an hour after he had gone.

Cardiff sent the amended article to the *London Magazine* with qualms. It was so unsuitable even then, that he hardly expected his name to do much for it, and the half-hour he devoted to persuading his literary conscience to let him send it was very uncomfortable indeed. Privately he thought any journalist would be rather an ass to print it, yet he sincerely hoped the editor of the *London Magazine* would prove himself such an ass. He selected the

London Magazine because it seemed to him that the quality of its matter had lately been slightly deteriorating. A few days later, when he dropped in at the office, impatient at the delay, to ask the fate of the article, he was distinctly disappointed to find that the editor had failed to approach it in the character he had mentally assigned to him. That gentleman took the manuscript out of the left-hand drawer of his writing-table, and fingered the pages over with a kind of disparaging consideration before handing it back.

"I'm very sorry, Cardiff, but we can't do anything with this, I'm afraid. We have—we have one or two things covering the same ground already in hand."

And he looked at his visitor with some curiosity. It was a queer article to have come through Lawrence Cardiff.

Cardiff resented the look more than the rejection. "It's of no consequence, thanks," he said drily. "Very good of you to look at it. But you print a great deal worse stuff, you know."

His private reflection was different, however, and led him to devote the following evening to making certain additions to the sense and alterations in the style of Elfrida's views on "The Nemesis of Romanticism," which enabled him to say, at about one o'clock in the morning, "*Enfin!* It is passable!" He took it to Elfrida on his way from his lecture next day. She met him at the door of her attic with expectant eyes; she was certain of success.

"Have they taken it?" she cried. "Tell me quick, quick!"

When he said no—the editor of the *London Magazine* had shown himself an idiot—he was very sorry, but they would try again, he thought she was going to cry. But her face changed as he went on, telling her frankly what he thought, and showing her what he had done.

"I've only improved it for the benefit of the Philistines," he said apologetically. "I hope you will forgive me."

"And now," she said at last, with a little hard air, "what do you propose?"

"I propose that if you approve these trifling alterations, we send the article to the *British Review*. And they are certain to take it."

Elfrida held out her hand for the manuscript, and he gave it to her. She looked at every page again. It was at least half re-written in Cardiff's small, cramped hand.

"Thank-you," she said slowly. "Thank-you very much. I have learned a great deal, I think, from what you have been kind enough to tell me, and to write here. But this, of course, so far as I am concerned in it, is a failure."

"Oh no!" he protested.

"An utter failure," she went on unnoticingly, "and it has served its purpose. There!" she cried with sudden passion, and in an instant the manuscript was flaming in the grate.

"Please—please go away," she sobbed, leaning against the mantel in a sudden betrayal of tears; and Cardiff, resisting the temptation to take her in his arms and bid her be comforted, went.

CHAPTER XXIII.

Mr. Rattray's proposal occurred as soon after the close of the season as he was able to find time to devote the amount of attention to it which he felt it required. He put it off deliberately till then, fearing that it might entail a degree of mental agitation on his part that would have an undesirable reflex action upon the paper. Mr. Rattray had never been really attracted toward matrimony before, although he had taken, in a discussion in the columns of the *Age* upon the careworn query, "Is Marriage a Failure?" a vigorous negative side under various pen-names which argued not only inclination, but experience. He felt, therefore, that he could not possibly predicate anything of himself under the circumstances, and that it would be distinctly the part of wisdom to wait until there was less going on. Mr. Rattray had an indefinite idea that in case of a rejection he might find it necessary to go out of town for some weeks to pull himself together again—it was the traditional course—and if such an exigency occurred before July the office would go to pieces under the pressure of events. So he waited, becoming every day more enthusiastically aware of the great advantage of having Miss Bell permanently connected with the paper under supervision which would be even more highly authorized than an editor's, and growing at the same time more thoroughly impressed with the unusual character of her personal charm. Elfrida was a "find" to Mr. Arthur Rattray from a newspaper point of view— a find he gave himself credit for sagaciously recognizing, and one which it would be expedient to obtain complete possession of before its market value should become known. And it was hardly possible for Mr. Rattray to divest himself of the newspaper point of view in the consideration of anything which concerned him personally. It struck him as uniquely fortunate that his own advantage and that of the *Age* should tally, as it undoubtedly might in this instance; and that, for Arthur Rattray, was putting the matter in a rather high, almost disinterested connection.

It is doubtful whether to this day Mr. Rattray fully understands his rejection, it was done so deftly, so frankly, yet with such a delicate consideration for his feelings. He took it, he assured himself afterward, without winking; but it is unlikely that he felt sufficiently indebted to the manner of its administration, in congratulating himself upon this point. It may be, too, that he left Miss Bell with the impression that her intention never to marry was not an immovable one, given indefinite time and indefinite abstention, on his part, from alluding to the subject. Certainly he found himself surprisingly little cast down by the event, and more resolved than ever to make the editor-in-chief admit that Elfrida's contributions were "the brightest things in the paper," and act accordingly. He realized, in the course of time, that he had never been very confident of any other answer; but nothing is more certain than that it acted as a curious stimulus to his interest in Elfrida's work. He found a co-enthusiast in Golightly Ticke, and on more than one occasion they agreed that something must be done to bring Miss Bell before the public, to put within her reach the opportunity of the success she deserved, which was of the order Mr. Rattray described as "screaming."

"So far as the booming is concerned," said Mr. Rattray to Mr. Ticke, "I will attend to that; but there must be something to boom. We can't sound the loud tocsin on a lot of our own paras. She must do something that will go between two covers."

The men were talking in Golightly's room over easeful Sunday afternoon cigars; and as Rattray spoke they heard a light step mount the stairs. "There she is now," replied Ticke. "Suppose we go up and propose it to her?"

"I wish I knew what to suggest," Rattray returned; "but we might talk it over with her—when she's had time to take off her bonnet."

Ten minutes later Elfrida was laughing at their ambitions. "A success?" she exclaimed. "Oh yes! I mean to have a success—one day! But not yet—oh no! First I must learn to write a line decently, then a paragraph, then a page. I must wait, oh, a very long time—ten years perhaps. Five, anyway."

"Oh, if you do that," protested Golightly Ticke, "it will be like decanted champagne. A success at nineteen—"

"Twenty-one," corrected Elfrida.

"Twenty-one if you like—is a sparkling success. A success at thirty-one is—well, it lacks the accompaniments."

"You are a great deal too exacting, Miss Bell," Rattray put in; "those things you do for us are charming, you know they are."

"You are very good to say so. I'm afraid they're only frivolous scraps."

"My opinion is this," Rattray went on sturdily. "You only want material. Nobody can make bricks without straw—to sell—and very few people can evolve books out of the air that any publisher will look at it. You get material for your scraps, and you treat it unconventionally, so the scraps supply a demand. It's a demand that's increasing every day—for fresh, unconventional matter. Your ability to treat the scraps proves your ability to do more sustained work if you could find it. Get the material for a book, and I'll guarantee you'll do it well."

Elfrida looked from one to the other with bright eyes. "What do you suggest?" she said, with a nervous little laugh. She had forgotten that she meant to wait ten years.

"That's precisely the difficulty," said Golightly, running his fingers through his hair.

"We must get hold of something," said Rattray. "You've never thought of doing a novel?"

Elfrida shook her head decidedly. "Not now," she said. "I would not dare. I haven't looked at life long enough—I've had hardly any experience at all. I couldn't conceive a single character with any force or completeness. And then for a novel one wants a leading idea—the plot, of course, is of no particular consequence. Rather I should say plots have merged into leading ideas; and I have none."

"Oh, distinctly!" observed Mr. Ticke finely. "A

plot is as vulgar at this end of the century as a—as a dress improver, to take a feminine simile."

Rattray looked seriously uncomprehending, and slowly scratched the back of his hand. "Couldn't you find a leading idea in some of the modern movements," he asked—"in the higher education of women, for instance, or the suffrage agitation?"

"Or University Extension, or Bimetallism, or Eight Hours' Labor, or Disestablishment!" Elfrida laughed. "No, Mr. Rattray, I don't think I could.

"I might do some essays," she suggested.

Rattray, tilting his chair back, with his forefingers in the arm-holes of his waistcoat, pursed his lips. "We couldn't get them read," he said. "It takes a well-established reputation to carry essays. People will stand them from a Lang or a Stevenson or that 'Obiter Dicta' fellow—not from an unknown young lady."

Elfrida bit her lip. "Of course I am not any of those."

"Miss Bell has done some idyllic verse," volunteered Golightly.

The girl looked at him with serious reprobation. "I did not give you permission to say that," she said gravely.

"No—forgive me!—but it's true, Rattray." He

searched in his breast pocket and brought out a diminutive pocket-book. "May I show those two little things I copied?" he begged, selecting a folded sheet of letter-paper from its contents. "This is serious, you know, really. We must go into all the chances."

Elfrida had a pang of physical distress.

"Oh," she said hastily, "Mr. Rattray will not care to see those. They weren't written for the *Age*, you know," she added, forcing a smile.

But Rattray declared that he should like it above all things, and looked the scraps gloomily over. One Elfrida had called "A Street Minstrel." Seeing him unresponsive, Golightly read it gracefully aloud.

"One late November afternoon
  I sudden heard a gentle rune.

"I could not see whence came the song,
  But, trancèd, stopped and listened long;

"And that drear month gave place to May,
  And all the city slipped away.

"The coal-carts ceased their din,—instead
  I heard a bluebird overhead;

"The pavements, black with dismal rain,
  Grew greenly to a country lane.

"Plainly as I see you, my friend,
  I saw the lilacs sway and bend,

"A blossoming apple-orchard where
The chimneys fret the foggy air,

"And wide mown fields of clover sweet
Sent up their fragrance at my feet,

"And once again dear Phyllis sat
The thorn beneath, and trimmed her hat.

. . . . .

"Long looked I for my wizard bard—
I found him on the boulevard.

"And now my urban hearth he cheers,
Singing all day of sylvan years,

"Right thankful for the warmer spot—
A cricket, by July forgot!"

Ticke looked inquiringly at Rattray when he had finished. Elfrida turned away her head, and tapped the floor impatiently with her foot.

"Isn't that dainty?" demanded Golightly.

"Dainty enough," Rattray responded, with a bored air. "But you can't read it to the public, you know. Poetry is out of the question. Poetry takes genius."

Golightly and Elfrida looked at each other sympathetically. Mr. Ticke's eyes said, "How hideously we are making you suffer," and Elfrida's conveyed a tacit reproach.

"Travels would do better," Rattray went on. "There's no end of a market for anything new in travels. Go on a walking tour through Spain, by yourself, disguised as a nun or something, and write about what you see."

Elfrida flushed with pleasure at the reckless idea. A score of situations rose before her thrilling, dangerous, picturesque, with a beautiful nun in the foreground. "I should like it above all things," she said, "but I have no money."

"I'm afraid it would take a good deal," Rattray returned.

"That's a pity."

"It disposes of the question of travelling, though, for the present," and Elfrida sighed with real regret.

"It's your turn, Ticke. Suggest something," Rattray went on. "It must be unusual and it must be interesting. Miss Bell must do something that no young lady has done before. That much she must concede to the trade. Granting that, the more artistically she does it the better."

"I should agree to that compromise," said Elfrida eagerly. "Anything to be left with a free hand."

"The book should be copiously illustrated," continued Rattray, "and the illustrations should draw their interest from you personally."

"I don't think I should mind that."

Her imagination was busy at a bound with press criticisms, pirated American editions, newspaper paragraphs describing the color of her hair, letters from great magazines asking for contributions. It leaped with a fierce joy at the picture of Janet reading these paragraphs, and knowing, whether she gave or withheld her own approval, that the world had pronounced in favor of Elfrida Bell. She wrote the simple note with which she would send a copy to Kendal, and somewhere in the book there would be things which he would feel so exquisitely that— The cover should have a French design and be the palest yellow. There was a moment's silence while she thought of these things, her knee clasped in her hands, her eyes blindly searching the dull red squares of the Llassa prayer-carpet.

"Rattray," said Golightly, with a suddenness that made both the others look up expectantly, "could Miss Bell do her present work for the *Age* anywhere?"

"Just now I think it's mostly book reviews—isn't it ?—and comments on odds and ends in the papers of interest to ladies. Yes—not quite so well out of London; but I dare say it could be done pretty much anywhere, reasonably near."

"Then," replied Golightly Ticke, with a repressed and guarded air, "I think I've got it."

CHAPTER XXIV.

THREE days later a note from Miss Cardiff in Kensington Square to Miss Bell in Essex Court, Fleet Street, came back unopened. A slanting line in very violet ink along the top read "*Out of town for the pressent. M. Jordan.*" Janet examined the line carefully, but could extract nothing further from it except that it had been written with extreme care, by a person of limited education and a taste for color. It occurred to her, in addition, that the person's name was probably Mary.

Elfrida's actions had come to have a curious importance to Janet; she realized how great an importance with the access of irritated surprise which came to her with this unopened note. In the beginning she had found Elfrida's passionate admiration so novel and so sweet that her heart was half won before they came together in completer intimacy, and she gave her new original friend a meed of affection which seemed to strengthen as it instinctively felt itself unreturned—at least in kind. Elfrida retracted none of her admiration, and she added to it, when she ceded her sympathy, the freedom of a fortified city; but Janet hungered for more. Inwardly she cried out for the something warm and human that was lacking to Elfrida's feeling for her, and sometimes she asked herself with grieved cynicism how her friend found it worth while to pretend to care so cleverly. More than once she had written to Elfrida with the deliberate purpose of soothing herself by provoking some tenderness in reply, and invariably the key she had struck had been that of homage, more or less whimsically unwilling. "*Don't* write such delicious things to me, *ma mie*," would come the answer. "You make me curl up with envy. What shall I do if malice and all uncharitableness follow? I admire you so horribly—there!" Janet told herself sorely that she was sick of Elfrida's admiration—it was not the stuff friendships were made of. And a keener pang supervened when she noticed that whatever savored most of an admiration on her own part had obviously the highest value for her friend. The thought of Kendal only heightened her feeling about Elfrida. She would be so much the stronger, she thought, to resist any—any strain —if she could be quite certain how much Elfrida cared—cared about her personally. Besides, the indictment that she, Janet, had against her seemed to make the girl's affection absolutely indispensable. And now Elfrida had apparently left London without a word. She had dined in Kensington Square the night before, and this was eleven o'clock in the morning. It looked very much as if she had deliberately intended to leave them in the dark as to her movements. People didn't go out of town indefinitely "for the present," on an hour's notice. The thought brought sudden tears to Janet's eyes, which she winked back angrily. "I am getting to be a perfect old maid!" she reflected. "Why shouldn't Frida go to Kamschatka, if she wants to, without giving us notice? It's only her eccentric way of doing things." And she frowned upon her sudden resolution to rush off to Fleet Street in a cab and inquire of Mrs. Jordan. It would be espionage. She would wait, quite calmly and indefinitely, till Frida chose to write, and then she would treat the escapade, whatever it was, with the perfect understanding of good-fellowship. Or perhaps not indefinitely—for two or three days—it was just possible that Frida might have had bad news and started suddenly for America by the early train to Liverpool, in which case she might easily not have had time to write. But in that case would not Mrs. Jordan have written "Gone to America"? Her heart stood still with another thought—could she have gone with Kendal? Granting that she had made up her mind to marry him, it would be just Elfrida's strange, sensational way. Janet walked the floor in a restless agony, mechanically tearing the note into little strips. She must know—she must find out. She would write and ask him for something—for what? A book, a paper—the *New Monthly*, and she must have some particular reason. She sat down to write, and pressed her fingers upon her throbbing eyes in the effort to summon a particular reason. It was as far from her as ever when the maid knocked and came in with a note from Kendal asking them to go to see Miss Rehan in "As You Like It" that evening—a note fragrant of tobacco, not an hour old.

"You needn't wait, Jessie," she said. "I'll send an answer later;" and the maid had hardly left the room before Janet was sobbing silently and helplessly with her head on the table. As the day passed however, Elfrida's conduct seemed less unforgivable, and by dinner-time she was able to talk of it with simple wonder, which became more tolerant still in the course of the evening, when she discovered that Kendal was as ignorant and as astonished as they themselves.

"She will write," Janet said hopefully; but a week passed and Elfrida did not write. A settled disquietude began to make itself felt between the Cardiffs. Accepting each other's silence for the statement that Elfrida had sent no word, they ceased to talk of her —as a topic her departure had become painful to both of them. Janet's anxiety finally conquered her scruples, and she betook herself to Essex Court to inquire of Mrs. Jordan. That lady was provokingly mysterious, and made the difficulty of ascertaining that she knew nothing whatever about Miss Bell's movements as great as possible. Janet saw an acquaintance with some collateral circumstance in her eyes, however, and was just turning away irritated by her vain attempts to obtain it, when Mrs. Jordan decided that the pleasure of the revelation would be, after all, greater than the pleasure of shielding the facts.

"Wether it 'as anything to do with Miss Bell or not, of course I can't say," Mrs. Jordan remarked, with conscientious hypocrisy, "but Mr. Ticke, *he* left town that same mornin'." She looked disappointed when Miss Cardiff received this important detail indifferently.

"Oh, nothing whatever," Janet replied, with additional annoyance that Elfrida should have subjected herself to such an insinuation. Janet had a thoroughgoing dislike to Golightly Ticke. On her way back in the omnibus she reflected on the coincidence, however, and in the end she did not mention it to her father.

The next day Lawrence Cardiff went to the *Age* office and had the good fortune to see Mr. Rattray, who was flattered to answer questions regarding Miss Bell's whereabouts, put by any one he knew to be a friend. Mr. Rattray undertook to apologize for their not hearing of the scheme, it had matured so suddenly. Miss Bell couldn't really have had time to do more than pack and start; in fact, there had been only three days in which to make all the arrangements. And of course the facts were confidential, but there was no reason why Miss Bell's friends should not be in the secret. Then Mr. Rattray imparted the facts, with a certain conscious gratification. There had been difficulties, but the difficulties had been surmounted, and he had heard from Miss Bell that morning that everything was going perfectly, and she was getting hold of magnificent copy. He was only sorry it wouldn't be quite suitable for serial publication in the *Age;* but, as Professor Cardiff was doubtless aware, the British public were kittle cattle to shoe behind, and he hardly thought the *Age* could handle it.

"Oh yes," Mr. Cardiff replied absently. "Cheynemouth, I think you said—for the next five days. Thanks. Successful? I dare say. The idea is certainly a novel one. Good-morning!" and he left the sub-editor of the *Illustrated Age* in a state of some uncertainty as to the wisdom of having disclosed so much. Half an hour later, when Kendal, who knew Rattray fairly well, called and asked him for Miss Bell's present address, he got it with some reluctance and fewer details.

Cardiff drove to his club, and wrote a note to Janet, asking her to send his portmanteau to the 3.45 train at Euston, as he intended to run down to Cheynemouth and might stay over night. He fastened up the envelope, then after a moment's hesitation tore it open and added, "Miss Bell is attempting a preposterous thing. I am going to see if it cannot be prevented." He fancied Janet would understand his not caring to go into particulars in the meantime. It was because of his aversion to going into particulars that he sent the note and lunched at the club, instead of driving home as he had abundance of time to do. Janet would have to be content with that; it would be bad enough to have to explain Rattray's intolerable "scheme" to her when it had been frustrated. After luncheon he went into the smoking-room and read through three leading articles with an occasional inkling of their meaning. At the end of the third he became convinced of the absurdity of trying to fix his attention upon anything, and smoked his next Havana with his eyes upon the toe of his boot, in profound meditation. An observant person might have noticed that he passed his hand once or twice lightly, mechanically, over the top of his head; but even an observant person would hardly have connected the action with Mr. Cardiff's latent idea that although his hair might be tinged in a damaging way there was still a good deal of it. Three o'clock found him standing at the club window with his hands in his pockets, and the firm-set lips of a man who has made up his mind, looking unseeingly into the street. At a quarter past he was driving to the station in a hansom, smiling at the rosette on the horse's head, which happened to be a white one.

"There's Cardiff," said a man who saw him taking his ticket. "More than ever the *joli garçon!*"

An hour and a half later one of the somewhat unprepossessing set of domestics attached to the Mansion Hotel, Cheynemouth, undertook to deliver Mr. Lawrence Cardiff's card to Miss Bell. She didn't remember no such name among the young ladies of the Peach Blossom Company, but she would h'inquire. They was a ladies' drawin'-room upstairs, if he would like to sit down. She conducted him to the ladies' drawing-room, which boasted two pairs of torn lace curtains, a set of dirty furniture with plush trimmings, several lithographs of mellow Oriental scenes somewhat undecidedly poised upon the wall, and a marble-topped centre-table around which were disposed at careful intervals three or four copies of last year's illustrated papers. "You can w'yt 'ere, sir," she said, installing him as it were. "I'll let you know direckly."

At the end of the corridor the girl met Elfrida herself, who took the card with that quickening of her pulse, that sudden commotion which had come to represent to her, in connection with any critical personal situation, one of the keenest possible sensations of pleasure. "You may tell the gentleman," she said quietly, "that I will come in a moment." Then she went back into her own room, closed the door, and sat down on the side of the bed with a pale face and eyes that comprehended, laughed, and were withal a little frightened. That was what she must get rid of, that feeling of fear, that scent of adverse criticism. She would sit still till she was perfectly calm, perfectly accustomed to the idea that Lawrence Cardiff had come to remonstrate with her, and had come because—because what she had been gradually becoming convinced of all these months was true. He was so clever, so distinguished, he had his eyes and his voice and his whole self so perfectly under control, that she never could be quite,

quite sure—but now! And in spite of herself her heart beat faster at the anticipation of what he might be waiting to say to her not twenty steps away. She hid her face in the pillow to laugh at the thought of how deliciously the interference of an elderly lover would lend itself to the piece of work which she saw in fascinating development under her hand, and she had an instantaneous flash of regret that she couldn't use it—no, she couldn't possibly. With fingers that trembled a little she twisted her hair into a knot that became her better, and gave an adjusting pat to the fluffy ends around her forehead. "Nous en ferons une comédie adorable!" she nodded at the girl in the glass; and then, with the face and manner of a child detected in some mischief who yet expects to be forgiven, she went into the drawing-room.

At the sight of her all that Cardiff was ready to say vanished from the surface of his mind. The room was already gray in the twilight. He drew her by both hands to the nearest window, and looked at her mutely, searchingly. It seemed to him that she, who was so quick of apprehension, ought to know why he had come without words, and her submission deepened his feeling of a complete understanding between them.

"I've washed it all off!" said she naïvely, lifting

her face to his scrutiny. "It's not an improvement by daylight, you know."

He smiled a little, but he did not release her hands. "Elfrida, you must come home."

"Let us sit down," she said, drawing them away. He had a trifle too much advantage, standing so close to her, tall and firm in the dusk, knowing what he wanted, and with that tenderness in his voice. Not that she had the most far-away intention of yielding, but she did not want their little farce to be spoiled by any complications that might mar her pleasure in looking back upon it. "I think," said she, "you will find that a comfortable chair," and she showed him one which stood where all the daylight that came through the torn curtains concentrated itself. From her own seat she could draw her face into the deepest shadow in the room. She made the arrangement almost instinctively, and the lines of intensity the last week had drawn upon Cardiff's face were her first reward.

"I have come to ask you to give up this thing," he said.

Elfrida leaned forward a little in her favorite attitude, clasping her knee. Her eyes were widely serious. "You ask me to give it up?" she repeated slowly. "But why do you ask me?"

"Because I cannot associate it with you—to me it is impossible that you should do it."

Elfrida lifted her eyebrows a little. "Do you know why I am doing it?" she asked.

"I think so."

"It is not a mere escapade, you understand. And these people do not pay me anything. That is quite just, because I have never learned to act and I haven't much voice. I can take no part, only just—appear."

"*Appear!*" Cardiff exclaimed. "Have you appeared?"

"Seven times," Elfrida said simply, but she felt that she was blushing.

Cardiff's anger rose up hotly within him, and strove with his love, and out of it there came a sickening sense of impotency which assailed his very soul. All his life he had had tangibilities to deal with. This was something in the air, and already he felt the apprehension of being baffled here, where he wrought for his heart and his future.

"So that is a part of it," he said, with tightened lips. "I did not know."

"Oh, I insisted upon that," Elfrida replied softly. "I am quite one of them—one of the young ladies of the Peach Blossom Company. I am learning all their sensations, their little frailties, their vocabulary, their ways of looking at things. I know how the novice feels when she makes her first appearance in the chorus of a spectacle—I've noted every vibration of her nerves. I'm learning all the little jealousies and intrigues among them, and all their histories and their ambitions. They are more moral than you may think, but it is not the moral one who is the most interesting. Her virtue is generally a very threadbare, common sort of thing. The—others—have more color in the fabric of their lives, and you can't think how picturesque their passions are. One of the chorus girls has two children. I feel a brute sometimes at the way she—" Elfrida broke off, and looked out of the window for an instant. "She brings their little clothes into my bedroom to make—though there is no need, they are in an asylum. She is divorced from their father," she went on coolly, "and he is married to the leading lady. Candidly," she added, looking at him with a courageous smile, "prejudice apart, is it not magnificent material?"

A storm of words trembled upon the verge of his lips, but his diplomacy instinctively sealed them up. "You can never use it," he said instead.

"Perfectly! I am not quite sure about the form —whether I shall write as one of them, or as myself, telling the story of my experience. But I never dreamed of having such an opportunity. If I didn't mean to write a word I should be glad of it—a look into another world, with its own customs and language and ethics and pleasures and pains. *Quelle chance!*

"And then," she went on, as if to herself, "to be of the life, the strange, unreal, painted, lime-lighted life that goes on behind the curtain! That is something—to act one's part in it, to know that one's own secret rôle is a thousand times more difficult than any in the *repertoire*. Can't you understand?" she appealed. "You are horribly unresponsive. We won't talk of it any longer," she added, with a little offended air. "How is Janet?"

"We must talk of it, Elfrida," Cardiff answered. "Let me tell you one thing," he added steadily. "Such a book as you propose writing would be classed as the lowest sensationalism. People would compare it with the literature of the police court."

Elfrida sprang to her feet, with her head thrown back and her beautiful eyes alight. "*Touché!*" Cardiff thought exultingly.

"You may go too far!" she exclaimed passionately. "There are some things that may not be said!"

Cardiff went over to her quickly and took her hand. "Forgive me," he said. "Forgive me—I am very much in earnest."

She turned away from him. "You had no right to say it. You know my work, and you know that the ideal of it is everything in the world to me—my religion. How dared you suggest a comparison between it and—*cette ordure là!*"

Her voice broke, and Cardiff fancied she was on the brink of tears. "Elfrida," he cried miserably, "let us have an end of this! I have no right to intrude my opinions—if you like, my prejudices—between you and what you are doing. But I have come to beg you to give me the right." He came a step closer and laid his free hand lightly on her shoulder. "Elfrida," he said unhesitatingly, "I want you to be my wife."

"And Janet's stepmother!" thought the girl swiftly. But she hoped he would not mention Janet; it would burlesque the situation.

"Your going away made me quite sure," he added simply. "I can never do without you altogether again. Instead I want to possess you altogether." He bent his fine face to the level of hers, and took both her hands in his. Elfrida thought that by that light he looked strangely young.

She slipped her hands away, but did not move. He was still very close to her—she could feel his breath upon her hair.

"Oh no!" she said. "Marriage is so absurd!" and immediately it occurred to her that she might have put this more effectively. "Cela n'est pas bien dit!" she thought.

"Let us sit down together and talk about it," he answered gently, and drew her toward the little sofa in the corner.

"But—I am afraid—there is nothing more to say. And in a quarter of an hour I must go."

Cardiff smiled masterfully. "I could marry you, little one, in a quarter of an hour," he said.

But at the end of that time Lawrence Cardiff found himself very far indeed from the altar, and more enlightened perhaps than he had ever been before about the radicalism of certain modern sentiments concerning it. She would change, he averred; might he be allowed to hope that she would change, and to wait—months, years? She would never change, Elfrida avowed, it was useless—quite useless—to think of that. The principle had too deep a root in her being—to tear it up would be to destroy her whole joy in life, she said, leaving Cardiff to wonder vaguely what she meant.

"I will wait," he said, as she rose to go; "but you will come back with me now, and we will write a book—some other book—together."

The girl laughed gaily. "All alone by myself I must do it," she answered. "And I must do *this* book. You will approve it when it is done. I am not afraid."

He had her hands again. "Elfrida," he threatened, "if you go on the stage to-night in the costume I see so graphically advertised—an Austrian hussar, isn't it?—I will attend. I will take a box," he added, wondering at his own brutality. But by any means he must prevail.

Elfrida turned a shade paler. "You will not do that," she said gravely. "Good-by. Thank you for having come to persuade me to give this up. And I wish I could do what you would like. But it is quite, quite impossible." She bent over him and touched his forehead lightly with her lips. "Good-by," she said again, and was gone.

An hour later he was on his way back to town. As the mail train whizzed by another, side-tracked to await its passing, Mr. Cardiff might have seen Kendal, if there had been time to look, puffing luxuriously in a smoking compartment, and unfolding a copy of the *Illustrated Age*.

CHAPTER XXV.

BEFORE he had been back in Norway a week Kendal felt his perturbation with regard to Elfrida remarkably quieted and soothed. It seemed to him, in the long hours while he fished and painted, that in the progress of the little drama, from its opening act at Lady Halifax's to its final scene at the studio, he had arrived at something solid and tangible as the basis of his relation toward the girl. It had precipitated in him a power of comprehending her and of criticising her which he had possessed before only, as it were, in solution. Whatever once held him from stating to himself the results of his study of her had vanished, leaving him no name by which to call it. He found that he could smile at her whimsicalities, and reflect upon her odd development, and regret her devouring egotism, without the vision of her making dumb his voluble thought; and he no longer regretted the incident that gave him his freedom. He realized her as he painted her, and the realization visited him less often, much less often, than before. Even the fact that she knew what he thought gradually became an agreeable one. There would be room for no hypocrisies between them. He wished that Janet Cardiff could have some such experience. It was provoking that she should be still so loyally *avenglé;* that he would not be able to discuss Elfrida with her, when he went back to London, from an impersonal point of view. He had a strong desire to say precisely what he thought of her friend to Janet, in which there was an obscure recognition of a duty of reparation—obscure because he had no overt disloyalty to Janet to charge himself with, but none the less present. He saw the intimacy between the two girls from a new point of view; he comprehended the change the months had made, and he had a feeling of some displeasure that Janet Cardiff should have allowed herself to be so subdued, so seconded in it.

Kendal came back a day or two before Elfrida's disappearance, and saw her only once in the meantime. That was on the evening—which struck him later as one of purposeless duplicity—before the Peach Blossom Company had left for the provinces, when he and Elfrida both dined at the Cardiffs'. With him that night she had the air of a chidden child; she was silent and embarrassed, and now and then he caught a glance which told him in so many words that she was very sorry, she hadn't meant to, she would never do it again. He did not for a moment suspect that it referred to the scene at Lady Halifax's, and was more than half real. It was not easy to know that even genuine feeling, with Elfrida, required a cloak of artifice. He put it down as a pretty pose, and found it as objectionable as the one he had painted. He was more curious, perhaps, but less disturbed than either of the Cardiffs as the days went by and Elfrida made no sign. He felt, however, that his curiosity was too irreligious to obtrude upon Janet; besides, his knowledge of her hurt anxiety kept him within the bounds of the simplest inquiry, while she, noting his silence, believed him to be eating his heart out. In the end it was the desire to relieve and to satisfy Janet that took him to the *Age* office. It might be impossible for her to make such inquiries, he told himself, but no obligation could possibly attach to him, except—and his heart throbbed affirmatively at this—the obligation of making Janet happier about it. He could have laughed aloud when he heard the scheme from Rattray's lips—it so perfectly filled out his picture, his future projection of Elfrida; he almost assured himself that he had imagined and expected it. But his desire to relieve Janet was suddenly lost in an upstarting brood of impulses that took him to the railway station with the smile still upon his lips. Here was a fresh development; his interest was keenly awake again, he would go and verify the facts. When his earlier intention reoccurred to him in the train, he dismissed it with the thought that what he had seen would be more effective, more disillusionizing, than what he had merely heard. He triumphed in advance over Janet's disillusion, but he thought more eagerly of the pleasure of proving, with his own eyes, another step in the working out of the problem which he believed he had solved in Elfrida.

"Big house to-night, sir. All the stalls taken," said the young man with the high collar in the box office when Kendal appeared before the window.

"Pit," replied Kendal, and the young man stared.

"Pit did you say, sir? Well, you'll 'ave to look slippy or you won't get a seat there either."

Kendal was glad it was a full house. He began to realize how very much he would prefer that Elfrida should not see him there. From his point of view it was perfectly warrantable—he had no sense of any obligation which would prevent his adding to his critical observation of her—but from Miss Bell's? He found himself lacking the assurance that no importance was to be attached to Miss Bell's point of view, and he turned up his coat collar and pulled his hat over his eyes, and seated himself as obscurely as possible, with a satisfactory sense that nobody could take him for a gentleman, mingled with a less agreeable suspicion that it was doubtful whether, under the circumstances, he had a complete right to the title. The overture strung him up more pleasureably than usual, however. He wondered if he should recognize her at once, and what part she would have. He did not know the piece, but of course it would be a small one. He wondered —for, so far as he knew, she had had no experience of the stage—how she could have been got ready in the time to take even a small one. Inevitably it would be a part with three words to say and nothing to sing—probably a maid-servant's. He smiled as he thought how sincerely Elfrida would detest such a personation. When the curtain rose at last Mr. John Kendal searched the stage more eagerly than the presence there of any mistress of her art had ever induced him to do before. The first act was full of gaiety, and the music was very tolerable; but Kendal, scanning one insistent figure and painted face after another, heard nothing, in effect, of what was said or sung—he was conscious only of a strong disappointment when it was over and Elfrida had not appeared.

The curtain went up again to a quick-step, to

clinking steel, and the sound of light marching feet. An instant after forty young women were rhythmically advancing and retreating before the footlights, picturesquely habited in a military costume comprising powdered wigs, three-cornered hats, gold-embroidered blue coats, flesh-colored tights, and kid top-boots, which dated uncertainly from the middle ages. . They sang, as they crossed their varyingly shapely legs, stamped their feet, and formed into figures no drill-book ever saw, a chorus of which the refrain was

> "Oh, it never matters, matters,
> Though his coat be tatters, tatters,
> His good sword rust-incrusted and his songs all sung,
> The maids will flatter, flatter,
> And foes will scatter, scatter,
> For a soldier is a soldier while his heart is young,"

the last line accompanied by a smiling flirt of their eyes over their shoulders and a kick to the rear as they wheeled, which evoked the unstinted appreciation of the house. The girls had the unvarying pink-and-white surfaces of their profession, but under it they obviously differed much, and the age and emaciation and ugliness among them had its common emphasis in the contrast of their smart masculine attire with the distressingly feminine outlines of their figures. "I should have thought it impossible to make a woman absolutely hideous by a dress that revealed her form," said Kendal to himself, as the jingling and the dancing and the music went on in the glare before him, "but, upon my word—" He paused suddenly. She wasn't absolutely hideous, that tall girl with the plume and the sword, who maneuvred always in front of the company—the lieutenant in charge. Indeed, she was comely every way, slight and graceful, and there was a singular strong beauty in her face, which was enhanced by the rouge and the powder, and culminated in the laugh in her eyes and upon her lips—a laugh which meant enjoyment, excitement, exhilaration.

It grew upon Kendal that none of the chorus girls approached Elfrida in the abandon with which they threw themselves into the representation—that all the others were more conscious than she of the wide-hipped incongruity of their rôle. To the man who beheld her there in an absolutely new world of light and color and coarse jest, it seemed that she was perfectly oblivious of any other, and that her personality was the most aggressive, the most ferociously determined to be made the most of, on the stage. As the chorus ceased a half-grown youth remarked to his companion in front, "But the orficer's the one, Dave! Ain't she fly!" and the words coming out distinctly in the moment of after-silence when the applause was over, set the pit laughing for two or three yards around. Whereat Kendal, with an assortment of feelings which he took small pleasure in analyzing later, got up and went out. People looked up angrily at him as he stumbled over their too numerous feet in doing so—he was spoiling a solo of some pathos by Mr. Golightly Ticke in the character of a princely refugee, a fur-trimmed mantle, and shoes with buckles.

Kendal informed himself with some severity that no possible motive could induce him to make any comment upon Miss Bell to Janet, and found it necessary to go down into Devonshire next day, where his responsibilities had begun to make a direct and persistent attack upon him. It was the first time he had yielded, and he could not help being amused by the remembrance, in the train, of Elfrida's solemn warning about the danger of his growing typical and going into Parliament. A middle-aged country gentleman with broad shoulders and a very red neck occupied the compartment with him, and handled the *Times* as if the privilege of reading it were one of the few the democratic spirit of the age had left to his class. Kendal scanned him with interest and admiration and pleasure. It was an excellent thing that England's backbone should be composed of men like that, he thought, and he half wished he were not so consciously undeserving of national vertebral honors himself—that Elfrida's warnings had a little more basis of probability. Not that he wanted to drop his work, but a man owed something to his country, especially when he had what they called a stake in it—to establish a home perhaps, to marry, to have children growing up about him. A man had to think of his old age. He told himself that he must be the lightest product of a flippant time, since these things did not occur to him more seriously; and he threw himself into all that had to be done upon "the place," when he arrived at it, with an energy that disposed its real administrators to believe that his ultimate salvation as a landlord was still possible.

He was talking to Janet Cardiff at one of Lady Halifax's afternoon teas a fortnight later, when their hostess advanced toward them interrogatively. "While I think of it, Janet," said she, laying a mittened hand on Miss Cardiff's arm, "what has become of your eccentric little American friend? I sent her a card a month ago, and we've neither heard nor seen anything of her."

"Elfrida Bell—oh, she's out of town, Lady Halifax, and I am rather desolate without her—we see so much of her, you know. But she will be back soon—I dare say I will be able to bring her next Thursday. How delicious this coffee is! I shall have another cup, if it keeps me awake for a week. Oh, you got my note about the concert, dear lady?"

Kendal noticed the adroitness of her chatter with amusement. Before she had half finished Lady Halifax had taken an initial step toward moving off, and Janet's last words received only a nod and a smile for reply.

"You know, then?" said he, when that excellent woman was safely out of earshot.

"Yes, I know," Janet answered, twisting the hanging end of her long-haired boa about her wrist. "I feel as if I oughtn't to, but daddy told me. Daddy went, you know, to try to persuade her to give it up. I *was* so angry with him for doing it. He might have known Elfrida better. And it was such a—such a criticism!"

"I wish you would tell me what you really think," said Kendal audaciously.

Janet sipped her coffee nervously. "I—I have no right to think," she returned. "I am not in Frida's confidence in the matter. But of course she is perfectly right, from her point of view."

"Ah!" Kendal said, "her point of view."

Janet looked up at him with a sudden perception of the coldness of his tone. In spite of herself it gave her keen happiness, until the reflection came that probably he resented her qualification, and turned her heart to lead. She searched her soul for words.

"If she wants to do this thing, she has taken, of course, the only way to do it well. She does not need any justification—none at all. I wish she were back," Janet went on desperately, "but only for my own sake—I don't like being out of it with her; not for any reason connected with what she is doing."

There was an appreciable pause between them. "Let me put down your cup," suggested Kendal.

Turning to her again, he said gravely, "I saw Miss Bell at Cheynemouth, too." Janet's hands trembled as she fastened the fur at her throat. "And I also wish she were back. But my reason is not, I am afraid, so simple as yours."

"Here is daddy," Janet answered, "and I know he wants to go. I don't think my father is looking quite as well as he ought to. He doesn't complain, but I suspect him of concealed neuralgia. Please give him a lecture upon over-doing—it's the predominant vice of his character!"

CHAPTER XXVI.

ELFRIDA spent five weeks with the Peach Blossom Company on their provincial tour, and in the end the manager was sorry to lose her. He was under the impression that she had joined them as an aspiring novice, presumably able to gratify that or any other whim. He had guessed that she was clever, and could see that she was extremely good-looking. Before the month was out he was congratulating himself upon his perception much as Rattray had a habit of doing, and was quite ready to give Elfrida every encouragement she wanted to embrace the burlesque stage seriously—it was a thundering pity she hadn't voice enough for comic opera. He had nothing to complain of; the arrangement had been for a few weeks only, and had cost him the merest trifle of travelling expenses; but the day Elfrida went back to town he was inclined to parley with her, to discuss the situation, and to make suggestions for her future plan of action. His attitude of visible regret added another thrill to the joy the girl had in the thought of her undertaking; it marked a point of her success, she thought, at least so far as preliminaries went. Already, as she shrank fastidiously into the corner of a third-class travelling-carriage, her project seemed to have reached its original and notable materialization. Chapters passed before her eyes as they do sometimes in dreams, full of charm and beauty; the book went through every phase of comedy and pathos, always ringing true. Little half-formed sentences of admirable art rose before her mind, and she hastily barred them out, feeling that she was not ready yet, and it would be mad misery to want them and to have forgotten them. The thought of what she meant to do possessed her wholly, though, and she resigned herself to dreams of the most effective arrangement of her material, the selection of her publisher, the long midnight hours alone with Buddha, in which she should give herself up to the enthralment of speaking with that voice which she could summon, that elusive voice which she lived only, only to be the medium for—that precious voice which would be heard one day, yes, and listened to.

She was so freshly impressed with the new lifelights, curious, tawdry, fascinating, revolting, above all sharp and undisguised, of the world she had left, that she saw them already projected with a verisimilitude which, if she had possessed the art of it, would have made her indeed famous. Her own power of realization assured her on this point—nobody could see, not divine but *see*, as she did, without being able to reproduce; the one implied the other. She fingered feverishly the strap of the little hand-bag in her lap, and satisfied herself by unlocking it with a key that hung on a string inside her jacket. It had two or three photographs of the women she knew among the company, another of herself in her stage uniform, a bill of the play, her powder-puff and rouge-box, a scrap of gold lace, a young Jew's letter full of blots and devotion, a rather vulgar sapphire bracelet, some artificial flowers, and a quantity of slips of paper of all sizes covered with her own enigmatically rounded handwriting. She put her hand in carefully and searched—everything was there; and up from the bag came a scent that made her shut her eyes and laugh with its power to bring her experiences back to her. She locked it carefully again with a quivering sigh—after all she would not have many hours to wait. Presently an idea came to her that she thought worth keeping, and she thrust her hand into her pocket for paper and pencil. She drew out a crumpled oblong scrap and wrote on the back of it, then unlocked the little bag again and put it carefully in. Before it had been only the check of the *Illustrated Age* for a fortnight's work; now it was the record of something valuable.

The train rolled into a black and echoing station as the light in the carriage began to turn from the uncertain grayness that came in at the window to the uncertain yellowness that descended from the roof. Boys ran up and down the length of the platform in the foggy gaslit darkness shouting Banbury cakes and newspapers. Elfrida hated Banbury cakes, but she had a consuming hunger and bought some. She also hated English newspapers, but lately some queer new notable Australian things had been appearing in the *St. George's Gazette*—Cardiff had sent them to her—and she selected this journal from the damp lot that hung over the newsboy's arm, on the chance of a fresh one. The doors were locked and the train hurried on. Elfrida ate two of her Banbury cakes with the malediction that only this British confection can inspire, and bestowed the rest upon a small boy who eyed her enviously over the back of an adjoining seat. She and the small boy and his mother had the carriage to themselves.

There was nothing from the unusual Australian contributor in this number of the *St. George's*, and Elfrida turned its pages with the bored feeling of knowing what else she might expect. "Parliamentary Debates," of course, and the news of London, five lines from America announcing the burning of a New York hotel with hideous loss of life, an article on the situation in Persia, and one on the cultivation of artichokes, "Money," "The Seer of Hawarden," the foreign markets—book reviews. Elfrida thought also that she knew what she might expect here, and that it would be nothing very absorbing. Still, with a sense of tasting criticism in advance, she let her eye travel over the column or two the paper devoted to three or four books of the week. A moment later Janet Cardiff's name in the second paragraph had sprung at her throat, it seemed to Elfrida, and choked her.

She could not see—she could not see! The print was so bad, the light was infernal, the carriage jolted so. She got up and held the paper nearer to the lamp in the roof, staying herself against the end of a seat. As she read she grew paler, and the paper shook in her hand. "One of the valuable books of the year," "showing grasp of character and keen dramatic instinct," "a distinctly original vein," "too slender a plot for perfect symmetry, but a treatment of situation at once nervous and strong," were some of the commonplaces that said themselves over and again in her mind as she sank back into her place by the window with the paper lying across her lap.

Her heart beat furiously, her head was in a whirl; she stared hard, for calmness, into the swift-passing night outside. Presently she recognized herself to be angry with an intense still jealous anger that seemed to rise and consume her in every part of her being. A success—of course it would be a success if Janet wrote it—she was not artistic enough to fail. Ah, should Janet's friend go so far as to say that? She didn't know—she would think afterward; but Janet was of those who succeed, and there were more ways than one of deserving success. Janet was a compromise; she belonged really to the British public and the class of Academy studies from the nude which were always draped, just a little. Elfrida found a bitter satisfaction in this simile, and elaborated it. The book would be one to be commended for *jeunes filles*, and her lips turned down mockingly in the shadow. She fancied some well-meaning critic saying, "It should be on every drawing-room table," and she almost laughed outright. She thought of a number of other little things that might be said, of the same nature and equally amusing. Her anger flamed up again at the thought of how Janet had concealed this ambition from her, had made her, in a way, the victim of it. It was not fair—not fair! She could have prepared herself against it; she might have got *her* book ready sooner, and its triumphant editions might at least have come out side by side with Janet's. She was just beginning to feel that they were neck and neck, in a way, and now Janet had shot so far ahead, in a night, in a paragraph. She could never, never catch up! And from under her closed eyelids two hot tears started and ran over her cold cheeks. It came upon her suddenly that she was sick with jealousy, not envy, but pure anger at being distanced, and she tried to attack herself about it. With a strong effort she heaped opprobrium and shame upon herself, denounced herself, tried to hate herself. But she felt that it was all a kind of dumb-show, and that under it nothing could change the person she was or the real feeling she had about this—nothing except being first. Ah! then she could be generous and loyal and disinterested; then she could be really a nice person to know, she derided herself. And as her foot touched the little hand-bag on the floor she took a kind of sullen courage, which deserted her when she folded the paper on her lap and was struck again in the face with Lash and Black's advertisement on the outside page announcing Janet's novel in letters that looked half a foot long.

Then she resigned herself to her wretchedness till the train sped into the glory of Paddington.

"I hope you're not bad, miss," remarked the small boy's mother as they pushed toward the door together; "them Banburys don't agree with everybody."

The effect upon Elfrida was hysterical. She controlled herself just long enough to answer with decent gravity, and escaped upon the platform to burst into a silent quivering paroxysm of laughter that brought her overcharged feeling delicious relief, and produced an answering smile on the face of a large, good-looking policeman. Her laugh rested her, calmed her, and restored something of her moral tone. She was at least able to resist the temptation of asking the boy at the book-stall where she bought "John Camberwell" whether the volume was selling rapidly or not. Buddha looked on askance while she read it, all night long and well into the morning. She reached the last page and flung down the book in pure physical exhaustion, with the framework of half a dozen reviews in her mind. When she awoke, at two in the afternoon, she decided that she must have another day or two of solitude; she would not let the Cardiffs know she had returned quite yet.

Three days afterward the *Illustrated Age* published a review of "John Camberwell" which brought an agreeable perplexity to Messrs. Lash and Black. It was too good to compress, and their usual advertising space would not contain it all. It was almost passionately appreciative; here and there the effect of criticism was obviously marred by the desire of the writer to let no point of beauty or of value escape divination. Quotations from the book were culled like flowers, with a delicate hand; and there was conspicuous care in the avoidance of any phrase that was hackneyed, any line of criticism that custom had impoverished. It seemed that the writer fashioned a tribute, and strove to make it perfect in every way. And so perfect it was, so cunningly devised and gracefully expressed, with such a self-conscious beauty of word and thought, that its extravagance went unsuspected, and the interest it provoked was its own.

Janet read the review in a glow of remorseful affection. She was appealed to less by the exquisite manipulation with which the phrases strove to say the most and the best, than by the loyal haste to praise she saw behind them, and she forgave their lack of blame in the happy belief that Elfrida had not the heart for it. She was not in the least angry that her friend should have done her the injustice of what would have been, less adroitly managed, indiscriminate praise; in fact, she hardly thought of the value of the critique at all, so absorbed was she in the sweet sense of the impulse that made Elfrida write it. To Janet's quick forgiveness it made up for everything; indeed, she found in it a scourge for her anger, for her resentment. Elfrida might do what she pleased, Janet would never cavil again; she was sure now of some real possession in her friend. But she longed to see Elfrida, to assure herself of the warm verity of this. Besides, she wanted to feel her work in her friend's presence, to extract the censure that was due, to take the essence of praise from her eyes and voice and hand. But she would wait. She had still no right to know that Elfrida had returned, and an odd sensitiveness prevented her from driving instantly to Essex Court to ask.

The next day passed, and the next. Lawrence Cardiff found no reason to share his daughter's scruples, and went twice, to meet Mrs. Jordan on the threshold with the implacable statement that Miss Bell had returned but was not at home. He found it impossible to mention Elfrida to Janet now.

John Kendal had gone back to Devonshire to look after the thinning of a bit of his woodlands—one thing after another claimed his attention there.

Janet had a gay note from him now and then, always *en camarade*, in which he deplored himself in the character of an intelligent land-owner, but in which she detected also a growing interest and satisfaction in all that he was finding to do. Janet saw it always with a throb of pleasure; his art was much to her, but the sympathy that bound him to the practical side of his world was more, though she would not have confessed it. She was unconsciously comforted by the sense that it was on the warm, bright, comprehensible side of his interest in life that she touched him—and that Elfrida did not touch him. The idea of the country house in Devonshire excluded Elfrida, and it was an exclusion Janet could be happy in conscientiously, since Elfrida did not care.

CHAPTER XXVII.

EVEN in view of her popular magazine articles and her literary name Janet's novel was a surprising success. There is no reason why we should follow the example of all the London critics except Elfrida Bell, and go into the detail of its slender story, and its fairly original, broadly human qualities of treatment, to explain this; the fact will, perhaps, be accepted without demonstration. It was a common phrase among the reviewers—though Messrs. Lash and Black carefully cut it out of their selections for advertisement—that the book with all its merits was in no way remarkable; and the publishers were as much astonished as anybody else when the first edition was exhausted in three weeks. Yet the agreeable fact remained that the reviewers gave it the amount of space usually assigned to books allowed to be remarkable, and that the *Athenian* announced the second edition to be had "at all book-sellers'" on a certain Monday. "When they say it is not remarkable," wrote Kendal to Janet, "they mean that it is not heroic, and that it is published in one volume, at six shillings. To be remarkable—to the trade—it should have dealt with epic passion, in three volumes, at thirty."

To him the book had a charm quite apart from its literary value in the revelation it made of its author. It was the first piece of work Janet had done from a seriously artistic point of view, into which she had thrown herself without fence or guard, and it was to him as if she had stepped from behind a mask. He wrote to her about it with the confidence of the new relation it established between them; he looked forward with warm pleasure to the closer intimacy which it would bring. To Janet, living in this new sweetness of their better understanding, only one thing was lacking—Elfrida made no sign. If Janet could have known, it was impossible. In her review Elfrida had done all she could. She had forced herself to write it before she touched a line of her own work, and now, persistently remote in her attic, she strove every night over the pile of notes which represented the ambition that sent its roots daily deeper into the fibre of her being. Twice she made up her mind to go to Kensington Square, and found she could not—the last time being the day the *Decade* said that a new and larger edition of "John Camberwell" was in preparation.

Ten days after her return the maid at Kensington Square, with a curious look, brought up Elfrida's card to Janet. Miss Bell was in the drawing-room, she said. Yes, she had told Miss Bell Miss Cardiff was up in the library, but Miss Bell said she would wait in the drawing-room.

Janet looked at the card in astonishment, debating with herself what it might mean—such a formality was absurd between them. Why had not Elfrida come up at once to this third-story den of theirs she knew so well? What new preposterous caprice was this? She went down gravely, chilled; but before she reached the drawing-room door she resolved to take it another way, as a whim, as matter for scolding. After all, she was glad Elfrida had come back to her on any terms. She went in radiant, with a quick step, holding the card at arm's length.

"To what," she demanded mockingly, "am I to attribute the honor of this visit?" but she seized Elfrida lightly and kissed her on both cheeks before it was possible for her to reply.

The girl disengaged herself gently. "Oh I have come, like the rest, to lay my homage at your feet," she said, with a little smile that put spaces between them. "You did not expect me to deny myself that pleasure?"

"Don't be absurd, Frida. When did you come back to town?"

"When did I come back?" Elfrida repeated slowly, watching for the effect of her words. "On the first, I think it was."

"And this is the tenth!" Janet exclaimed; adding helplessly, "You *are* an enigma! Why didn't you let me know?"

"How could I suppose that you would care to know anything just now—except what the papers tell you."

Janet regarded her silently, saying nothing. Under her look Elfrida's expression changed a little, grew uncomfortable. The elder girl felt the chill, the seriousness with which she received the card upstairs, return upon her suddenly, and she became aware that she could not, with self-respect, fight it any longer.

"If you thought that," she said gravely, "it was a curious thing to think. But I believe I am indebted to you for one of the pleasantest things the papers have been telling me," she went on, with constraint. "It was very kind—much too kind. Thank you very much."

Elfrida looked up, half frightened at the revulsion of her tone. "But—but your book is delightful. I was no more charmed than everybody must be. And it has made a tremendous hit, hasn't it?"

"Thanks, I believe it is doing a fair amount of credit to its publishers. They are very pushing people."

"How delicious it must feel!" Elfrida said. Her words were more like those of their ordinary relation, but her tone and manner had the aloofness of the merest acquaintance. Janet felt a slow anger grow up in her. It was intolerable, this dictation of their relation. Elfrida desired a change—she should have it, but not at her caprice. Janet's innate dominance rose up and asserted a superior right to make the terms between them, and all the hidden jar, the unacknowledged contempt, the irritation, the hurt and the stress of the year that had passed rushed in from banishment and gained possession of her. She took just an appreciable instant to steady herself, and then her gray eyes regarded Elfrida with a calm remoteness in them which gave the other girl a quick impression of having done more than she meant to do, gone too far to return. Their glances met, and Elfrida's eyes, unquiet and undecided, dropped before Janet's. Already she had a vibrant regret.

"You enjoyed being out of town, of course," Janet said. "It is always pleasant to leave London for a while, I think."

There was a cool masterfulness in the tone of this that arrested Elfrida's feeling of half-penitence, and armed her instantly. Whatever desire she had felt to assert and indulge her individuality at any expense, in her own attitude there had been the consciousness of what they owed one another. She had defied it, perhaps, but it had been there. In this it was ignored; Janet had gone a step further—her tone expressed the blankest indifference. Elfrida drew herself up.

"Thanks, it was delightful. An escape from London always is, as you say. Unfortunately, one is obliged to come back."

Janet laughed lightly. "Oh, I don't know that I go so far as that. I rather like coming back too. And you have missed one or two things, you know, by being away."

"The Lord Mayor's Show?" asked Elfrida, angry that she could not restrain the curl of her lip.

"Oh dear, no! That comes off in November—don't you remember? Things at the theatres chiefly. Oh, Jessie, Jessie!" she went on, shaking her head at the maid who had come in with the tray, "you're a quarter of an hour late with tea! Make it for us now, where you are, and remember that Miss Bell doesn't like cream."

The maid blushed and smiled under the easy reproof, and did as she was told. Janet chatted on pleasantly about the one or two first nights she had seen, and Elfrida felt for a moment that the situation was hopelessly changed. She had an intense, unreasonable indignation. The maid had scarcely left the room when her blind search for means of retaliation succeeded.

"But one is not necessarily wholly without diversions in the provinces. I had, for instance, the pleasure of a visit from Mr. Cardiff."

"Oh yes, I heard of that," Janet returned, smiling. "My father thought that we were being improperly robbed of your society, and went to try to persuade you to return, didn't he? I told him I thought it a shocking liberty; but you ought to forgive him—on the ground of his disappointment."

The cup Elfrida held shook in its saucer, and she put it down to silence it. Janet did not know, did not suspect, then. Well, she should; her indifference was too maddening.

"Under the circumstances it was not a liberty at all. Mr. Cardiff wanted me to come back to marry him."

There! It was done, and as brutally as possible.

Her vanity was avenged—she could have her triumphs too. And instant with its gratification came the cold recoil of herself upon herself, a sense of shame, a longing to undo.

Janet took the announcement with the very slightest lifting of her eyebrows. She bent her head and stirred her teacup meditatively, then looked up gravely at Elfrida.

"Really?" she said. "And may I ask—whether you *have* come back for that?"

"I—I hardly know," Elfrida faltered. "You know what I think about marriage—there is so much to consider."

"Doubtless," Janet returned. Her head was throbbing with the question why this girl would not go—go—*go!* How had she the hardihood to stay another instant? At any moment her father might come in, and then how could she support the situation? But all she added was, "I am afraid it is a matter which we cannot very well discuss." Then a bold thought came to her, and without weighing it she put it into words. The answer might put everything definitely—so definitely—at an end.

"Mr. Kendal went to remonstrate with you, too, didn't he? It must have been very troublesome and embarrassing—"

Janet stopped. Elfrida had turned paler, and her

eyes greatened with excitement. "*No*," she said, "I did not see Mr. Kendal. What do you mean? Tell me!"

"Perhaps I have no right. But he told me that he had seen you, at Cheynemouth."

"He must have been in the audience," Elfrida returned, in a voice that was hardly audible.

"Perhaps."

For a moment there was silence between them—a natural silence, and no dumbness. They had forgotten about themselves in the absorption of other thoughts.

"I must go," Elfrida said, with an effort, rising. What had come to her with this thing Janet had told her? Why had she this strange fullness in the beating of her heart, this sense, part of shame, part of fright, part of happiness, that had taken possession of her? What had become of her strained feeling about Janet? For it had gone, gone utterly, and with it all her pride, all her self-control. She was conscious only of a great need of somebody's strength, of somebody's thought and interest—of Janet's. Yet how could she unsay anything? She held out her hand, and Janet took it. "Good-by, then," she said.

"Good-by; I hope you will escape the rain."

But at the door Elfrida turned and came back.

Janet was mechanically stirring the coals in the grate.

"Listen!" she said. "I want to tell you something about myself."

Janet looked up with an inward impatience. She knew these little repentant self-revealings so well.

"I know I'm a beast—I can't help it. Ever since I heard of your success I've been hating it! You can laugh if you like, but I've been *jealous*—oh, I'm not deceived; very well, we are acquainted, myself and I! It's pure jealousy—I admit it. I despise it, but there it is. You have everything; you succeed in *all* the things you do—you suffocate me—do you understand? *Always* the first place, always the attention, the consideration, wherever we go together. And your pretence—your *lie*—of believing my work as good as yours! I believe it—yes, I do, but you *do not*. Oh, I know you through and through, Janet Cardiff! And altogether," she went on passionately, "it has been too much for me. I have not been able to govern it. I have yielded, *misérable* that I am. But just now I felt it going away from me, Janet—" She paused, but there was no answer. Janet was looking contemplatively into the fire.

"And I made up my mind to say it straight out. It is better so, don't you think?"

"Oh yes, it is better so."

"I hate you sometimes—when you suffocate me with your cleverness—but I admire you *tremendously* always. So I suppose we can go on, can't we?

"Ah!" Elfrida cried, noting Janet's hesitation with a kind of wonder—how should it be exacted of her to be anything more than frank? "I will go a step further to come back to you, my Janet. I will tell you a secret—the first one I ever had. Don't be afraid that I shall become your stepmother and hate me in advance. That is too absurd!" and the girl laughed ringingly. "Because—I believe I am in love with John Kendal!"

For answer Janet turned to her with the look of one pressed to the last extremity. "Is it true that you are going to write your own experiences in the *corps de ballet?*" she asked ironically.

"Quite true. I have done three chapters already. What do you think of it? Isn't it a good idea?"

"Do you really want to know?"

"Of course!"

"I think," said Janet slowly, looking into the fire, "that the scheme is a contemptible one, and that you are doing a very poor sort of thing in carrying it out."

"Thanks," Elfrida returned. "We are all pretty much alike, we women, aren't we, after all? Only some of us say so and some of us don't. But I shouldn't have thought you would have objected to my small rivalry *before the fact!*"

Janet sighed wearily, and looked out of the window. "Let me lend you an umbrella," she said; "the rain has come."

"It won't be necessary, thanks," Elfrida returned. "I hear Mr. Cardiff coming upstairs. I shall ask him to take care of me as far as the omnibuses. Good-by!"

CHAPTER XXVIII.

"Oh but—but," cried Elfrida, tragic-eyed, "you don't understand, my friend. And these pretences of mine are unendurable—I won't make another. This is the real reason why I can't go to your house: Janet knows—everything there is to know. I told her—I myself—in a fit of rage ten days ago, and then she said things and I said things, and—and there is nothing now between us any more!"

Lawrence Cardiff looked grave. "I am sorry for that," he said.

A middle-aged gentleman in apparently hopeless love does not confide in his grown-up daughter, and Janet's father had hardly thought of her seriously in connection with this new relation, which was to him so precarious and so sweet. Its realization had never been close enough for practical considerations; it was an image, something in the clouds; and if he still hoped and longed for its materialization there were times when he feared even to regard it too closely lest it should vanish. His first thought at this announcement of Elfrida's was of what it might signify of change, what bearing it had upon her feeling, upon her intention. Then he thought of its immediate results, which seemed to be unfortunate. But in the instant he had for reflection he did not consider Janet at all.

"Ah, yes! It was contemptible—but *contemptible!* I did it partly to hurt her, and partly, I think, to gratify my vanity. You would not have thought anything so bad of me perhaps?" She looked up at him childishly. They were strolling about the quiet spaces of the Temple Courts. It was a pleasant afternoon in February, the new grass was pushing up. They could be quite occupied with one another—they had the place almost to themselves. Elfrida's well-fitting shabby little jacket hung unbuttoned, and she swung Cardiff's light walking-stick as they sauntered. He, with his eyes on her delicately flushed face and his hands unprofessorially in his pockets, was counting the minutes that were left them.

"You wouldn't have, would you?" she insisted.

"I would think any womanly fault you like of you," he laughed, "but one—the fear to confess it."

Elfrida shut her lips with a little proud smile. "Do you know," she said confidingly, "when you say things like that to me I like you very much— but *very much!*"

"But not enough," he answered her quickly, "never enough, Frida?"

The girl's expression changed. "You are not to call me 'Frida,'" she said, frowning a little. "It has an association that will always be painful to me. When people—disappoint me, I try to forget them in every way I can." She paused, and Cardiff saw that her eyes were full of tears. He had an instant of intense resentment against his daughter. What brutality had she been guilty of toward Elfrida in that moment of unreasonable jealousy that surged up between them? He would fiercely like to know. But Elfrida was smiling again, looking up at him in wilful disregard of her wet eyes.

"Say 'Elfrida' please—all of it."

They had reached the Inner Temple Hall. "Let us go in there and sit down," he suggested. "You must be tired—dear child."

She hesitated and submitted. "Yes, I am," she said. Presently they were sitting on one of the long dark polished wooden benches in the quiet and the rich light the ages have left in this place, keeping a mutual moment of silence. "How splendid it is!" Elfrida said restlessly, looking at the great carved wooden screen they had come through. "The man who did that had a joy in his life, hadn't he? To-day is very cheap and common, don't you think?"

He had hardly words to answer her vague question, so absorbed was he in the beauty and the grace and the interest with which she had suddenly invested the high-backed corner she sat in. He felt no desire to analyze her charm. He did not ask himself whether it was the poetry of her eyes and lips, or her sincerity about herself, or the joy in art that was the key to her soul, or all of these, or something that was none of them. He simply allowed himself to be possessed by it, and Elfrida saw his pleasure in his eager look and in every line of his delicate features. It was delicious to be able to give such pleasure, she thought. She felt like a thrice spiritualized Hebe, lifting the cup, not to Jove, but to a very superior mortal. She wished in effect, as she looked at him, that he were of her essence—she might be cup-bearer to him always then. It was a graceful and unexacting occupation. But he was not, absolutely, and the question was how long— She started as he seemed to voice her thought.

"This can't go on, Elfrida!"

Cardiff had somehow possessed himself of her hand as it lay along the polished edge of the wooden seat. It was a privilege she permitted him sometimes, with the tacit understanding that he was not to abuse it.

"And why not—for a little while? It is pleasant, I think."

"If you were in love you would know why. You are not, I know—you needn't say so. But it will come, Elfrida—only give it the chance. I would stake my soul on the certainty of being able to make you love me." His confidence in the power of his own passion was as strong as a boy's of twenty.

"If I were in love!" Elfrida repeated slowly, with an absent smile. "And you think it would come afterward. That is an exploded idea, my friend. I should feel as if I were acting out an old-fashioned novel—an old-fashioned *second-rate* novel."

She looked at him with eyes that invited him to share their laughter, but the smile he gave her was pitiful, if she could have known it. The strain she had been putting upon him, and promised indefinitely to put upon him, was growing greater than he could bear.

"I am afraid I must ask you to decide," he said. "You have been telling me two things, dear. One thing with your lips and another thing with your eyes—and ways of doing. You tell me that I must go, but you make it possible for me to stay. For God's sake let it be one or the other."

"I am so sorry. We could be friends of a sort, I think, but I can't marry you."

"You have never told me why."

"Shall I tell you truly, literally—brutally?"

"Of course!"

"Then it is not only because I don't love you—that there is not for me the common temptation to enter a form of bondage which, as I see it, is hateful. That is enough, but it is not all; it is not even the principal thing. It is"—she hesitated—"it is that—that we are different, you and I. It would be preposterous," she went on hastily, "not to admit that you are infinitely superior—of course—and cleverer and wiser and more important in the world. And that will make me absurd in your eyes when I tell you that my whole life is wrapped up in a sense which I cannot see or feel that you have at all. You have much —oh, a great deal—outside of it, and I have nothing. My life is swayed in obedience to laws that you do not even know of. You can hardly be my friend, completely. As your wife I should suffer and you would suffer, in a false position which could never be altered."

She paused and looked at him seriously, and he felt that she believed what she had said. She had, at all events, given him full permission to go. And he was as far from being able to avail of himself of it as he had been before—further, for every moment those slender fingers rested in his made it more impossible to relinquish them, for always. So, he persisted, with a bitter sense of failure that would not wholly, honestly recognize itself.

"Is Golightly Ticke your friend—completely?"

"More—pardon me—than you could ever be," she answered him, undaunted by the contempt in his tone.

There was silence for a moment between them. Elfrida's wide-eyed gaze wandered appreciatively over the dusky interior, which for the man beside her barely existed.

"What a lot of English character there is here," she said softly. "How dignified it is, and conscientious, and restrained!"

It was as if she had not spoken. Cardiff stared with knit brows into the insoluble problem she had presented to him a moment longer. "*How* are we so different, Elfrida?" he broke out passionately. "You are a woman and I am a man; the world has dealt with us, educated us, differently, and I am older than I dare say I ought to be to hope for your love. But these are not differences that count, whatever their results may be. It seems to me trivial to speak of such things in this connection, but we like very much the same books, the same people. I grant you I don't know anything about pictures; but surely," he pleaded, "these are not the things that cut a man off from the happiness of a lifetime!"

"I'm afraid—" she began, and then she broke off suddenly. "I *am* sorry—sorrier than I have ever been before, I think. I should have liked so well to keep your friendship; it is the most chivalrous I know. But if you feel like—like this about it I suppose I must not. Shall we say good-by here and now? Truly I am sorry."

She had risen, and he could find no words to stay her. It seemed that the battle to possess her was over, and that he had lost. Her desire for his friendship had all the mockery of freedom in it to him—in the agony of the moment it insulted him. With an effort he controlled himself—there should be no more of the futility of words. He must see the last of her some time—let it be now, then. He bent his head over the slender hand he held, brought his lips to it, and then, with sudden passion, kissed it hotly again and again, seeking the warm, uncovered little spot above the fastening. Elfrida snatched it away with a little shiver at the contact, a little angry shiver of surprised nerves. He looked at her piteously, struggling for a word, for any word to send away her repulsion, to bring her back to the mood of the moment before. But he could not find it; he seemed to have drifted hopelessly from her, to have lost all his reckonings.

"Well?" she said. She was held there partly by her sense of pity and partly by her desire to see the last, the very last of it.

"Go!" he returned, with a shrinking of pain at the word, "I cannot."

"*Pauvre ami!*" she said softly, and then she turned, and her light steps sounded back to him through the length of the hall.

She walked more slowly when she reached the pavement outside, and one who met her might have thought she indulged in a fairly pleasant reverie. A little smile curved about the corners of her mouth, half compassionate, half amused and triumphant. She had barely time to banish it when she heard Cardiff's step beside her, and his voice.

"I had to come after you," he said; "I've let you carry off my stick."

She looked at him in mischievous challenge of his subterfuge, and he added frankly, with a voice that shook a little notwithstanding—

"It's of no use—I find I must accept your compromise. It is very good of you to be willing to make one. And I can't let you go altogether, Elfrida."

She gave him a happy smile. "And now," she said, "shall we talk of something else?"

CHAPTER XXIX.

MARCH brought John Kendal back to town with a few Devonshire studies and a kindling discontent with the three subjects he had in hand for the May exhibitions. It spread over everything he had done for the last six months when he found himself alone with his canvases and whole-hearted toward them. He recognized that he had been dividing his interest, that his ambition had suffered, that his hand did not leap as it had before at the suggestion of some lyric or dramatic possibility of color. He even fancied that his drawing, which was his vulnerable point, had worsened. He worked strenuously for days without satisfying himself that he had recovered ground appreciably, and then came desperately to the conclusion that he wanted the stimulus of a new idea, a subject altogether disassociated with anything he had done. It was only, he felt, when his spirit was wholly in bondage to the charm of his work that he could do it well, and he needed to be bound afresh. Literally, he told himself, the only thing he had painted in months that pleased him was that mere sketch, from memory, of the Halifax drawing-room episode. He dragged it out and looked at it, under its damaging red stripes, with enthusiasm. Whatever she did with herself, he thought, Elfrida Bell was curiously satisfying from an artistic point of view. He fell into a train of meditation, which quickened presently into a practical idea that set him striding up and down the room.

"I believe she would be delighted!" he said aloud, coming to a sudden standstill; "and, by Jove, it would be a kind of reparation!"

He delved into an abysmal cupboard for a crusted pen and a cobwebby bottle of ink, and was presently sitting among the fragments of three notes addressed, one after the other, to "Dear Miss Bell." In the end he wrote a single line without any formality whatever, and when Elfrida opened it an hour later she read:

"Will you let me paint your portrait for the Academy?
"JOHN KENDAL.

"P.S.—Or any other exhibition you may prefer."

The last line was a stroke of policy. "She abhors Burlington House," he had reflected.

The answer came next day, and he tore it open with rapid fingers. "I can't think why—but if you wish it, yes. But why not for the Academy, since you are disposed to do me that honor?"

"Characteristic," thought Kendal grimly, as he tore up the note. "She can't think why. But I'm glad the Academy doesn't stick in her pretty throat—I was afraid it would. It's the potent influence of the Private View."

He wrote immediately in joyful gratitude to make an appointment for the next day, went to work vigorously about his preparations, and when he had finished smoked a series of pipes to calm the turbulence of his anticipations. As a neighboring clock struck five he put on his coat. Janet must know about this new idea of his; he longed to tell her, to talk about it over the old-fashioned Spode cup of tea she would give him—Janet was a connoisseur in tea. He realized as he went downstairs how much of the pleasure of his life was centering in these occasional afternoon gossips with her, in the mingled delight of her interest and the fragrance and the comfort of that half-hour over the Spode tea-cup. The association brought him a reminiscence that sent him smiling to the nearest confectioner's shop, where he ordered a supply of Italian cakes against the next day that would make an ample provision for the advent of half a dozen unexpected visitors to the studio. He would have to do his best with afternoon sittings, Elfrida was not available in the morning; and he thought compassionately that his sitter must not be starved. "I will feed her first," he thought ironically, remembering her keen childish enjoyment of sugared things. "She will pose all the better for some tea." And he walked on to Kensington Square.

CHAPTER XXX.

"JANET," said Lawrence Cardiff a week later at breakfast, "the Halifaxes have decided upon their American tour. I saw Lady Halifax last night and she tells me they sail on the twenty-first. They want you to go with them. Do you feel disposed to do it?"

Mr. Cardiff looked at his daughter with eyes from which the hardness that entered them weeks before in the Temple Courts had never quite disappeared. His face was worn and thin, its delicacy had sharpened, and he carried about with him an habitual abstraction. Janet, regarding him day after day in the light of her secret knowledge, gave herself up to an inward storm of anger and grief and anxiety. Elfrida's name had been tacitly dropped between them, but to Janet's sensitiveness she was constantly and painfully to be reckoned with in their common life. Lawrence Cardiff's moods were accountable to his daughter obviously by Elfrida's influence. She noted bitterly that his old evenness of temper, the gay placidity that made so delightful a basis for their joint happiness, had absolutely disappeared. Instead, she found her father either irritable or despondent, or inspired by a gaiety which she had no hand in producing, and which took no account of her. That was the real pain. Janet was keenly distressed at the little drama of suffering that unfolded itself daily before her, but her disapproval of its cause very much blunted her sense of its seriousness. She had, besides, a grown-up daughter's repulsion and impatience for a parental love-affair, and it is doubtful whether she would have brought her father's to a happy conclusion without a very severe struggle if she had possessed the power to do it. But this exclusion gave her a keener pang; she had shared so much with him before, had been so important to him always. And now he could propose, with perfect equanimity that she should go to America with the Halifaxes.

"But you could not get away by the twenty-first," she returned, trying to take it for granted that the idea included him.

"Oh, I don't propose going," Mr. Cardiff returned from behind his newspaper.

"But, daddy, they intend to be away for a year."

"About that. Lady Halifax has arranged a capital itinerary. They mean to come back by India."

"And pray what would become of you all by yourself for a year, sir?" asked Janet brightly. "Besides, we were always going to do that trip together." She had a stubborn inward determination not to recognize this difference that had sprung up between them. It was only a phase, she told herself, of her father's miserable feeling just now; it would last another week, another fortnight, and then things would be as they had been before. She would not let herself believe in it, hurt as it might.

Mr. Cardiff lowered his paper. "Don't think of that," he said over the top of it. "There is really no occasion. I shall get on very well. There is always the club, you know. And this is an opportunity you ought not to miss."

Janet said nothing, and Lawrence Cardiff went back to his newspaper. She tried to go on with her breakfast, but scalding tears stood in her eyes, and she could not swallow. She was unable to command herself far enough to ask to be excused, and she rose abruptly and left the room with her face turned carefully away.

Cardiff followed her with his eyes and gave an uncomprehending shrug. He looked at his watch; there was still half an hour before he need leave the house. It brought him an uncomfortable thought that he might go and comfort Janet—it was evident that something he had said had hurt her—she was growing absurdly hypersensitive. He dismissed the idea—Heaven only knew into what complications it might lead them. He spent the time instead in a restless walk up and down the room, revolving whether Elfrida Bell would or would not be brought to reconsider her refusal to let him take her to "Faust" that night—he never could depend upon her.

Janet had not seen John Kendal since the afternoon he came to her radiant with his intention of putting all of Elfrida's elusive charm upon canvas, full of its intrinsic difficulties, eager for her sympathy, depending on her enthusiastic interest. She had disappointed him—she did her best, but the sympathy and enthusiasm and interest would not come. She could not tell him why—her broken friendship was still sacred to her for what it had been. Besides, explanations were impossible. So she listened and approved with a strained smile, and led him, with a persistence he did not understand, to talk of other things. He went away chilled and baffled, and he had not come again. She knew that he was painting with every nerve tense and eager, in oblivion to all but his work and the face that inspired it. Elfrida, he told her, was to give him three sittings a week, of an hour each, and he complained of the scantiness of the dole. She could conjure up those hours, all too short for his delight in his model and his work. Surely it would not be long now! Elfrida cared, by her own confession— Janet felt, dully, there could now be no doubt of that—and since Elfrida cared, what could be more certain than the natural issue? She fought with herself to accept it; she spent hours in seeking for the indifference that might come of accustoming herself to the fact. And when she thought of her father she hoped that it might be soon.

There came a day when Lawrence Cardiff gave his daughter the happiness of being almost his other self again. He had come downstairs with a headache and a touch of fever, and all day long he let her take care of him submissively, with the old pleasant gratitude that seemed to re-establish their comradeship. She had a joyful secret wonder at the change, it was so sudden and so complete; but their sympathetic relation reasserted itself naturally and at once, and she would not let herself question it. In the evening he sent her to her room for a book of his, and when she brought it to him where he lay upon the lounge in the library he detained her a moment.

"You mustn't attempt to read without a lamp now, daddy," she said, touching his forehead lightly with her lips. "You will damage your poor old eyes."

"Don't be impertinent about my poor old eyes, miss," he returned, smiling. "Janet, there is something I think you ought to know."

"Yes, daddy." The girl felt herself turning rigid.

"I want you to make friends with Elfrida again. I have every reason to believe—at all events some reason to believe—that she will become my wife." Her knowing already made it simpler to say.

"Has—has she promised, daddy?"

"Not exactly. But I think she will, Janet." His tone was very confident. "And of course you must forgive each other any little heart-burnings there may have been between you."

Any little heart-burnings! Janet had a quivering moment of indecision. "Oh, daddy! she won't! she won't!" she cried tumultuously, and hurried out of the room. Cardiff lay still, smiling pityingly. What odd ideas women managed to get into their heads about one another! Janet thought Elfrida would refuse her overtures if she made them. How little she knew Elfrida—his just, candid, generous Elfrida!

Janet flung herself upon her bed and faced the situation, dry-eyed, with burning cheeks. She could always face a situation when it admitted the possibility of anything being done, when there was a chance for resolution and action. Practical difficulties nerved her; it was only before the blankness of a problem of pure abstractness that she quailed—such a problem as the complication of her relation to John Kendal and to Elfrida Bell. She had shrunk from that for months, had put it away habitually in the furthest corner of her consciousness, and had done her best to make it stay there. She discovered how sore its fret had been only with the relief she felt when she simplified it at a stroke that afternoon on which everything came to an end between her and Elfrida. Since the burden of obligation their relation imposed had been removed Janet had analyzed her friendship, and had found it wanting in many ways to which she had been wilfully blind before. The criticism she had always silenced came forward and spoke boldly; and she recognized the impossibility of a whole-hearted intimacy where a need for enforced dumbness existed. All the girl's charm she acknowledged with a heart wrung by the thought that it was no longer for her. She dwelt separately and long upon Elfrida's keen sense of justice, her impulsive generosity, her refined consideration for other people, the delicacy of some of her personal instincts, her absolute sincerity toward herself and the world, her passionate exaltation of what was to her the ideal in art. Janet exacted from herself the last jot of justice toward Elfrida in all these things; and then she listened, as she had not done before, to the voice that spoke to her from the very depths of her being, it seemed, and said, "Nevertheless, *no!*" She only half comprehended, and the words brought her a sadness that would be long, she knew, in leaving her; but she listened and agreed.

And now it seemed to her that she must ignore it again, that the wise, the necessary, the expedient thing to do was to go to Elfrida and re-establish, if she could, the old relation, cost what it might. She must take up her burden of obligation again in order that it might be mutual. Then she would have the right to beg Elfrida to stop playing fast and loose with her father, to act decisively. If Elfrida only knew, only realized, the difference it made, and how little right she had to control, at her whim, the happiness of any human being—and Janet brought a strong hand to bear upon her indignation, for she had resolved to go, and to go that night.

Lawrence Cardiff bade his daughter an early good-night after their unusually pleasant dinner. "Do you think you can do it?" he asked her before he went. Janet started at the question, for they had not mentioned Elfrida again, even remotely.

"I think I can, daddy," she answered him gravely, and they separated. She looked at her watch; by half-past nine she could be in Essex Court.

Yes, Miss Bell was in, Miss Cardiff could go straight up, Mrs. Jordan informed her, and she mounted the last flight of stairs with a beating heart. Her mission was important—oh, so important! She had compromised with her conscience in planning it, and now if it should fail! Her hand trembled as she knocked. In answer to Elfrida's "Come in!" she pushed the door slowly open. "It is I, Janet," she said; "may I?"

"But of course!"

Elfrida rose from a confusion of sheets of manuscript upon the table and came forward, holding out her hand with an odd gleam in her eyes, and an amused, slightly excited smile about her lips.

"How do you do?" she said, with rather ostentatiously suppressed wonder. "Please sit down, but not in that chair. It is not quite reliable. This one, I think, is better. How are—how are *you*?"

The slight emphasis she placed on the last word was airy and regardless. Janet would have preferred to have been met by one of the old affectations; she would have felt herself taken more seriously.

"It's very late to come, and I interrupt you," she said awkwardly, glancing at the manuscript.

"Not at all. I am very happy—"

"But of course I had a special reason for coming. It is serious enough, I think, to justify me."

"What can it be?"

"*Don't*, Elfrida," Janet cried passionately. "Listen to me. I have come to try to make things right again between us—to ask you to forgive me for speaking as I—as I did about your writing that day. I am sorry—I am, indeed."

"I don't quite understand. You ask me to *forgive* you—but what question is there of forgiveness? You had a perfect right to your opinion, and I was glad to have it at last from you, frankly."

"But it offended you, Elfrida. It is what is accountable for the—the rupture between us."

"Perhaps. But not because it hurt my feelings," Elfrida returned scornfully, "in the ordinary sense. It offended me truly, but in quite another way. In what you said you put me on a different plane from yourself in the matter of artistic execution. Very well. I am content to stay there—in your opinion. But why this talk of forgiveness? Neither of us can alter anything. Only," Elfrida breathed quickly, "be sure that I will not be accepted by you upon those terms."

"That wasn't what I meant in the least."

"What else could you have meant? And more than that," Elfrida went on rapidly—her phrases had the patness of formed conclusions—"what you said betrayed a totally different conception of art, as it expresses itself in the nudity of things, from the one I supposed you to hold. And, if you will pardon me for saying so, a much lower one. It seems to me that we cannot hold together there—that our aims and creeds are different, and that we have been comrades under false pretences. Perhaps we are both to blame for that; but we cannot change it, or the fact that we have found it out."

Janet bit her lip. The "nudity of things" brought her an instant's impulse toward hysteria—it was so characteristic a touch of candid exaggeration. But her need for reflection helped her to control it. Elfrida had taken a different ground from the one she expected—it was less simple, and a mere apology, however sincere, would not meet it. But there was one thing more which she could say, and with an effort she said it.

"Elfrida, suppose that, even as an expression of opinion—putting it aside as an expression of feeling toward you—what I said that day was not quite sincere. Suppose that I was not quite mistress of myself—I would rather not tell you why—"

"Is that true?" asked Elfrida directly.

"Yes, it is true. For the moment I wanted more than anything else in the world to break with you. I took the surest means."

The other girl regarded Janet steadfastly. "But if it is only a question of the *degree* of your sincerity," she persisted, "I cannot see that the situation alters much."

"I was not altogether responsible, believe me, Elfrida. I don't remember now what I said, but—but I am afraid it must have taken all its color from my feeling."

"Of course." Elfrida hesitated, and her tone showed her touched. "I can understand that what I told you about—about Mr. Cardiff must have been a shock. For the moment I became an animal, and turned upon you—upon you who had been to me the very soul of kindness. I have hated myself for it—you may be sure of that."

Janet Cardiff had a moment's inward struggle, and yielded. She would let Elfrida believe it had been that. After all it was partly true, and her lips refused absolutely to say the rest.

"Yes, it must have hurt you—more, perhaps, than I can guess." Elfrida's eyes grew wet and her voice shook. "But I can't understand your retaliating *that way*, if you didn't believe what you said. And if you believed it, what more is there to say?"

Janet felt herself possessed by an intense sensation of playing for stakes, unusual, exciting, and of some personal importance. She did not pause to regard her attitude from any other point of view; she succumbed at once, not without enjoyment, to the necessity for diplomacy. Under its rush of suggestions her conscience was only vaguely restive. To-morrow it would assert itself; unconsciously she put off paying attention to it until then. Elfrida must come back to her. For the moment the need was to choose her plea.

"It seems to me," she said slowly, "that there is something between us which is indestructible, Frida. We didn't make it, and we can't unmake it. For my part, I think it is worth our preserving, but I don't believe we could lose it if we tried. You may put me away from you for any reason that seems good to you, as far as you like, but so long as we both live there will be that something, recognized or unrecognized. All we can do arbitrarily is to make it a joy or a pain of it. Haven't you felt that?"

The other girl looked at her uncertainly. "I have felt it sometimes," she said, "but now it seems to me that I can never be sure that there is not some qualification in it—some hidden flaw."

"Don't you think it's worth making the best of? Can't we make up our minds to have a little charity for the flaws?"

Elfrida shook her head. "I don't think I'm capable of a friendship that demands charity," she said.

"And yet, whether we close each other's lips or not, we will always have things to say, the one to the other, in this world. Is it to be dumbness between us?"

There was a moment's silence in the room—a crucial moment, it seemed to both of them. Elfrida sat against the table with her elbows among its litter of paged manuscript, her face hidden in her hands. Janet rose and took a step or two toward her. Then she paused, and looked at the little bronze image on the table instead. Elfrida was suddenly shaken by deep, indrawn, silent sobs.

"It is finished, then," Janet said softly; "we are to separate for always, Buddha, she and I. She will not know any more of me nor I of her—it will be, so far as we can make it, like the grave. You must belong to a strange world, Buddha, always to smile!" She spoke evenly, quietly, with restraint, and still she did not look at the convulsively silent figure in the chair. "But I am glad you will always keep that face for her, Buddha. I hope the world will, too, our world that is sometimes more bitter than you can understand. And I say good-by to you, for to her I cannot say it." And she turned to go.

Elfrida stumbled to her feet and hurried to the

door. "No!" she said, holding it fast. "No! You must not go that way—I owe you too much, after all. We will—we will make the best of it."

"Not on that ground," Janet answered gravely. "Neither your friendship nor mine is purchasable, I hope."

"No, no! That was bad. On any ground you like. Only stay a little—let us find ourselves again!"

Elfrida forced a smile into what she said, and Janet let herself be drawn back to a chair.

It was nearly midnight when she found herself again in her cab, driving through the empty lamp-lit Strand toward Kensington. She had prevailed, and now she had to scrutinize her methods. That necessity urged itself beyond her power to turn away from it, and left her sick at heart. She had prevailed—Elfrida, she believed, was hers again. They had talked as candidly as might be of her father. Elfrida had promised nothing, but she would bring matters to an end, Janet knew she would, in a day or two, when she had had time to think how intolerable the situation would be if she didn't. Janet remembered with wonder, however, how little Elfrida seemed to realize that it need make any difference between them compared with other things, and what a trivial concession she thought

it beside the restoration of the privileges of her friendship. The girl asked herself drearily how it would be possible that she should ever forget the frank cynical surprise with which Elfrida had received her entreaty, based on the fact of her father's unrest and the wretchedness of his false hopes—
"You have your success; does it really matter—so very much?"

CHAPTER XXXI.

"To-day, remember. You promised that I should see it to-day," Elfrida reminded Kendal, dropping instantly into the pose they had jointly decided on. "I know I'm late, but you will not punish me by another postponement, will you?"

Kendal looked sternly at his watch. "A good twenty minutes, mademoiselle," he returned aggrievedly. "It would be only justice—poetic justice—to say no. But I think you may, if we get on to-day."

He was already at work, turning from the texture of the rounded throat which occupied him before she came in, to the more serious problem of the nuances of expression in the face. It was a whim of his, based partly upon a cautiousness, of which he was hardly aware, that she should not see the portrait in its earlier stages, and she had made a great concession of this. As it grew before him, out of his consciousness, under his hand, he became more and more aware that he would prefer to postpone her seeing it, for reasons which he would not pause to define. Certainly they were not connected with any sense of having failed to do justice to his subject. Kendal felt an exulting mastery over it which was the most intoxicating sensation his work had ever brought him. He had, as he painted, a silent, brooding triumph in his manipulation, in his control. He gave himself up to the delight of his insight, the power of his reproduction, and to the intense satisfaction of knowing that out of the two there grew something of more than usually keen intrinsic interest within the wide creed of his art. He worked with every nerve tense upon his conception of what he saw, which so excluded other considerations that now and then, in answer to some word of hers that distracted him, he spoke to her almost roughly. At which Elfrida, with a little smile of forgiving comprehension, obediently kept silence. She saw the artist in him dominant, and she exulted for his sake. It was to her delicious to be the medium of his inspiration, delicious and fit and sweetly acceptable. And they had agreed upon a charming pose.

Presently Kendal lowered his brush impatiently. "Talk to me a little," he said resentfully, ignoring his usual preference that she should not talk because what she said had always power to weaken the concentration of his energy. "There is a little muteness about the lips. Am I very unreasonable?

But you don't know what a difficult creature you are."

She threw up her chin in one of her bewitching ways and laughed. "I wouldn't be too simple," she returned. She looked at him with the light of her laughter still in her eyes, and went on: "I know I must be difficult—tremendously difficult; because I, whom you see as an individual, am so many people. Phases of character have an attraction for me—I wear one to-day and another to-morrow. It is very flippant, but you see I am honest about it. And it must make me difficult to paint, for it can be only by accident that I am the same person twice."

Without answering Kendal made two or three rapid strokes. "That's better," he said, as if to himself. "Go on talking, please. What did you say?"

"It doesn't seem to matter much," she answered, with a little pout. "I said 'Baa, baa, black sheep, have you any wool?'"

"No, you didn't," returned Kendal as they laughed together. "You said something about being like Cleopatra, a creature of infinite variety, didn't you? About having a great many disguises—" absently. "But—"

Kendal fell into the absorbed silence of his work

again, leaving the sentence unfinished. He looked up at her with a long, close, almost intimate scrutiny, under which and his careless words she blushed hotly.

"Then I hope you have chosen my most becoming disguise," she cried imperiously, jumping up. "Now, if you please, I will see."

She stood beside the canvas with her eyes upon his face, waiting for a sign from him. He, feeling, without knowing definitely why, that a critical moment had come between them, rose and stepped back a pace or two, involuntarily pulling himself together to meet what she might say. "Yes, you may look," he said, seeing that she would not turn her head without his word; and waited.

Elfrida took three or four steps beyond the easel and faced it. In the first instant of her gaze her face grew radiant. "Ah," she said softly, "how unconscionably you must have flattered me! I can't be so pretty as that."

A look of relief shot across Kendal's face. "I'm glad you like it," he said briefly. "It's a capital pose."

The first thing that could possibly be observed about the portrait was its almost dramatic loveliness. The head was turned a little, and the eyes regarded something distant, with a half wishful, half deprecating dreaminess. The lips were plaintively courageous, and the line of the lifted chin and throat helped the pathetic eyes and annihilated the heaviness of the other features. It was as if the face made an expressive effort to subdue a vitality which might otherwise have been aggressive; but while the full value of this effect of spiritual pose was caught and rendered, Kendal had done his work in a vibrant significant chord of color that strove for the personal force beneath it and brought it out.

Elfrida dropped into the nearest chair, clasped her knees in her hands, and bending forward, earnestly regarded the canvas with a silence that presently became perceptible. It seemed to Kendal at first, as he stood talking to her of its technicalities, that she tested the worth of every stroke; then he became aware that she was otherwise occupied, and that she did not hear him. He paused and stepped over to where, standing behind her chair, he shared her point of view. ' Even the exaltation of his success did not prevent his impatient wonder why his relation with this girl must always be so uncomfortable.

Then as he stood in silence looking with her, it seemed that he saw with her, and the thing that he had done revealed itself to him for the first time fully, convincingly, with no appeal. He looked at it with curious, painful interest, but without remorse, even in the knowledge that she saw it too, and suffered. He realized exultingly that he had done better work than he thought—he might repent later, but for the moment he could feel nothing but that. As to the girl before him, she was simply the source and the reason of it—he was particularly glad he had happened to come across her.

He had echoed her talk of disguises, and his words embodied the unconscious perception under which he worked. He had selected a disguise, and, as she wished, a becoming one. But he had not used it fairly, seriously. He had thrown it over her face like a veil, if anything could be a veil which rather revealed than hid, rather emphasized than softened, the human secret of the face underneath. He realized now that he had been guided by a broader perception, by deeper instincts, in painting that. It was the real Elfrida.

There was still a moment before she spoke. He wondered vaguely how she would take it, and he was conscious of an anxiety to get it over. At last she rose and faced him, with one hand, that trembled, resting on the back of the chair. Her face wore a look that was almost profound, and there was an acknowledgment in it, a degree of submission, which startled him.

"So that is how you have read me," she said,

looking again at the portrait. "Oh, I do not find fault; I would like to, but I dare not. I am not sure enough that you are wrong—no, I am too sure that you are right. I am, indeed, very much preoccupied with myself. I have always been—I shall always be. Don't think I shall reform after this moral shock as people do in books. I am what I am. But I acknowledge that an egotist doesn't make an agreeable picture, however charmingly you apologize for her. It is a personality of stone, isn't it?—implacable, unchangeable. I've often felt that."

Kendal was incapable of denying a word of what she said. "If it is any comfort to you to know it," he ventured, "hardly any one will see in it what you—and I—see."

"Yes," she said, with a smile, "that's true. I shan't mind its going to the Academy."

She sat down again and looked fixedly at the picture, her chin propped in her hand. "Don't you feel," she said, looking up at him with a little childish gesture of confidence, "as if you had stolen something from me?"

"Yes," Kendal declared honestly, "I do. I've taken something you didn't intend me to have."

"Well, I give it you—it is yours quite freely and ungrudgingly. Don't feel that way any more. You have a right to your divination," she added bravely.

"I would not withhold it if I could. Only—I hope you find *something* good in it. I think, myself, there is something."

Her look was a direct interrogation, and Kendal flinched before it. "Dear creature," he murmured, "you are very true to yourself."

"And to you," she pleaded, "always to you too. Has there ever been anything but the clearest honesty between us? Ah, my friend, that is valuable— there are so few people who inspire it."

She had risen again, and he found himself shamefacedly holding her hand. His conscience roused itself and smote him mightily. Had there always been this absolute single-mindedness between them?

"You make it necessary for me to tell you," he said slowly, "that there is one thing between us you do not know. I saw you at Cheynemouth on the stage."

"I know you did," she smiled at him. "Janet Cardiff let it out, by accident. I suppose you came, like Mr. Cardiff, because you—disapproved. Then why didn't you remonstrate with me? I've often wondered." Elfrida spoke softly, dreamily. Her happiness seemed very near. Her self-surrender was so perfect and his understanding, as it always had been, so sweet, that the illusion of the moment was cruelly perfect. She raised her eyes to Kendal's with an abandonment of tenderness in them that quickened his heart-beats, man that he was.

"Tell me, do *you* want me to give it up—my book —last night I finished it—my ambition?"

She was ready with her sacrifice, or for the instant she believed herself to be, and it was not wholly without an effort that he put it away. On the pretence of picking up his palette knife he relinquished her hand.

"It is not a matter upon which I have permitted myself a definite opinion," he said, more coldly than he intended, "but for your own sake I should advise it."

For her own sake! The room seemed full of the echo of his words. A blank look crossed the girl's face; she turned instinctively away from him and picked up her hat. She put it on and buttoned her gloves without the faintest knowledge of what she was doing; her senses were wholly occupied with the comprehension of the collapse that had taken place within her. It was the single moment of her life when she differed, in any important way, from the girl Kendal had painted. Her self-consciousness was a wreck, she no longer controlled it; it tossed at the mercy of her emotion. Her face was very white and painfully empty, her eyes wandered uncertainly around the room, unwilling above all things to meet Kendal's again. She had forgotten about the portrait.

"I will go, then," she said simply, without looking at him, and this time, with a flash, Kendal comprehended again. He held the door open for her mutely, with the keenest pang his pleasant life had ever brought him, and she passed out and down the dingy stairs.

On the first landing she paused and turned. "I will never be different," she said aloud, as if he were still beside her, "I will never be different!" She swiftly unbuttoned one of her gloves and fingered the curious silver ring that gleamed uncertainly on her hand in the shabby light of the staircase. The alternative within it, the alternative like a bit of brown sugar, offered itself very suggestively at the moment. She looked around her at the dingy place she stood in, and in imagination threw herself across the lowest step. Even at that miserable moment she was aware of the strong, the artistic, the effective thing to do. "And when he came down he might tread on me," she said to herself, with a little shudder. "I wish I had the courage. But no—it might hurt, after all. I am a coward, too."

She had an overwhelming realization of impotence in every direction. It came upon her like a burden;

under it she grew sick and faint. At the door she stumbled, and she was hardly sure of her steps to her cab, which was drawn up by the curbstone, and in which she presently went blindly home.

By ten o'clock that night she had herself, in a manner, in hand again. Her eyes were still wide and bitter, and the baffled, uncomprehending look had not quite gone out of them, but a line or two of cynical acceptance had drawn themselves round her lips. She had sat so long and so quietly regarding the situation that she became conscious of the physical discomfort of stiffened limbs. She leaned back in her chair and put her feet on another, and lighted a cigarette.

"No, Buddha," she said, as if to a confessor, "don't think it of me. It was a lie, a pose to tempt him on. I would never have given it up—never! It is more to me—I am *almost* sure—than he is. It is part of my soul, Buddha, and my love for him— oh, I cannot tell!"

She threw the cigarette away from her and stared at the smiling image with heavy eyes in silence. Then she went on:

"But I always tell you everything, little bronze god, and I won't keep back even this. There was a moment when I would have let him take me in his arms and hold me close, close to him. And I wish he had—I should have had it to remember. Bah! why is my face hot! I might as well be ashamed of wanting my dinner!"

Again she dropped into silence, and when next she spoke her whole face had hardened.

"But no! He thinks that he has read me finally, that he has done with me, that I no longer count! He will marry some red-and-white cow of an Englishwoman who will accept herself in the light of a reproductive agent and do her duty by him accordingly. As I would not—no! Good heavens, no! So perhaps it is as well, for I will go on loving him, of course, and some day he will come back to me, in his shackles, and together, whatever we do, we will make no vulgar mess of it. In the meantime, Buddha, I will smile, like you.

"And there is always this, which is the best of me. You agree, don't you, that it is the best of me?" She fingered the manuscript in her lap. "All my power, all my joy, the quintessence of my life! I think I shall be angry if it has a common success, if the people like it too well. I only want recognition for it—recognition and acknowledgment and admission. I want George Meredith to ask to be introduced to me!" She made rather a pitiful effort to smile. "And that, Buddha, is what will happen."

Mechanically she lighted another cigarette and turned over her first rough pages—a copy had gone to Rattray—looking for passages she had wrought most to her satisfaction. They left her cold as she read them, but she was not unaware that the reason of this lay elsewhere; and when she went to bed she put the packet under her pillow and slept a little better for the comfort of it.

CHAPTER XXXII.

IN the week that followed Janet Cardiff's visit to Elfrida's attic, these two young women went through a curious reapproachment. At every step it was tentative, but at every step it was also enjoyable. They made sacrifices to meet on most days; they took long walks together, and arranged lunches at out-of-the-way restaurants; they canvassed eagerly such matters of interest in the world that supremely attracted them as had been lying undiscussed between them until now. The intrinsic pleasure that was in each for the other had been enhanced by deprivation, and they tasted it again with a keenness of savor which was a surprise to both of them. Their mutual understanding of most things, their common point of view, reasserted itself more strongly than ever as a mutual possession; they could not help perceiving its value. Janet made a fairly successful attempt to drown her sense of insincerity in the recognition. She, Janet, was conscious of a deliberate effort to widen and deepen the sympathy between them. An obscure desire to make reparation, she hardly knew for what, combined itself with a great longing to see their friendship the altogether beautiful and perfect thing its mirage was, and pushed her on to seize every opportunity to fortify the place she had retaken. Elfrida had never found her so considerate, so appreciative, so amusing, so prodigal of her gay ideas, or so much inclined to go upon her knees at shrines before which she sometimes stood and mocked. She had a special happiness in availing herself of an opportunity which resulted in Elfrida's receiving a letter from the editor of the *St. George's* asking her for two or three articles on the American Colony in Paris, and only very occasionally she recognized, with a subtle thrill of disgust, that she was employing diplomacy in every action, every word, almost every look which concerned her friend. She asked herself then despairingly how it could last and what good could come of it, whereupon fifty considerations, armed with whips, drove her on.

Perhaps the most potent of these was the consciousness that in spite of it all she was not wholly successful, that as between Elfrida and herself things were not entirely as they had been. They were cordial, they were mutually appreciative, they had moments of expansive intercourse; but Janet could not disguise to herself the fact that there was a difference, the difference between fit and fusion. The impression was not a strong one, but she half suspected her friend now and then of intently watching her, and she could not help observing how reticent the girl had become upon certain subjects that touched her personally. The actress in Elfrida was nevertheless constantly supreme, and interfered with the trustworthiness of any single impression. She could not resist the pardoning rôle; she played it intermittently, with a pretty impulsiveness that would have amused Miss Cardiff more if it had irritated her less. For the certainty that Elfrida would be her former self for three days together Janet would have dispensed gladly with the little Bohemian dinner in Essex Court in honor of her book, or the violets that sometimes dropped out of Elfrida's notes, or even the sudden but premeditated occasional offer of Elfrida's lips.

Meanwhile the Halifaxes were urging their western trip upon her, Lady Halifax declaring roundly that she was looking wretchedly, Miss Halifax suggesting playfully the possibility of an American heroine for her next novel. Janet, repelling both publicly, admitted both privately. She felt worn out physically, and when she thought of producing another book her brain responded with a helpless negative. She had been turning lately with dogged conviction to her work as the only solace life was likely to offer her, and anything that hinted at loss of power filled her with blank dismay. She was desperately weary and she wanted to forget, desiring, besides, some sort of stimulus as a flagging swimmer desires a rope.

One more reason came and took possession of her common sense. Between her father and Elfrida she felt herself a complication. If she could bring herself to consent to her own removal, the situation, she could not help seeing, would be considerably simplified. She read plainly in her father that the finality Elfrida promised had not yet been given—doubtless an opportunity had not yet occurred; and Janet was willing to concede that the circumstances might require a rather special opportunity. When it should occur she recognized that delicacy, decency almost, demanded that she should be out of the way. She shrank miserably from the prospect of being a daily familiar looker-on at the spectacle of Lawrence Cardiff's pain, and she had a knowledge that there would be somehow an aggravation of it in her person. In a year everything would mend itself more or less, she believed dully and tried to feel. Her father would be the same again, with his old good-humor and criticism of her enthusiasms, his old interest in things and people, his old comradeship for her.

John Kendal would have married Elfrida Bell—
what an idyll they would make of life together!—and
she, Janet, would have accepted the situation. Her
interest in the prospective pleasures on which Lady
Halifax expatiated was slight; she was obliged to
speculate upon its rising, which she did with all the
confidence she could command. She declined absolutely to read Bryce's "American Commonwealth,"
or Miss Bird's account of the Rocky Mountains, or
anybody's travels in the Orient, upon all of which
Miss Halifax had painstakingly fixed her attention;
but one afternoon she ordered a blue serge travelling-dress and refused one or two literary engagements
for the present, and the next day wrote to Lady
Halifax that she had decided to go. Her father received her decision with more relief than he meant
to show, and Janet had a bitter half-hour over it.
Then she plunged with energy into her arrangements, and Lawrence Cardiff made her inconsistently happy again with the interest he took in them,
supplemented by an extremely dainty little travelling-clock. He became suddenly so solicitous for her
that she sometimes quivered before the idea that he
guessed all the reasons that were putting her to
flight, which gave her a wholly unnecessary pang,
for nothing would have astonished Lawrence Cardiff
more than to be confronted, at the moment, with
any passion that was not his own.

CHAPTER XXXIII.

KENDAL, as the door closed behind Elfrida on the afternoon of her last sitting, shutting him in with himself and the portrait on the easel, and the revelation she had made, did his best to feel contrition, and wondered that he was so little successful. He assured himself that he had been a brute; yet in an uncompromising review of all that he had ever said or done in connection with Elfrida he failed to satisfy his own indignation with himself by discovering any occasion upon which his brutality had been particularly obvious. He remembered with involuntary self-justification how distinctly she had insisted upon *camaraderie* between them, how she had spurned everything that savored of another standard of manners on his part, how she had once actually had the curious taste to want him to call her "old chap," and how it had grated. He remembered her only half-veiled invitation, her challenge to him to see as much as he cared, and to make what he could of her. He was to blame for accepting, but he would have been a conceited ass if he had thought of the danger of a result like this. In the midst of his reflections an idea came to him about the portrait, and he observed, with irritation, after giving it a few touches, that the light was irretrievably gone for the day.

Next morning he worked for three hours at it without a pang, and in the afternoon, with relaxed nerves and a high heart, he took his hat and turned his face toward Kensington Square. The distance was considerable, but he walked lightly, rapidly, with a conscious enjoyment of that form of relief to his wrought nerves, his very limbs drawing energy from the knowledge of his finished work. Never before had he felt so completely the divine sense of success, and though he had worked at the portrait with passionate concentration from the beginning, this realization had come to him only the day before, when, stepping back to look with Elfrida, he saw what he had done. Troubled as the revelation was, in it he saw himself a master. He had for once escaped, and he felt that the escape was a notable one, from the tyranny of his brilliant technique. He had subjected it to his idea, which had grown upon the canvas obscure to him under his own brush until that final moment, and he recognized with astonishment how relative and incidental the truth of the treatment seemed in comparison with the truth of the idea.

With the modern scornful word for the literary value of paintings on his lips, Kendal was forced to admit that in this his consummate picture, as he very truly thought it, the chief significance lay elsewhere than in the brushing and the color—they were only its dramatic exponents—and the knowledge of this brought him a new and glorious sense of control. It had already carried him further in power, this portrait, it would carry him further in place, than anything he had yet done; and the thought gave a sparkle to the delicious ineffable content that bathed his soul. He felt that the direction of his walk intensified his eager physical joy in it. He was going to Janet with his success, as he had always gone to her. As soon as the absorbing vision of his work had admitted another perception, it was Janet's sympathy, Janet's applause, that had mingled itself with his certain reward. He could not say that it had inspired him in the least, but it formed a very essential part of his triumph. He could wish her more exacting, but this time he had done something that should make her less easy to satisfy in the future. Unconsciously he hastened his steps through the gardens, switching off a daisy head now and then with his stick as he went, and pausing only once, when he found himself, to his utter astonishment, asking a purely incidental errand boy if he wanted sixpence.

Janet, in the drawing-room, received him with hardly a quickening of pulse. It was so nearly over now; she seemed to have packed up a good part of her tiresome heart-ache with the warm things Lady Halifax had dictated for the Atlantic. She had a vague expectation that it would reappear, but not until she unlocked the box, in mid-ocean, where it wouldn't matter so much. She knew that it was only reasonable and probable that she should see him again before they left for Liverpool. She had been expecting this visit, and she meant to be unflinching with herself when she exchanged farewells with him. She meant to make herself believe that the occasion was quite an ordinary one—also until afterward, when her feeling about it would be of less consequence.

"Well," she asked directly, with a failing heart as she saw his face, "what is your good news?"

Kendal laughed aloud; it was delightful to be anticipated. "So I am unconsciously advertising it," he said. "Guess!"

His tone had the vaunting glory of a lover's—a lover new to his lordship, with his privileges still sweet upon his lips. Janet felt a little cold contraction about her heart, and sank quickly into the nearest arm-chair. "How can I guess," she said, looking beyond him at the wall, which she did not see, "without anything to go upon? Give me a hint."

Kendal laughed again. "It's very simple, and you know something about it already."

Then she was not mistaken—there was no chance of it. She tried to look at him with smiling, sympathetic intelligence, while her whole being quivered in anticipation of the blow that was coming. "Does it—does it concern another person?" she faltered.

Kendal looked grave, and suffered an instant's compunction. "It does—it does indeed," he assured her. "It concerns Miss Elfrida Bell very much, in a way. Ah!" he went on impatiently, as she still sat silent, "why are you so unnaturally dull, Janet? I've finished that young woman's portrait, and it is more—satisfactory—than I ever in my life dared hope that any picture of mine would be."

"Is that all?"

The words escaped her in a quick breath of relief. Her face was crimson, and the room seemed to swim.

"*All!*" she heard Kendal say reproachfully. "Wait until you see it!" He experienced a shade of dejection, and there was an instant's silence between them, during which it seemed to Janet that the world was made over again. "That young woman!" She disloyally extracted the last suggestion of indifference out of the phrase, and found it the sweetest she had heard for months. But her brain whirled with the effort to decide what it could possibly mean.

"I hope you have made it as beautiful as Elfrida is," she cried, with sharp self-reproof. "It must have been difficult to do that."

"I have made it—what she is, I think," he answered, again with that sudden gravity. "It is so like my conception of her which I have never felt permitted to explain to you, that I feel as if I had stolen a march upon her. You must see it. When will you come? It goes in the day after to-morrow, but I can't wait for your opinion till it's hung."

"I like your calm reliance upon the Committee," Janet laughed. "Suppose—"

"I won't. It will go on the line," Kendal returned confidently. "I did nothing last year that I will permit to be compared with it. Will you come to-morrow?"

"Impossible; I haven't two consecutive minutes to-morrow. We sail, you know, on Thursday."

Kendal looked at her blankly. "You *sail?* On Thursday?"

"I am going to America, Lady Halifax and I. And Elizabeth, of course. We are to be away a year. Lady Halifax is buying tickets, I am collecting light literature, and Elizabeth is in pursuit of facts. Oh, we are deep in preparation. I thought you knew."

"How could I possibly know?"

"Elfrida didn't tell you, then!"

"Did she know?"

"Oh yes, ten days ago."

"Odd that she didn't mention it."

Janet told herself that it was odd, but found with some surprise that it was not more than odd. There had been a time when the discovery that she and her affairs were of so little consequence to her friend would have given her a wondering pang; but that time seemed to have passed. She talked lightly on about her journey; her voice and her thoughts had suddenly been freed. She dilated upon the pleasures she anticipated as if they had been real, skimming over the long spaces of his silence, and gathering gaiety as he grew more and more sombre. When he rose to go their moods had changed: the brightness and the flush were hers, and his face spoke only of a puzzled dejection, an anxious uncertainty.

"So it is good-by," he said, as she gave him her hand, "for a year!"

Something in his voice made her look up suddenly, with such an unconscious tenderness in her eyes as he had never seen in any other woman's. She dropped them before he could be quite certain he recognized it, though his heart was beating in a way which told him there had been no mistake.

"Lady Halifax means it to be a year," she answered—and surely, since it was to be a year, he might keep her hand an instant longer.

The full knowledge of what this woman was to him seemed to descend upon John Kendal then, and he stood silent under it, pale and grave-eyed, baring his heart to the rush of the first serious emotion life had brought him, filled with a single conscious desire—that she should show him that sweetness in her eyes again. But she looked wilfully down, and he could only come closer to her, with a sudden muteness upon his ready lips, and a strange newborn fear wrestling for possession of him. For in that moment Janet, hitherto so simple, so approachable, as it were so available, had become remote, difficult, incomprehensible. Kendal invested her with the change in himself, and quivered in uncertainty as to what it might do with her. He seemed to have nothing to trust to but that one glance for knowledge of the girl his love had newly exalted; and still she stood before him looking down. He took two or three vague steps into the middle of the room, drawing her with him. In their nearness to each other the silence between them held them intoxicatingly, and he had her in his arms before he found occasion to say, between his lingering kisses upon her hair, "You can't go, Janet. You must stay—and marry me."

*   *   *   *   *

"I don't know," wrote Lawrence Cardiff in a postscript to a note to Miss Bell that evening, "that Janet will thank me for forestalling her with such all-important news, but I can't resist the pleasure of telling you that she and Kendal got themselves engaged, without so much as a 'by your leave' to me, this afternoon. The young man shamelessly stayed to dinner, and I am informed that they mean to be married in June. Kendal is full of your portrait; we are to see it to-morrow. I hope he has arranged that we shall have the advantage of comparing it with the original."

CHAPTER XXXIV.

"Miss Cardiff's in the lib'ry, sir," said the housemaid, opening the door for Kendal next morning with a smile which he did not find too broadly sympathetic. He went up the stairs two steps at a time, whistling like a schoolboy.

"Lady Halifax says," he announced, taking immediate possession of Janet where she stood, and drawing her to a seat beside him on the lounge, "that the least we can do by way of reparation is to arrange our wedding-trip in their society. She declares she will wait any reasonable time; but I assured her delicately that her idea of compensation was a little exaggerated."

Janet looked at him with an absent smile. "Yes, I think so," she said, but her eyes were preoccupied, and the lover in him resented it.

"What is it?" he asked. "What has happened, dear?"

She looked down at an open letter in her hand, and for a moment said nothing. "I don't know whether I ought to tell you; but it would be a relief."

"Can there be anything you ought not to tell me?" he insisted tenderly.

"Perhaps, on the other hand, I ought," she said reflectively. "It may help you to a proper definition of my character, and then—you may think less of me. Yes, I think I ought."

"Darling, for Heaven's sake don't talk nonsense!"

"I had a letter—this letter—a little while ago, from Elfrida Bell." She held it out to him. "Read it."

Kendal hesitated and scanned her face. She was smiling now; she had the look of half-amused dismay that might greet an ineffectual blow. He took the letter.

"If it is from Miss Bell," he said at a suggestion from his conscience, "I fancy, for some reason, it is not pleasant."

"No," she replied, "it is not pleasant."

He unfolded the letter, recognizing the characteristic broad margins and the repressed rounded perpendicular hand with its supreme effort after significance, and his thought reflected a tinge of his old amused curiosity. It was only a reflection, and yet it distinctly embodied the idea that he might be on the brink of a further discovery. He glanced at Janet again: her hands were clasped in her lap, and she was looking straight before her with smilingly grave lips and lowered lids, which nevertheless gave him a glimpse of retrospection. He felt the beginnings of indignation, yet he looked back at the letter acquisitively; its interest was intrinsic.

"I feel that I can no longer hold myself in honor," he read, "if I refrain further from defining the personal situation between us as it appears to me. That I have let nearly three weeks go by without doing it you may put down to my weakness and selfishness, to your own charm, to what you will; but I shall be glad if you will not withhold the blame that is due me in the matter, for I have wronged you, as well as myself, in keeping silence.

"Look, it is all here in a nutshell. *Nothing is changed.* I have tried to believe otherwise, but the truth is stronger than my will. My opinion of you is a naked, uncompromising fact. I cannot drape it or adorn it, or even throw around it a mist of charity. It is unalterably there, and in any future intercourse with you, such intercourse as we have had in the past, I should only dash myself forever against it. I do not clearly see upon what level you accepted me in the beginning, but I am absolutely firm in my belief that it was not such as I would have tolerated if I had known. To-day at all events I am confronted with the proof that I have not had your confidence—that you have not thought it worth while to be single-minded in your relation to me. From a personal point of view there is more that I might say, but perhaps that is damning enough, and I have no desire to be abusive. It is on my conscience to add, moreover, that I find you a sophist, and your sophistry a little vulgar. I find you compromising with your ambitions, which in themselves are not above reproach from any point of view. I find you adulterating what ought to be the pure stream of ideality with muddy considerations of what the people are pleased to call the moralities, and with the feebler contamination of the conventionalities—"

"I *couldn't* smoke with her," commented Janet, reading over his shoulder. "It wasn't that I objected in the least, but it made me so very—uncomfortable, that I would never try a second time."

Kendal's smile deepened, and he read on without answering, except by pressing her finger-tips against his lips.

"I should be sorry to deny your great cleverness and your pretensions to a certain sort of artistic interpretation. But to me the *artist bourgeois* is an outsider, who must remain outside. He has nothing to gain by fellowship with me, and I—pardon me—have much to lose.

"So, if you please, we will go our separate ways, and doubtless will represent, each to the other, an experiment that has failed. You will believe me when I say that I am intensely sorry. And perhaps you will accept, as sincerely as I offer it, my wish that the future may bring you success even more brilliant than you have already attained." Here a line had been carefully scratched out. "What I have written I have written under compulsion. I am sure you will understand that.

"Believe me,
"Yours sincerely,
"ELFRIDA BELL.

"P. S.—I had a dream once of what I fancied our friendship might be. It is a long time ago, and the days between have faded all the color and sweetness out of my dream—still, I remember that it was beautiful. For the sake of that vain imagining, and because it was beautiful, I will send you, if you will allow me, a photograph of a painting which I like, which represents art as I have learned to kneel to it."

Kendal read this communication through with a look of keen amusement until he came to the postscript. Then he threw back his head and laughed outright. Janet's face had changed; she tried to smile in concert, but the effort was rather piteous. "Oh, Jack," she said, "please take it seriously." But he laughed on, irrepressibly.

She tried to cover his lips. "*Don't* shout so!" she begged, as if there were illness in the house or a funeral next door, and he saw something in her face which stopped him.

"My darling, it can't hurt—it doesn't, does it?"

"I'd like to say no, but it does, a little. Not so much as it would have done a while ago."

"Are you going to accept Miss Bell's souvenir of her shattered ideal? That's the best thing in the letter—that's really supreme!" and Kendal, still broadly mirthful, stretched out his hand to take it again; but Janet drew it back.

"No," she said, "of course not; that was silly of her. But a good deal of the rest is true, I'm afraid, Jack."

"It's damnably impudent," he cried, with sudden anger. "I suppose she believes it herself, and that's the measure of its truth. How dare she dogmatize to you about the art of your work! *She* to *you!*"

"Oh, it isn't that I care about. It doesn't matter

to me how little she thinks of my aims and my methods. I'm quite content to do my work with what artistic conception I've got without analyzing its quality—I'm thankful enough to have any. Besides, I'm not sure about the finality of her opinion—"

"You needn't be!" Kendal interrupted, with scorn.

"But what hurts—like a knife—is that part about my insincerity. I *haven't* been honest with her—I haven't! From the very beginning I've criticised her privately. I've felt all sorts of reserves and qualifications about her, and concealed them—for the sake of—of I don't know what—the pleasure I had in knowing her, I suppose."

"It seems to me pretty clear, from this precious communication, that she was quietly reciprocating," Kendal said bluntly.

"That doesn't clear me in the least. Besides, when she had made up her mind she had the courage to tell me what she thought; there was some principle in that. I—I admire her for doing it, but I couldn't, myself."

"Thank the Lord, no. And I wouldn't be too sure, if I were you, darling, about the unmixed heroism that dictates her letter. I dare say she fancied it was that, but—"

Janet's head leaped up from his shoulder. "Now you are unjust to her," she cried. "You don't know Elfrida, Jack. If you think her capable of assuming a motive—"

"Well, do you know what I think?" said Kendal, with an irrelevant smile, glancing at the letter in her hand. "I think she has kept a copy."

Janet looked at him with reproachful eyes, which nevertheless had the relief of amusement in them. "Don't you?" he insisted.

"I—dare say."

"And she thoroughly enjoyed writing as she did. The phrases read as if she had rolled them under her tongue. It was a *coup*, don't you see?—and the making of a *coup*, of any kind, at any expense, is the most refined joy which life affords that young woman."

"There's sincerity in every line."

"Oh, she means what she says. But she found an exquisite gratification in saying it which you cannot comprehend, dear. This letter is a flower of her egotism, as it were—she regards it with natural ecstasy, as an achievement."

Janet shook her head. "Oh no, no!" she cried miserably. "You can't realize the—the sort of thing there was between us, dear, and how it should have been sacred to me beyond all tampering and cavilling, or it should not have been at all. It isn't that I didn't know all the time that I was disloyal to her, while she thought I was sincerely her friend. I did! And now she has found me out, and it serves me perfectly right—perfectly."

Kendal reflected for a moment, and then he brought comfort to her from his last resource.

"Of course the intimacy between two girls is a wholly different thing, and I don't know whether the relation between Miss Bell and myself affords any parallel to it—"

"Oh, Jack! And I thought—"

"What did you think, dearest?"

"I thought," said Janet, in a voice considerably muffled by contact with his tweed coat collar, "that you were perfectly *madly* in love with her."

"Heavens!" Kendal cried, as if the contingency had been physically impossible. "It is a man's privilege to fall in love with a woman, darling—not with an incarnate idea."

"It's a very beautiful idea."

"I'm not sure of that—it looks well from the outside. But it is quite incapable of any growth or much change," Kendal went on musingly, "and in the end—Lord, how a man would be bored!"

"You are incapable of being fair to her," came from the coat collar.

"Perhaps. I have something else to think of—since yesterday. Janet, look up!"

She looked up, and for a little space Elfrida Bell found oblivion as complete as she could have desired between them. Then—

"You were telling me—" Janet said.

"Yes. Your Elfrida and I had a sort of friendship too—it began, as you know, in Paris. And I was quite aware that one does not have an ordinary friendship with her—it accedes and it exacts more than the common relation. And I've sometimes made myself uncomfortable with the idea that she gave me credit for a more faultless conception of her than I possessed; for the honest, brutal truth is, I'm afraid, that I've only been working her out. When the portrait was finished I found that somehow I had succeeded. She saw it, too, and so I fancy my false position has righted itself. So I haven't been sincere to her either, Janet. But my conscience seems fairly callous about it. I can't help reflecting that we are to other people pretty much what they deserve that we shall be. We can't control our own respect."

"I've lost hers," Janet repeated, with depression, and Kendal gave an impatient groan.

"I don't think you'll miss it," he said.

"And, Jack, haven't you any—compunctions about exhibiting that portrait?"

"Absolutely none." He looked at her with candid eyes. "Of course if she wished me to I would destroy it. I respect her property in it so far as that. But so long as she accepts it as the significant truth it is, I am entirely incapable of regretting it. I have painted her, with her permission, as I saw her, as she is. If I had given her a squint or a dimple, I could accuse myself; but I have not wronged her or gratified myself by one touch of misrepresentation."

"I am to see it this afternoon," said Janet. Unconsciously she was looking forward to finding some measure of justification for herself in the portrait; why, it would be difficult to say.

"Yes; I put it into its frame with my own hands yesterday. I don't know when anything has given me so much pleasure. And so far as Miss Bell is concerned," he went on, "it is an unpleasant thing to say, but one's acquaintance with her seems more and more to resolve itself into an opportunity for observation, and to be without significance other than that. I tell you frankly I began to see that when I found I shared what she called her friendship with Golightly Ticke. And I think, dear, with people like you and me, any more serious feeling toward her is impossible."

"Doesn't it distress you to think that she believes you incapable of speaking of her like this?"

"I think," said Kendal slowly, "that she knows how I would be likely to speak of her."

"Well," Janet returned, "I'm glad you haven't reason to suffer about her as I do. And I don't know at all how to answer her letter."

"I'll tell you," Kendal replied. He jumped up and brought her a pen and a sheet of paper and a blotting-pad, and sat down again beside her, holding the ink bottle. "Write 'My dear Miss Bell.'"

"But she began her letter without any formality."

"Never mind; that's a cheapness that you needn't imitate, even for the sake of politeness. Write 'My dear Miss Bell.'"

Janet wrote it.

"'I am sorry to find,'" Kendal dictated slowly, a few words at a time, "'that the flaws in my regard for you are sufficiently considerable—to attract your attention as strongly as your letter indicates. The right of judgment in so personal a matter—is indisputably yours, however—and I write to acknowledge, not to question it.'"

"Dear, that isn't as I feel."

"It's as you will feel," Kendal replied ruthlessly. "Now add: 'I have to acknowledge the very candid expression of your opinion of myself—which does not lose in interest—by the somewhat exaggerated idea of its value which appears to have dictated it,

—and to thank you for your extremely kind offer to send me a picture. I am afraid, however—even in view of the idyllic considerations you mention—I cannot allow myself to take advantage of that—'

"On the whole I wouldn't allude to the shattered ideal—"

"Oh no, dear. Go on."

"Or the fact that you probably wouldn't be able to hang it up," he added grimly. "Now write 'You may be glad to know that the episode in my life—which your letter terminates—appears to me to be of less importance than you perhaps imagine it—notwithstanding a certain soreness over its close.'"

"It doesn't, Jack."

"It will. I wouldn't say anything more, if I were you; just 'yours very truly, Janet Cardiff.'"

She wrote as he dictated, and then read the letter slowly over from the beginning. "It sounds very hard, dear," she said, lifting eyes to his which he saw were full of tears, "and as if I didn't care."

"My darling," he said, taking her into his arms, "I hope you don't—I hope you won't care, after to-morrow. And now, don't you think we've had enough of Miss Elfrida Bell for the present?"

CHAPTER XXXV.

AT three o'clock, an hour before he expected the Cardiffs, John Kendal ran up the stairs to his studio. The door stood ajar, and with a jealous sense of his possession within, he reproached himself for his carelessness in leaving it so. He had placed the portrait the day before where all the light in the room fell upon it, and his first hasty impression of the place assured him that it stood there still. When he looked directly at it he instinctively shut the door, made a step or two forward, closed his eyes and so stood for a moment, with his hands before them. Then, with a groan, "Damnation!" he opened them again and faced the fact. The portrait was literally in rags. They hung from the top of the frame and swung over the bottom of it. Hardly enough of the canvas remained unriddled to show that it had represented anything human. Its destruction was absolute—fiendish, it seemed to Kendal.

He dropped into a chair and stared with his knee locked in his hands.

"Damnation!" he repeated, with a white face.

"I'll never approach it again;" and then he added grimly, still speaking aloud, "Janet will say I deserved it."

He had not an instant's doubt of the author of the destruction, and he remembered with a flash in connection with it the little silver-handled Algerian dagger that pinned one of Nádie Palicsky's studies against the wall of Elfrida's room. It was not till a quarter of an hour afterward that he thought it worth while to pick up the note that lay on the table addressed to him, and then he opened it with a nauseated sense of her unnecessary insistence.

"I have come here this morning," Elfrida had written, "determined to either kill myself or IT. It is impossible, I find, notwithstanding all that I said, that both should continue to exist. I cannot explain further, you must not ask it of me. You may not believe me when I tell you that I struggled hard to let it be myself. I had such a hideous doubt as to which had the best right to live. But I failed there—death is too ghastly. So I did what you see. In doing it I think I committed the unforgivable sin—not against you, but against art. It may be some satisfaction to you to know that I shall never wholly respect myself again in consequence." A word or two scratched out, and then: "Understand that I bear no malice toward you, have no blame for you, only honor. You acted under the very highest obligation—you could not have done otherwise. * * * * And I am glad to think that I do not destroy with your work the joy you had in it. * * * "

Kendal noted the consideration of this final statement with a cynical laugh, and counted the asterisks. Why the devil hadn't he locked the door? His confidence in her had been too ludicrous. He read the note half through once again, and then with uncontrollable impatience tore it into shreds. To have done it at all was hideous, but to try and impress herself in doing it was disgusting. He reflected, with a smile of incredulous contempt, upon what she had said about killing herself, and wondered, in his anger, how she could be so blind to her own disingenuousness. Five asterisks—she had made them carefully—and then the preposterousness about what she had destroyed and what she hadn't destroyed; and then more asterisks. What had she thought they could possibly signify—what could anything she might say possibly signify?

In a savage rudimentary way he went over the ethical aspect of the affair, coming to no very clear conclusion. He would have destroyed the thing himself if she had asked him, but she should have asked him. And even in his engrossing indignation he could experience a kind of spiritual blush as he recognized how safe his concession was behind the improbability of its condition. Finally he wrote a line to Janet, informing her that the portrait had sustained an injury, and postponing her and her father's visit to the studio. He would come in the morning to tell her about it, he added, and despatched the missive by the boy downstairs, posthaste, in a cab. It would be to-morrow, he reflected, before he could screw himself up to talking about it, even to Janet. For that day he must be alone with his discomfiture.

* * * * *

In the days of his youth and adversity, long before he and the public were upon speaking terms, Mr. George Jasper had found encouragement of a substantial sort with Messrs. Pittman, Pitt & Sanderson, of Ludgate Hill, which was a well-known explanation of the fact that this brilliant author clung, in the main, to a rather old-fashioned firm of publishers when the dimensions of his reputation gave him a proportionate choice. It explained also the circumstance that Mr. Jasper's notable critical acumen was very often at the service of his friend Mr. Pitt—Mr. Pittman was dead, as at least one member of a London publishing firm is apt to be—in cases where manuscripts of any curiously distinctive character, from unknown authors, puzzled his perception of the truly expedient thing to do. Mr. Arthur Rattray, of the *Illustrated Age*, had personal access to Mr. Pitt, and had succeeded in confusing him very much indeed as to the probable success of a book by an impressionistic young lady friend of his, which he called "An Adventure in Stage-Land," and which Mr. Rattray declared to have every element of unconventional interest. Mr. Pitt distrusted unconventional interest, distrusted impressionistic literature, and especially distrusted books by young lady friends. Rattray, nevertheless, showed a suspicious indifference to its being accepted, and an irritating readiness to take it somewhere else, and Mr. Pitt knew Rattray for a sagacious man. And so it happened that, returning late from a dinner where he had taken refuge from being bored entirely to extinction in two or three extremely indigestible dishes, Mr. George Jasper found Elfrida's manuscript in a neat, thick, oblong paper parcel, waiting for him on his dressing-table. He felt himself particularly wide awake, and he had a consciousness that the evening had made a very small inroad upon his capacity for saying clever things. So he went over "An Adventure in Stage-Land" at once, and in writing his opinion of it to Mr. Pitt, which he did with some elaboration, a couple of hours later, he had all the relief of a revenge upon a well-meaning hostess, without the reproach of having done her the slightest harm. It is probable that if Mr. Jasper had known that the opinion of the firm's "reader" was to find its way to the author, he would have expressed himself in terms of more guarded commonplace, for we cannot believe that he still cherished a sufficiently lively resentment at having his hand publicly kissed by a pretty girl to do otherwise; but Mr. Pitt had not thought it necessary to tell him of this condition, which Rattray, at Elfrida's express desire, had exacted. As it happened, nobody can ever know precisely what he wrote, except Mr. Pitt, who has forgotten, and Mr. Arthur Rattray, who tries to forget; for the letter, the morning after it had been received, which was the morning after the portrait met its fate, lay in a little charred heap in the fireplace of Elfrida's room, when Janet Cardiff pushed the screen aside at last and went in.

Kendal had come as he promised, and told her everything. He had not received quite the measure of indignant sympathy he had expected, and Janet had not laughed at the asterisks. On the other hand, she had sent him away, with unnatural gravity of demeanor, rather earlier than he meant to go, and without telling him why. She thought, as she directed the cabman to Essex Court, Fleet Street, that she would tell him why afterward; and all the way there she thought of the most explicit terms in which to inform Elfrida that her letter had been the product of hardness of heart, that she really felt quite differently, and had come to tell her, purely for honesty's sake, how she did feel.

After a moment of ineffectual calling on the other side of the screen, her voice failed her, and in dumb terror that would not be reasoned away it seemed that she saw the outlines of the long, still, slender figure under the bed draperies, while she still looked helplessly at a flock of wild geese flying over Fugi Yama. Buddha smiled at her from the table with a kind of horrid expectancy, and the litter of papers round him, in Elfrida's handwriting, mixed their familiarity with his mockery. She had only to drag her trembling limbs a little further to know that the room was pregnant with the presence of death. Some white tuberoses in a vase seemed to make it palpable with their fragrance. She ran wildly to the window and drew back the curtain; the pale sunlight flooding in gave a little white nimbus to a silver ring upon the floor.

The fact may not be without interest that six months afterward "An Adventure in Stage-Land" was published by Messrs. Lash and Black, and met with a very considerable success. Mr. Arthur Rattray undertook its disposal, with the consent of Mr. and Mrs. Leslie Bell, who insisted, without much difficulty, that he should receive a percentage of the profits for his trouble. Mr. Rattray was also of assistance to them when, as soon as the expense could be managed, these two middle-aged Americans, whose grief was not less impressive because of its twang, arrived in London to arrange that their daughter's final resting-place should be changed to her native land. Mr. Bell told him in confidence that while he hoped he was entirely devoid of what you may call race prejudice against the English people, it didn't seem as if he could let anybody belonging to him lie under the British flag for all time, and found it a comfort that Rattray understood. Sparta is divided in its opinion whether the imposing red granite monument they erected in the cemetery, with plenty of space left for the final earthly record of Leslie and Margaret Bell, is not too expensive considering the Bells' means, and too conspicuous considering the circumstances. It has hitherto occurred to nobody, however, to doubt the appropriateness of the texts inscribed upon it, in connection with three little French words which Elfrida, in the charmingly apologetic letter which she left for her parents, commanded to be put there—"*Pas femme-artiste.*" Janet, who once paid a visit to the place, hopes in all seriousness that the sleeper underneath is not aware of the combination.

Miss Kimpsey boards with the Bells now, and her relation to them has become almost daughterly. The three are swayed, to the extent of their several capacities, by what one might call a cult of Elfrida —her death has long ago been explained by the fact that a grandaunt of Mrs. Bell's suffered from melancholia.

Mr. and Mrs. John Kendal's delightful circle of friends say that they live an idyllic life in Devonshire. But even in the height of some domestic joy a silence sometimes falls between them still. Then, I fancy, he is thinking of an art that has slipped away from him, and she of a loyalty she could not hold. The only person whose equanimity is entirely undisturbed is Buddha. In his place among the mournful Magdalens of Mrs. Bell's drawing-room in Sparta, Buddha still smiles.

THE END.

D. APPLETON & CO.'S PUBLICATIONS.

NOVELS BY MAARTEN MAARTENS.

THE GREATER GLORY. A Story of High Life. By MAARTEN MAARTENS, author of "God's Fool," "Joost Avelingh," etc. 12mo. Cloth, $1.50.

"Until the Appletons discovered the merits of Maarten Maartens, the foremost of Dutch novelists, it is doubtful if many American readers knew that there were Dutch novelists. His 'God's Fool' and 'Joost Avelingh' made for him an American reputation. To our mind this just published work of his is his best. . . . He is a master of epigram, an artist in description, a prophet in insight."—*Boston Advertiser.*

"It would take several columns to give any adequate idea of the superb way in which the Dutch novelist has developed his theme and wrought out one of the most impressive stories of the period. . . . It belongs to the small class of novels which one can not afford to neglect."—*San Francisco Chronicle.*

"Maarten Maartens stands head and shoulders above the average novelist of the day in intellectual subtlety and imaginative power."—*Boston Beacon.*

GOD'S FOOL. By MAARTEN MAARTENS. 12mo. Cloth, $1.50.

"Throughout there is an epigrammatic force which would make palatable a less interesting story of human lives or one less deftly told."—*London Saturday Review.*

"Perfectly easy, graceful, humorous. . . . The author's skill in character-drawing is undeniable."—*London Chronicle.*

"A remarkable work."—*New York Times.*

"Maarten Maartens has secured a firm footing in the eddies of current literature. . . . Pathos deepens into tragedy in the thrilling story of 'God's Fool.'"—*Philadelphia Ledger.*

"Its preface alone stamps the author as one of the leading English novelists of to-day."—*Boston Daily Advertiser.*

"The story is wonderfully brilliant. . . . The interest never lags; the style is realistic and intense; and there is a constantly underlying current of subtle humor. . . . It is, in short, a book which no student of modern literature should fail to read."—*Boston Times.*

"A story of remarkable interest and point."—*New York Observer.*

JOOST AVELINGH. By MAARTEN MAARTENS. 12mo. Cloth, $1.50.

"So unmistakably good as to induce the hope that an acquaintance with the Dutch literature of fiction may soon become more general among us."—*London Morning Post.*

"In scarcely any of the sensational novels of the day will the reader find more nature or more human nature."—*London Standard.*

"A novel of a very high type. At once strongly realistic and powerfully idealistic."—*London Literary World.*

"Full of local color and rich in quaint phraseology and suggestion."—*London Telegraph.*

"Maarten Maartens is a capital story-teller."—*Pall Mall Gazette.*

"Our English writers of fiction will have to look to their laurels."—*Birmingham Daily Post.*

New York: D. APPLETON & CO., 1, 3, & 5 Bond Street.

D. APPLETON & CO.'S PUBLICATIONS.

MANY INVENTIONS. By RUDYARD KIPLING. Containing fourteen stories, several of which are now published for the first time, and two poems. 12mo, 427 pages. Cloth, $1.50.

"The reader turns from its pages with the conviction that the author has no superior to-day in animated narrative and virility of style. He remains master of a power in which none of his contemporaries approach him—the ability to select out of countless details the few vital ones which create the finished picture. He knows how, with a phrase or a word, to make you see his characters as he sees them, to make you feel the full meaning of a dramatic situation."—*New York Tribune.*

"'Many Inventions' will confirm Mr. Kipling's reputation. . . . We would cite with pleasure sentences from almost every page, and extract incidents from almost every story. But to what end? Here is the completest book that Mr. Kipling has yet given us in workmanship, the weightiest and most humane in breadth of view."—*Pall Mall Gazette.*

"Mr. Kipling's powers as a story-teller are evidently not diminishing. We advise everybody to buy 'Many Inventions,' and to profit by some of the best entertainment that modern fiction has to offer."—*New York Sun.*

"'Many Inventions' will be welcomed wherever the English language is spoken. . . . Every one of the stories bears the imprint of a master who conjures up incident as if by magic, and who portrays character, scenery, and feeling with an ease which is only exceeded by the boldness of force."—*Boston Globe.*

"The book will get and hold the closest attention of the reader."—*American Bookseller.*

"Mr. Rudyard Kipling's place in the world of letters is unique. He sits quite aloof and alone, the incomparable and inimitable master of the exquisitely fine art of short-story writing. Mr. Robert Louis Stevenson has perhaps written several tales which match the run of Mr. Kipling's work, but the best of Mr. Kipling's tales are matchless, and his latest collection, 'Many Inventions,' contains several such."—*Philadelphia Press.*

"Of late essays in fiction the work of Kipling can be compared to only three—Blackmore's 'Lorna Doone,' Stevenson's marvelous sketch of Villon in the 'New Arabian Nights,' and Thomas Hardy's 'Tess of the D'Urbervilles.' . . . It is probably owing to this extreme care that 'Many Inventions' is undoubtedly Mr. Kipling's best book."—*Chicago Post.*

"Mr. Kipling's style is too well known to American readers to require introduction, but it can scarcely be amiss to say there is not a story in this collection that does not more than repay a perusal of them all."—*Baltimore American.*

"As a writer of short stories Rudyard Kipling is a genius. He has had imitators, but they have not been successful in dimming the luster of his achievements by contrast. . . . 'Many Inventions' is the title. And they are inventions—entirely original in incident, ingenious in plot, and startling by their boldness and force."—*Rochester Herald.*

"How clever he is! This must always be the first thought on reading such a collection of Kipling's stories. Here is art—art of the most consummate sort. Compared with this, the stories of our brightest young writers become commonplace."—*New York Evangelist.*

"Taking the group as a whole, it may be said that the execution is up to his best in the past, while two or three sketches surpass in rounded strength and vividness of imagination anything else he has done."—*Hartford Courant.*

"Fifteen more extraordinary sketches, without a tinge of sensationalism, it would be hard to find. . . . Every one has an individuality of its own which fascinates the reader."—*Boston Times.*

New York: D. APPLETON & CO., 1, 3, & 5 Bond Street.

D. APPLETON & CO.'S PUBLICATIONS.

BENEFITS FORGOT. By WOLCOTT BALESTIER, author of "Reffey," "A Common Story," etc. 12mo. Cloth, $1.50.

"A credit to American literature and a monument to the memory of the author."—*Boston Beacon.*

"The author places his reader at the very pulse of the human machine when that machine is throbbing most tumultuously."—*London Chronicle.*

"The author manages a difficult scene in a masterly way, and his style is brilliant and finished."—*Buffalo Courier.*

"An ambitious work. . . . The author's style is clear and graceful."—*New York Times.*

"Mr. Balestier has done some excellent literary work, but we have no hesitation in pronouncing this, his latest work, by far his best."—*Boston Advertiser.*

DUFFELS. By EDWARD EGGLESTON, author of "The Faith Doctor," "Roxy," "The Hoosier Schoolmaster," etc. 12mo. Cloth, $1.25.

"A collection of stories each of which is thoroughly characteristic of Dr. Eggleston at his best."—*Baltimore American.*

"Destined to become very popular. The stories are of infinite variety. All are pleasing, even fascinating, studies of the character, lives, and manners of the periods with which they deal."—*Philadelphia Item.*

THE FAITH DOCTOR. By EDWARD EGGLESTON, author of "The Hoosier Schoolmaster," "The Circuit Rider," etc. 12mo. Cloth, $1.50.

"One of *the* novels of the decade."—*Rochester Union and Advertiser.*

"The author of 'The Hoosier Schoolmaster' has enhanced his reputation by this beautiful and touching study of the character of a girl to love whom proved a liberal education to both of her admirers."—*London Athenæum.*

"'The Faith Doctor' is worth reading for its style, its wit, and its humor, and not less, we may add, for its pathos."—*London Spectator.*

"Much skill is shown by the author in making these 'fads' the basis of a novel of great interest. . . . One who tries to keep in the current of good novel-reading must certainly find time to read 'The Faith Doctor.'"—*Buffalo Commercial.*

"LA BELLA" AND OTHERS. By EGERTON CASTLE, author of "Consequences." Paper, 50 cents; cloth, $1.00.

"The stories will be welcomed with a sense of refreshing pungency by readers who have been cloyed by a too long succession of insipid sweetness and familiar incident."—*London Athenæum.*

"The author is gifted with a lively fancy, and the clever plots he has devised gain greatly in interest, thanks to the unfamiliar surroundings in which the action for the most part takes place."—*London Literary World.*

"Eight stories, all exhibiting notable originality in conception and mastery of art, the first two illustrating them best. They add a dramatic power that makes them masterpieces. Both belong to the period when fencing was most skillful, and illustrate its practice."—*Boston Globe.*

New York: D. APPLETON & CO., 1, 3, & 5 Bond Street.

D. APPLETON & CO.'S PUBLICATIONS.

BEATRICE WHITBY'S NOVELS.

THE AWAKENING OF MARY FENWICK. 12mo. Paper, 50 cents; cloth, $1.00.

"Miss Whitby is far above the average novelist.... This story is original without seeming ingenious, and powerful without being overdrawn."—*New York Commercial Advertiser.*

"An admirable portrayal of the development of human character under novel experiences."—*Boston Commonwealth.*

PART OF THE PROPERTY. 12mo. Paper, 50 cents; cloth, $1.00.

"The book is a thoroughly good one. The theme is the rebellion of a spirited girl against a match which has been arranged for her without her knowledge or consent. ... It is refreshing to read a novel in which there is not a trace of slipshod work."—*London Spectator.*

A MATTER OF SKILL. 12mo. Paper, 50 cents; cloth, $1.00.

"A very charming love-story, whose heroine is drawn with original skill and beauty, and whom everybody will love for her splendid if very independent character."—*Boston Home Journal.*

"Told in a gracefully piquant manner, and with a frank freshness of style that makes it very attractive in the reading. It is uncommonly well written."—*Boston Saturday Evening Gazette.*

ONE REASON WHY. 12mo. Paper, 50 cents; cloth, $1.00.

"A remarkably well-written story.... The author makes her people speak the language of every-day life, and a vigorous and attractive realism pervades the book, which provides excellent entertainment from beginning to end."—*Boston Saturday Evening Gazette.*

IN THE SUNTIME OF HER YOUTH. 12mo. Paper, 50 cents; cloth, $1.00.

"The story has a refreshing air of novelty, and the people that figure in it are depicted with a vivacity and subtlety that are very attractive."—*Boston Beacon.*

The above five volumes, 12mo, cloth, in box, $5.00.

ON THE LAKE OF LUCERNE, and other Stories. 16mo. Half cloth, with specially designed cover, 50 cents.

"Six short stories carefully and conscientiously finished, and told with the graceful ease of the practiced *raconteur.*"—*Literary Digest.*

"Very dainty, not only in mechanical workmanship but in matter and manner."—*Boston Advertiser.*

New York: D. APPLETON & CO., 1, 3, & 5 Bond Street.

www.ingramcontent.com/pod-product-compliance
Lightning Source LLC
Chambersburg PA
CBHW030426300426
44112CB00009B/875